Garbo
and the
Night Watchmen

Cinema Two

Garbo

GARBO AND THE NIGHT WATCHMEN

A Selection made in 1937 from the writings of
British and American Film Critics

Assembled and Edited by
Alistair Cooke

McGraw-Hill Book Company
New York · St. Louis · San Francisco

Library of Congress Catalog Card Number: 79-135303
07–012490–6

Printed in Great Britain

Contents

Acknowledgements

The publishers express their thanks to the editors of the following periodicals, whose permission in 1937 to reprint these pieces made the collection possible: in the United States, *The New Republic*, *The New Masses*, *Life*, *Variety*, *Esquire*; and in Great Britain, *The Spectator*, *Life and Letters Today*, *The London Mercury*, *The Listener*, *The New Statesman and Nation*, and *The Manchester Guardian*.

Stills by courtesy of the original production companies and distributors of the films discussed in the text: Albatros Film, British Commercial Gas Association, British International Pictures, Capitol Film, Columbia, Famous Players-Lasky, Les Films Fernand Rivers, First National, Gaumont Pictures, G.B. Productions, GPO Film Unit, Lenfilm, London Film Productions, Mejrabpom Film, M-G-M, Paramount, Pickford-Lasky, Praesens Film, Republic Pictures, RKO-Radio, Samuel Goldwyn, Société Générale de Films, Société Nouvelle de Cinématographie, Twentieth Century-Fox, United Artists, Universal, Warner Brothers.

Preface to 1971 Edition

A recent tour of the cluttered bookshops along what used to be called Fourth Avenue disclosed the interesting sociological item that whereas the advanced thinkers among the young of the 1930s bought books – mostly indignant – about the Soviet utopia and its prophets, the same types today are mad for books by or about film directors. It is hardly to be believed. It is further testimony to the sad fact that prophecy is the last gift given to man, and to the complementary fact that no bright boy in his own generation believes he is without it. Everybody who latches on, in his youth, to the reigning intellectuals of course has his favourites and his villains, but somewhere between the grave jargon of Marcuse and the papal bulls of the exiled Eldridge Cleaver the young radical of today knows some things for sure: that the investment banker and the haircut are doomed, that the universities will soon be run by the freshmen, that Vietnam is the white man's last adventure in Asia, that ecology is the new religion and the 'people' will rise and cleanse the earth and the heavens and the waters that are under the heavens.

May I, as the English judges say, take leave to doubt? I was brought up on the certain guarantee, sworn to by such double-domes as Bernard Shaw, H. G. Wells, Bertrand Russell, Count Keyserling and Havelock Ellis that marriage was on its last legs, that Eugenic Breeding was as inevitable as it was right, that world government was just around the corner because another world war would promptly extinguish the human race in a cloud of poison gas. None of these things has happened. Eugenic Breeding, as naïve a fetish as ever obsessed the intelligentsia, has now to be looked up in books of social history that record the rise and fall of flagpole sitting, the Charleston and Social Credit.

Way back there when this book was published it was inconceivable that any English or American film director would want to expound his 'philosophy of film' in a book; more unbelievable still, that anyone would want to read it. (I hold to this prejudice all the more having dipped into the recent confessionals of Antonioni and Fellini, to go no further). As the farthest reach of the improbable, I should not have guessed that anybody in the dim apocalypse of 1971 would want to reprint this book. Plato's *Dialogues*, yes. Mrs Beeton, certainly (it has just been done). Harold Nicolson's *Public Faces*, a bizarre pre-vision – by the unlikeliest author – of the dropping of the atomic bomb. But *Garbo And The Night Watchmen*, a casual chronicle of pleasure and pain in the movies, put together by eight youngish men and one gorgeous woman in the 1930s! The book had its first and only edition in the autumn of 1937. Even a year later C. A. Lejeune, the film critic of the *Observer* (whose omission from this collection I now regret), told as a joke about an earnest schoolboy who wanted this book for a school prize 'if any copies could still be found.' In short, it was warmly reviewed (though not by the critics who had been left out), and it died. Why it should now excite a publisher sufficiently to arrange for its reincarnation is a mystery I have no intention of probing. Naturally, a beginning author believes that his first born is incomparably precious. And it is flattering indeed to see a child of the '30s dolled up in this handsome way.

The old hands at preface-reading will guess what comes next: the editor's admission that, on second thoughts, perhaps there is after all something fresh and valuable to be got from salvaging these notes. I will not bore the reader with this bit of regulation hypocrisy. I can only say that the original criterion for choosing these particular critics was a lucky one.

Like jurymen, they were chosen not as specialists in the law but as 'twelve of the ordinary men looking on.' The shops that dealt in books on the drama were already beginning to groan under histories of film and monographs on montage, usually written by Eisenstein and the denser Germans, that are unreadable to this day.

What I admired, and admire, most in a critic is a personal point of view and the ability to express it crisply, or passionately, or drolly or entertainingly, but above all intelligibly. I could name half a dozen eminent contemporary critics who would never have been invited into the company of these night watchmen because in various wordy ways they illustrate the grinding solemnity which Otis Ferguson so richly parodied in his piece here on *Three Songs Of Lenin*: 'The appreciation of pictures is much like all other forms; but there is the sad fact of its having thus far got so little intelligent consideration that intelligence, when it appears, tends to become the high priest guarding marvels. Everyone goes to the movies, to laugh or delight his heart; they are a part of common experience – and very common at that, usually. Now and then one is good, but thinking of it we do not think of art. It's just a movie; we only went for the fun. So when someone comes along and says down his nose, Art in the cinema is largely in the hands of artists in cinematographic experimentation, we think, Mm, fancy such a thing, I wonder what *that* is like. . . . As for pure cinema, we would not praise a novel (in which field by this time you must, to be intelligent, be intelligible or perish) by saying merely that it was pure *roman*. I do not wish to pull rabbits out of the hat, but here is a fact: you too can make pure cinema.'

If I had a prejudice, then, in choosing my co-authors it was for people who showed, first, an appetite for life and, second, a liking for the movies as a warming part of it. Each of the nine was true to a different background and so had an honestly different point of view. They all loved the movies yet did not feel called on to claim for their love that it was about to replace religion, sex, the Supreme Court or interstate commerce. They all wrote long after the art-for-art's-sake delusion of the 1890s and long before it was resurrected in a maniacal form in the 1960s. They were all gifted and intelligent people, none of them educated to compulsory polysyllables, all of them with their own brand of humour. I do not believe this book contains a single 'meaningful' gasp of 'empathy', the 'thrust' of a 'relevant' argument, or a plea for 'alienation.' Plots (and there were plots) were plotted and not 'structured'. James Cagney was quietly recognised as an engaging scamp, with no call to be proclaimed as the symbolic 'anti-hero' who ought to run Franklin Roosevelt out of the White House. Mae West was not (I quote) 'a puritanistic degradation symbol of the American female'. She was a riot. Or, if you wanted to be sociological with Robert Forsythe, 'the middle class matron in her hour of license'.

The more I fight through the knotty prose of admittedly serious critics whose lives seem to lurch, one way or another, between the bed and the theatre, the more I approve of James Agate's remark that 'it is an enormous advantage when theatre and film critics are authorities on something else besides plays and films. Though I place confidence in the judgments of Mr B. I should like to feel that he was also expert in aeronautics and water polo. I could wish that Mr C. had been a flyweight boxer or ridden Derby winners.'

This presumption of catholicity is something that did not cross my mind when the invitations went out, but I see now that it was there as an insurance against the occult and the esoteric. Robert Herring has been a novelist, editor, mountaineer, amateur cook and interplanetary buff. Don Herold was a professional cartoonist, humorist and advertising man. John Marks, a notable linguist, was in his time a publisher's reader, magazine editor, translator and the best Anglo-Saxon authority on bullfighting. Meyer Levin, the author of the best-selling *Compulsion*, has been a reporter, painter, and an expert manipulator of marionettes. Robert Forsythe's radical convictions were strongly planted in the poverty of his childhood and the grim years in the coal mines and steel factories of Pennsylvania. Otis Ferguson was a sailor, a boxer, a considerable man with the bottle, and the best jazz critic of the 1930's on his off-nights from the movies. Cecelia Ager was an early feminist and later *aficionado* of popular songs, Democratic politics, women's fashions and *bonsai* cultivation. It is surely gratuitous so late in the day to elaborate on Graham Greene's insatiable interest in the human animal from Brighton to Cuba. And I hope it may be added without coyness that yours truly is happy indeed that he gave only a little of his life to the movies and most of it to American politics, the landscape of the West, music, golf, fishing, and every known indoor game excepting only bridge.

Anthologies are famous graveyards of literature, and in a literal sense the contributors to this one are now divided between the quick and the dead. Otis Ferguson was the first to go: he returned to the sea after Pearl Harbor and was torpedoed in the Atlantic. John Marks was the last. In between, Don Herold died and so did Kyle Crichton, an ingratiating hind let loose who at one and the same time was an accomplished Establishment journalist and also Robert Forsythe, the raging Anglophobe and Russophile of the *New Masses*. If the rest of us are asked what we did in the revolutionary era that separates Mr Deeds from Myra Breckinridge, I suppose we should say, with the Abbé Sieyès, 'we existed.'

A.C.

Preface to 1937 Edition

There have been many books about the movies but not many kinds. Maybe it's as well that people with a prejudice against abstract writing on the movies should be told that at no stage of its making was this book likely to be called *Montage Today* or *The Future of Celluloid*. It is not meant to compete with the notable work of historians and theoretical critics.

This is a book about the movies by people who earn their bread and butter by dashing from meals to movies. It is probably the first book about the movies by writers who are so busy seeing them that they have no time to write books. Perhaps at another time, and in a better life, they can sit down at leisure and consider *The Film* and weigh trends. If that sentence carries a whiff of sour grapes it should be admitted that there is no reason why one sort of critic should be some other sort. But even if he can do both kinds of criticism, pure and applied, in these pages he is a professional star-gazer, a night watchman who must rush away at midnight to state a heartache or a preference against the dawn's deadline (the fact that some of these critics write for weeklies and even a monthly makes no difference, all periodical writers loaf away thirty days and then scribble through to sunrise of press day, failing in February to produce any copy at all). This collection cannot pretend to be exhaustive, there are probably a dozen critics writing somewhere in the English-speaking world whose work has an equal right to go on record. Nor is this a history of movie reviewing. It starts late, but no later than the day the movies grew up – almost any day after *The Singing Fool*. It puts between covers, I believe for the first time, several ways of looking at the movies, since the time they turned into talkies. In this day and age, which has seen remarkable theoretical criticism in many arts, there has been a tendency, and especially in movie criticism, for the academic critic to stake a claim on critical fields which are still open to the squatter. The movies are sometimes fine and sometimes foul, trivial and memorable, as inconsequential and maddening and unforgettable as a part of life. They are primarily put out, with successful cunning, to appeal to two hundred million people a year. So it would not be surprising if there were all sorts of ways of writing about them, if they encouraged all types of minds to browse. And I have not searched only in the files of 'intelligent weeklies'. In the United States especially, editors don't seem to demand that the critics should write like the rest of the paper, and good criticism sports in strange places. In both countries it makes a brave effort to keep alive in the columns of some daily newspapers. But the critic of a daily newspaper has many cloying duties which do not make his writing any easier to read after a year or so. He has to recount to a thousand words last night's weary plot for this morning's alert breakfast table. He has to respect, however tactfully, his paper's advertisers. There are many good daily critics who still make glamorous these chores, but criticism is nothing if not free, and it would be unfair to those critics to lump them with writers who may write as they please. Even when left to himself a critic finds himself to be many other things than the pure judge he prays to be. The most strenuous seekers for truth, when they want advice about the movies, do not ask for a noble piece of editing or continuity. They say they'd like to see a good movie. And the critic in his time becomes tipster, narrator, propagandist, father-confessor, and when he is left alone – a fan. Perhaps only the beautiful finality of Miss Ager's writing, and her special assignment to judge only the women in films, uniquely qualifies her to be called the cinema's recording angel.

The first test of these pieces was that they should be entertaining writing. And the second that they should be, on the whole, about particular movies and not on 'subjects'. I hope that a book like this has enough uses, as Groucho might say, to make it welcome to several sorts of reader. The searcher after *montage* will track down many a valuable thought. On the other hand, it can be used as a bed book.

A.C.

July 1937

Robert Herring

Born London, 1903. Started in Fleet Street, 1925, became film critic for *The London Mercury* in 1926, and subsequently for *The Manchester Guardian* (1928–38), as well as being London correspondent to the international film magazine *Close Up* (1927–34). Editor of *Life and Letters Today* (1935–50), and author of *The President's Hat, Adam and Evelyn at Kew,* and *Cactus Coast.*

The Virginian: Gary Cooper, Mary Brian

1. Robert Herring

The Way of All Flesh

Father wakes, stretches, gets up. (This takes some time.) The children wake. There are six of them, so this also takes some time. The last two, as their cot shows, are quite young. But Father is quite old. He has a beard. Germans have beards, however, when they are quite young. Yet Father's knees are stiff, so Father must be quite old. Where is Mother? She would explain, but she is not here.

Perhaps there is no Mother? Or perhaps she has a Heart of Stone and does not love her children well. Which is it?

They are all in the bathroom now, Father superintending. Brush, spit, gargle, spit. Very pretty. The Mother must be – but no, here she is saying breakfast is ready. You remember her from *Stella Dallas*, the woman who put the Love in Mother. So if Belle Bennett is kept downstairs with the breakfast while the camera follows her husband's nursemaid activities in the bathroom, something stronger than mother-love must be at work. It is father-love. All that business with the children was not the Smile that Hides an Aching Heart. It was Father feeling holy, ritualizing the tooth-brushing and ear-washing. Father is a Simple Soul.

But why that old man's walk, as if he were bowed by the cares of the world? Well, he is a big man, and that is the way of all flesh upon the knees. Also, Father is Jannings and Jannings is Preparing the Way for something. The walk and the beard – they have been made to catch our eye, so we must wait. But we wish the walk were not so irritating. It has caught our eye by being unlovely and it is a pity we must wait until some significance atones for it. The director has not succeeded here. He is Victor Fleming and he is doing his best for Jannings. America can appreciate a Great Artist, too. America can be German, too. That is why the film is taking too long, why we are watching so much. You remember *Vaudeville*. It is like that; pounding, pounding. The method gives a number of 'moments', and we admire Jannings for taking longer, say to light a cigar, than we had believed possible. He has control, he can draw out details to their breaking point. But what is it all leading up to? Where is that inner quality that makes these details, if not aesthetic, expressive?

We are too restless. It isn't, is it, that we are quick, can see things more easily? that for us one symbol, not six, suffices? One child, as it were, being washed, not six. No; it is that we are so used to the quick-lunch counter, we cannot appreciate a banquet when we get it. *That* is what the film is saying – taste the finer essences. Watch Jannings.

We must. That is why the film was made; and in order that we must watch him, the duties of father and mother, the smacking and sanitation of his children, are combined in him, while his wife is left as a rather fidgety governess whose gestures consist of flicking her hands. You have to imagine a ruler at the end of them, and then they are rebuking. Or a handkerchief and they are waving goodbye. But the ruler and the handkerchief are called into play not by the hands but by the surroundings – and by our need for them to be doing something when they flick. Belle Bennett can be better than this. But watch Jannings. Breakfast is over. One child has been smacked and one has been carried out with the usual apprehensive gestures. You simply must not think of Chaplin now, it would be fatal. The children are given their satchels and Father sets off with his attaché case. The point illustrated by the satchels and case is that the Little Men will one day be Big Men like Dad; also, if you like, that August Schilling is a Child at Heart. A Simple Soul.

Father goes with that click-clack step to his Respected Position at the bank. He puts on his working coat, takes off his cuffs. By these

The Way of All Flesh: Emil Jannings

signs shall ye know the man. He pats his beard. This beard is the symbol of respectability, of pride in being a Family Man. When it goes – but stop, stop, you are anticipating. There is quite enough you cannot help seeing, don't, I beg you, let your imagination go on ahead. Jannings is rebuking an office boy for stealing sixpence. He explains that one step may cause one's downfall. Home truths? Rubbish; home chat. All this is supposed to give an air of reality. We *are* seeing how he lives, aren't we? But it is a series of acting tricks. Where *is* that inner quality? Don't be in a hurry. We're not with Segrave; we're on a steam-roller. It moves slowly but it grinds everything. Everything that is in its direct path it grinds exceeding small, like the mills of God. Yes, it must be a good picture to make you think of that.

   Jannings is home again, asking his favourite son to play his favourite tune. You think, at once, this is the last time Father will see his home. That *Wiegenlied* is dramatic. See, he is going out! Perhaps he Leads a Double Life. Again the film reproves you for the filmishness of your mind. He is at his club, bowling. He wins. He pats his beard. We have seen Werner Krauss bowling, too, in *Die Hose.* Perhaps we like him better, though his play wasn't so spectacular. Now they are having drinks. Father enjoys his victory. (Krauss was good, wasn't he?) They want Jannings to have more beer. He won't, he says, thank you. Just one, they urge. Will he, won't he?

His wife is on the telephone. Clearly, he did. He will come home drunk. Happy, honest Father will come home drunk. You are wrong; this film is not a bad film. Why won't you realize that? Wifie was answering the bank. You must not go thinking ahead like this. Watch Jannings. It's all very slow, but there's plenty of it. Why isn't your mind occupied? It finds it easy to disconnect from the eye, does it? Yes, I know; but Watch Jannings. He is being sent to Chicago with important bonds. This is the train. A Bad Woman is opposite Jannings. Ear-rings and feather boa and picture hat – you know. This is before the war. She wouldn't take us in, but she takes herself in and, more important, she takes Father in – finally. Not at once. Nothing happens at once. That is where they think they've psychological subtlety, but they haven't. Jannings has lost his ticket. Ah! it is in his case with the bonds. We, entrusted with the bonds, would button them up, sit on them, hide them – we wouldn't put them with our ticket that we are going to bring out in a crowded carriage. But August is a Simple Soul. Although he makes proverbs to the office boy, what does he know of the Wicked World?

The hussy is after the bonds. She captures August. She laughs a great deal, throwing her head back, wagging one forefinger. She wouldn't take us in, but she takes Father in.

When this film is shown, people will probably say that Belle Bennett and Phyllis Haver are too 'stagey' compared with Jannings's *marvellous naturalism* – 'out of the picture'. But the picture *is* Jannings; his wife and this woman are seen through his eyes (that is why they are so obvious). These images are not representational, but expressive, and that must be remembered. It is one of the few technical subtleties of the film. Elsewhere the camera records, and that is enough.

The minx flatters Father into having his beard off. (She does not want to be suspected nor to have him recognized.) They go to a Haunt. They Drink Too Much. Watch Jannings. Do you remember the elephants in *Chang*? They trampled the houses, broke them into bits (I am watching Jannings) – they made everything clear, but they left nothing standing.

Jannings's beard has gone. As he joins her, his walk is different. So that was what it was – that we should see how different he looked when it was off. It is thus a Great Character-Study. *If* he must look (not seem but look) young and abandoned at one point, make him look older before and after. What art! The film has been conceived from the wrong end.

Jannings waking up in a sordid room is good. Jannings dazed and bewildered is good Jannings. And so is Jannings seized with fury at finding the bonds stolen. He fights the thief on the railway track. By a very clumsy accident the man is killed. Father stumbles off. He looks at the river. He sees in the lights flaming accusations; he sees them too often, once or twice was enough to change Murgatroyd to Murdered. A newspaper reports August's death 'in defence of his trust'. So he can never go home again. He takes to selling chestnuts. He grows a Beard again. You see he is regretting The Past.

Years later, a placard announces 'August Schilling, the great violinist'. We were right about the *Wiegenlied*. Father gets a place in the gallery. His son is not so great that a beggar cannot, without waiting, walk into the front seat. (Camera considerations.) The encore is 'a Piece my Father taught me'. Jannings weeps over the gallery rails. Dirty, dishevelled, heartbroken.

It is moving? So was Old Bill. It is also funny, watching the new devices of prolonging emotion. Father creeps about after his family, watching them leave church. Snow is falling. Hazy effect on the old man's shoulders and hair, contrasting with the sharpness of Belle Bennett's mourning. He peers in at his own home (O *Stella Dallas*!). There is, we knew there would be, a Christmas Tree. The children are very kind to their old Mother. Father is seen by a policeman. Comerlongerme. But the violinist intervenes. Spirit of Christmas, constable. We are spared the fade-out to Bethlehem, but the feeling is there. Young August has his dad's Kind Heart, he offers Jannings warm coffee, but he does not recognize him. Father can bear it no longer. He stumbles down the street. Is the snow feathers or salt?

There was a prison scene once. They cut it, but that is how the film was made. Everything you can think of. Pile it on. Happy home . . . too much to drink . . . the spirit of Christmas . . . poor old dad . . . touch of a vanished hand. What I mean is, it becomes funny after a time. There is a hint of tears behind the deepest laughter, but positive guffaws lie behind this grief. Give that Gulpy Feeling, and you're an artist.

Well, now really! This is the Great Piece of Acting. But what is the use and where is the beauty of it? We do not need the films for this. It 'made the directors cry'. I don't wonder. And isn't that a very easy thing to do, to make people cry? Easier than making them laugh, or exhilarating them by the beauty of the flow of images.

Jannings's acting intensifies, it does not transfigure. That is what I say about Jannings. He can impress himself on the general atmosphere. Put him in water and he will swim; put him in mud and he sinks, he becomes mud. *The Way of All Flesh* may deceive because of the air of reality the cinema gives, but it is only too truly all flesh. There is no spirit. Don't blame the movies. Blame our minds. We're not ready yet. Here is the instrument, and that is what we make of it. *There* is the reason for tears.

Les Nouveaux Messieurs

Not a single one of these films is as good as it ought to be, yet there is something to be said for all of them. They are, in fact, distressing examples of the tendency of the whole cinema, which is evolving an alloy that it is still a little hard to reject entirely. In those old days which we are now hearing so much about, films were so bad that one could reject them, whilst seeing through to what they hinted at. Then came a few one could accept. There is now none among the average releases that one can either refuse or welcome. That is why, among other reasons, talkies are welcome. They set us back again to the days of out-and-out vulgarity and stupidity, sometimes avoiding both, and one still has hope that the next phase of efficient mediocrity may be leapt. But the general run of films shows them to be all so competent and so hopelessly un-worth-while, and that is a sign of loss of youth. Youth may be vulgar and it may not know how to do what it wants to do, but it *does* want to do something, and it *has* got spirits. The cinema today has not, and instead of grace it has graciousness.

The curse of the box-office, in short, is over all these films. One expects it from America, because one has got used to it. It is a pity that Germany now does the same in the endeavour to complete her Americanization, and as for France, M. Feyder was asked to Hollywood after *Les Nouveaux Messieurs*, and he will doubtless succeed very well there; he had his eye on Hollywood most of the time whilst making this film, and it prevented his tongue being sufficiently in his cheek. It is quite a pleasant film; that is what is the trouble, for it might have been so much more than pleasant.

Here is a theme of a dancer who is to be raised to the position of star by her protector, when there is a change of ministry. She transfers what are known as attentions to the electrician at the Opéra, who has become a Minister. But this new left-wing Ministry is speedily overthrown, and her original protector comes back to power. His first step is to send the electrician to a post abroad, and the ex-Minister is so

Les Nouveaux Messieurs; Brigitte Helm in *Crisis*

flattered that he misses the reason and does not see that the dancer has come not to say farewell, but, had he realized it, to go with him. All this 'real love despite everything' weakens the film, though it makes it popular. But it takes the edge off the satire, and reduces the stylization of the whole theme. One has again the old, queer French conception of women, and it is not even tilted to satire. This is the film which was banned by the French Government on account of its irreverence towards the Chamber of Deputies.

Crisis (Abwege)
Pabst's new film is unlike any other he has made, and one is left wondering why he made it, and why, for once, he did not make more of it. That perhaps he was himself bored by it seems the only conclusion and explanation. *Crisis* tells the story of a young wife who is neglected by her husband. She has that kind of friend that husbands dislike. She 'goes gay'. She tries to elope with an artist (Jack Trevor, who has to smoke a pipe, because he is English), but it is her husband who turns up at the station. He then, not knowing what can be done about it, leaves her to herself, and she flings off to a cabaret, which she loathes, and finally tries to compromise herself with a boxer in the artist's flat, and is found by her husband. All of which is ridiculous.

Brigitte Helm is, however, marvellous as the wife, and her performance is undoubtedly due to Pabst. She is electric, dynamic, pent-up as only she can be, with suggestions of enormous forces behind her. More than this, she gives the impression that she could control these forces if she liked, but that just for once she is going to let them have their way. She is deliberate, always, and in this unlike Asta Nielsen, to whom it has occurred to few people to compare her.

L'Age Dangereux
There are indeed few points of comparison. Age, type, style of acting are different, but there is just this one quality of hidden forces which they both have the power of suggesting. *L'Age Dangereux* is in many ways a better film than *Crisis*, though it owes nothing to its direction, and has none of Pabst's cutting, and was made cheaply, in rooms that are long, dark, and over-furnished. The theme is the same, though in this case the wife is middle-aged. Her husband is a professor, who is intent on his work. His favourite pupil calls one day, and the professor tells his wife that he plays the piano. The professor being Bernard Goetzke, who possesses one of the best screen masks in the world, the gesture with which he shuts the door so as to be undisturbed by the

playing is memorable. And Asta Nielsen feels what is happening to her. She goes away, but the young man insists on her coming with him. In the flat above is a girl, also studying, who has been his childhood's friend. Slowly Asta Nielsen visualizes what will happen when he finds she is really so much older; slowly she sees the girl above as a rival. She goes into the country.

Being Asta Nielsen, she proceeds to take the covers off the chairs. She wastes no time. She sets quite quietly about the business of forgetting. When she comes in, she sinks into a chair, and you think now there is going to be a conventional scene of longing for the absent loved one. She goes to put her bag on the table, it is covered with dust, and she opens her bag, wipes her fingers on a handkerchief. You see her clutching gratefully and consciously at a detail that will give her something to do. The young man comes to look for her. She welcomes him, but she sends him away. Then she runs after him, and collapses, ill, and is feverish. The acting here is Nielsen at her best. It is not easy to express an ageing woman sick with longing; and yet, though you see that that is what she is and what it is, Asta Nielsen is such an actress that you find yourself seeing someone showing you, as you yourself, how by far the most frightful thing it is to want someone very much – the mere fact of their presence. After this point, the film falls off. There is a good deal of to-and-fro, taking place in those nests of rooms the Germans love, and finally her husband returns and says, 'To me you will always be young, for we will grow old together', which I positively cannot believe was the real end of the film. I believe the box-office entered in again. But except for that, *L'Age Dangereux* is a serious film; it is really, I think, nearly a film, which I doubt if *Crisis* is, because Asta Nielsen's acting is definitely screen stylization. You watch her hands, her slow, blank face with terrific things happening behind it, and you realize that she has developed something quite new on the screen.

Lonesome

Whilst Pabst is made to busy himself with the most primitive forms of sex, America is indulging in the new game of simplicity. We had it in *Four Devils*; now *Lonesome* comes and is hailed as an important film. It is hard to see why, except that we are so starved by the need for box-office appeal that when we do get something approaching truth, we lose our heads. The theme of *Lonesome* had possibilities. It might be a big theme – the problem of the utter inability of town-dwellers, feeding machinery all day, to do anything with leisure when they get it. But Fejos made nothing of this. Instead, he told his theme with the story of

Lonesome; White Shadows in the South Seas

a boy and girl who were both hopelessly alone in New York and met by chance at Coney Island. That might have been all right, but what happened?

Well, there had to be action. So the switchback car in which she was riding caught fire, and when she was rescued, they were separated. And each of them returned home lonesome, humming the tune they had danced to. And the boy put it on his phonograph, and someone played it next door to the girl's room, and of course you have guessed that when she beat on the wall and told the neighbour to stop it, it turned out to be the boy, so they weren't lonesome any more, and any point anyone might have found in the film was nullified, and no one sees that simplicity is a matter of selection, not reduction.

It would be a good thing if some educationist or sociologist would turn his attention to making films that deal with problems of modern life. The cinema is a more or less modern thing, and it ought to be used, now and again, as a means of getting something clear about the life that takes hold of us, and our attempts to pretend that the hold is a handshake.

Hungarian Rhapsody

It is doing nothing at all to make films like *Hungarian Rhapsody*, which is only unpleasant, and could have been done better as a series of tableaux in a Parisian revue. The musical basis of the film was technically interesting, but there was not even, as in *Crisis*, good acting to compensate for a wickedly retrogressive story. It was pleasant to look at but that did not make one feel happier. Stevenson observed that there was good and so on in everything, but Stevenson was *fin de siècle*, and when one is trying hard to get at the good and coagulate it, it is annoying to have unnecessary evil put before one.

White Shadows in the South Seas

There is not very much sex in *White Shadows in the South Seas*, but there is sympathy, and that is the next surest box-office draw. Indeed, as Chaplin has shown, it is almost the best. The sympathy in *White Shadows* is for the gay and innocent Polynesians who are being wiped out by the greedy, grasping, white people. There is something here, but the scales are too heavily tilted. Here is another film which might have meant so much, and would have meant more if the maker of *Nanook* had gone on with it. Its chief interest now is in the documentary scenes, though most of the native life is prettified, and in the sound accompaniment.

Garbo and the Night Watchmen

This film taught me that I prefer canned music for films, and some-one explained this to me by saying that that was because an orchestra in front of the screen was in the wrong dimension. Certainly, when the orchestra at the Regal ceased playing the theme song, and the synchronization took it up, I looked to see where this new and more fitting noise came from. Others may not agree with me, but it is a point to be considered: indeed it is a platitude, that reproduced music goes better with reproduced images.

The Four Feathers

Two years were spent by Messrs Schoedsack and Cooper, filming in Africa. This was after the great success of their *Chang*. The results were brought back, and you would have thought that enough footage would have been shot in that time to make a picture long enough even for von Stroheim. But what do we see? A film 'based on the novel by A. E. W. Mason', in which the African record is used as realistic back-ground. There is not very much of Africa in the film, but one would willingly have seen more. It is very good, despite the fondness of Schoedsack and Cooper for testing the credulousness of the public. But for once, in these few scenes, we are seeing mass on the screen, moving mass, which is what the film exists to mould. And this mass is to do with animals and natives, scenery and how to live, which once again is the material *par excellence* of the film. In the story part of the picture, two soldiers are escaping from captivity; their captors, in order to smoke them out, set fire to the bush, and we then see animals flying before the fire. A family of baboons flying, reaching a river bridge, which, with the cruelty peculiar to the makers of *Chang*, breaks, plunging the animals in the river. Hippopotami stampeding before the flames . . . and then after this we are asked to take interest in the escape of two Hollywood actors disguised as soldiers disguised as something else. It is not hard to imagine that this forest-fire was to be the core of the film as devised by the travelling cameramen. And it is not hard to imagine that the Hollywood powers thought an 'interest' film would not hold a talkie-mad public, and that in any case they wanted a vehicle for Richard Arlen, and so once again what we have gained is only a tombstone for what is lost.

Finis Terrae

But *Finis Terrae* is pure gain, and pure cinema. It is not without faults. M. Epstein may be thought to be a little slow, as he is also a little senti-mental. In the original version, which I saw in Paris, the film had a

White Shadows in the South Seas; Finis Terrae

weakly sentimental ending; the doctor was called away from operating on the boy to another case, the implication being that for the doctor there is no rest, he is at the service of mankind. Besides being sentimental, this ending was bad because it suddenly switched the interest on to the doctor, and one wondered why one had hitherto been concerned with the life of the fishermen, to whom the doctor was incidental.

There is nothing sensational about the film. No big issues are involved, no questions of death and honour, and though this is its virtue – that it expresses ordinary life as it flies – it is also the cause for the film being almost perfect in a small style, rather than striking out for the big things. Just off Ouessant, four fishermen are on a wild wind-swept island harvesting seaweed; two of them are men, two boys. By the smoke that rises from the seaweed, the people on the mainland know how they are faring. One day, one of the boys thinks of a bottle of wine he has in his locker, and sends the other to fetch it. On his way back, over the beach, he stumbles and smashes it. Jean-Marie, the elder, is angry, and in his annoyance drops his knife. They watch the last of the wine sink in the sand, and then Jean-Marie finds he has lost his knife. He accuses Ambrose of having taken it. 'You have dropped my last bottle of wine; you might at least let me have my knife.' Small things, a knife and a bottle of wine. But they are on a bare island; such things are precious. The mainland is not so far away, but they cannot leave their work. By these little things we feel the life of these fishermen and all like them. The story reaches out to others besides fishermen. The wine causes ripples as it falls. Ambrose has cut his thumb on the broken bottle, and does not answer about the knife. The boys quarrel, and when the thumb grows worse, there is no one to look after Ambrose. He is unable to take his share in the work. They think he is sulking and shirking. Jean-Marie's cart is bowing beneath its load. There is only a little well on the island and water is precious. Ambrose, drawing some to cool his finger, is seen. These are little incidents which, in telling the story, enlarge the conception of life.

The difference between such films as *Finis Terrae* and the majority of pictures is the same as the difference between the work of novelists of feeling and imagination and of those who go out to look for 'life' in rough quarters, disguised with a mackintosh and blue spectacles. For life is round us all the time, there is no need to go out to look for it. Life is in the brain, and if the brain is not conscious of it, there is no use in seeking the docks, in ranging exotic slices of 'real life' before one. It is the same with the camera, which does not exist to have scenes and stories enacted before it. It is a mechanical extension of eyes, hands, brain and heart, and goes round, catching life where it finds it, and moulding it according to the sense and appreciation of the man behind it. M. Epstein has this sense, and the films he makes are all expressions of his feeling of life moulded in the plastic forms of cinema.

Jungle Rhythm; Laurel and Hardy; Secrets of Nature; British Movietone News
Mickey is the first child of the marriage of microphone and movie; all the others were stepchildren or illegitimate. But in Mickey, the microphone justifies itself, and in doing so raises the short film to its right importance on the screen. With the exception of the Chaplin two-reelers, the short film has never been treated very respectfully by the cinemas. It was a filler, a stop-gap – nothing more. Then came Mickey, and with Mickey came the audiences – for the short film.

The laughter in the houses that show Mickey is new laughter, something quite different from any that has gone before. Athene Seyler once lamented to me that people don't laugh in cinemas. 'There is all that material', she said, 'and yet the actors can only raise a smile. They are not flesh and blood.' But even Athene Seyler couldn't be as funny as Mickey, and he is not flesh and blood. Yet he strikes that personal note, he establishes that contact and wins that response which is alleged to be the prerogative of flesh and blood. Mickey isn't even an image of something actual. He is only a drawing, and never the same drawing for long. He is a song made plastic, a dance that is graphic (instead of choreographic), and above all he is almost all the gaiety in our minds that has never been satisfied. He is like a really good and inane nursery rhyme, and even a good nursery rhyme isn't Mickey. Take, for instance, *Jungle Rhythm*, which has been showing at the Plaza before *The Virginian*, and is now preceding *The Love Parade* at the Carlton. This mad cartoon, this piece of cardboard and crayon magic, is nothing more tangible than what its title says; it is a rhythm, a jungle rhythm. How did its maker know that with nothing more to offer, though he had everything else, his film would make thousands of people roar (themselves like a jungle) with laughter? I put in that clumsy parenthesis because it hints at an explanation of what the mouse does. He takes a piece of our mind that we have probably never been conscious of, and gives it to us to recognize and rejoice over, with all the relief at finding something we had not known

Big Business: Laurel and Hardy

was lost. This mouse in *Jungle Rhythm* is exploring, as mice will, and he is in a jungle, which gives him an advantage over everyday, hole-and-corner mice. Naturally he meets a lion, and naturally the lion is fierce. A bear is even more so. Mickey is between them. So he whistles, to show he doesn't care. He whistles and whistles, because he daren't stop, and the lion and the bear can't resist it; they dance. And all the animals in the jungle dance, and Mickey makes instruments of those that don't. The jungle rhythm is in full swing, and it is a perfectly authentic jungle. When one sees this film, one knows that it is quite right for two monkeys to glide across the screen in an entirely un-believable dance, and the fact that the music that moves them is the 'Blue Danube' only adds to the authenticity of this jungle. You have to see the film to be convinced; it had probably never struck you before that a Strauss waltz was real jungle music, but that is because you have been brought up on cinema tom-toms, and in any case have probably never seen monkeys dance. There is a lion that does a hula-hula, and there are two storks whose bodies very obligingly do all that their minds suddenly think would be appropriate, and there is a row of tigers that emit satisfactory and original noises when hit in the stomach by Mickey, and all this flows on in a marvellous symphony of movement, like the 'Tiger Rag' itself.

Laurel and Hardy are two comedians whose films have the same metaphysical quality of presenting in the vocabulary of slapstick a truer expression of man's inner thoughts on his outer life than pretentious productions such as *Atlantic* or *The Lost Zeppelin*. One of these men is stout and voluble, the other silent, thin, and put-upon. He is always about to leave the other one, but he never does, and he always very honestly tries to improve the other one's ideas, so as to make life easier for them. They are excellent ideas, but something goes wrong with them. For instance, what could have been better, after you have been turned away from one house where you have tried to sell a Christmas tree, than to go into the next street? There is reasoning behind such an idea, a knowledge of the law of averages, pioneer spirit and courage. It is not your fault that, with all these qualities, you overlook the fact that the house at the corner has two approaches, one in each street, and that you thus get turned away from what is the same house again. This occurs in *Big Business*, which was shown at the Empire with *Hallelujah*. Laurel and Hardy appear in *The Hollywood Revue*, in the best number in that dismal production, and they can be seen all over the country, both talking and silent. Wherever Laurel and Hardy are to be found, there will be a picture which I myself find funnier, because it is truer, than the old Chaplins.

A short of a different nature which to me is always one of the best films in any programme is British Movietone News, to which can also be added the other synchronized gazettes. Here you see such things as Japanese wrestling (Gaumont), the Naval delegates (British Movietone), the religious excitements in Russia (Pathé). The recording of British Movietone News always seems to me the best there is to be heard. It is the only talkie I know where the letter 'S' comes out. In *Rookery Nook*, despite the connection of H.M.V. with the production, the recording is bad; not only are the various letters muffled, but there is a hollow ring about the voices. Even in *The Virginian*, we have to listen to Gary Cooper making love to the 'thoolmiththreth'.

The Virginian
This is a small detail in a film that otherwise does so much that is excellent. The advent of the microphone to this picture, which was made seven years ago as a silent film, means that it is something more than a 'Western'. The fact that this subject has been chosen for the

Atlantic; Jeanette MacDonald and Maurice Chevalier in *The Love Parade*

microphone means that for once we get away from stage and drawing-room melodramas. Even as a 'Western' this film would be good, acted as it is by the screen's best cowboys, and being replete with the sound of iron on rock, of foot on ground, bellowing cattle, and rushing streams. But, having all this round it and woven into it, *The Virginian* becomes surrounded with the implications of life, and, though I do not know Virginia, something about this film rings true; I feel it is an authentic picture of pioneer days in Virginia, with more reality than glamour.

Atlantic; The Love Parade

I do not know shipwrecks, I have not yet been in one, but I am equally convinced that not only would neither I nor (I hope) anyone I know behave like the characters in *Atlantic*, but that the behaviour of such characters is not interesting enough to make a good film-scenario. It may be impressive; lots of people are moved by it – but people are very easily moved. It may be true – but these people are too good to be true. Who can care about a snarling wife who, together with a petulant daughter, spends the voyage asking male passengers where her husband is? Who is very interested in honeymoon couples who remain just that? Or in that most tiresome of literary conventions, the cynical author who, of course, is the best man of them all? There are others, a clergyman, a tippler, a valet, and the philandering husband. They all gather in the smoking-room, and the drama focuses on their not very important reactions. One cannot be very interested in the fate of people presented in such a way that one knows they would be the first one would shun on the voyage, and Herr Dupont ought to have found a way of making his bores artistically interesting. Lubitsch's characters are all unimportant, rather cheap people, yet *The Love Parade* holds one's interest from start to finish. That film has, of course, the advantage of being a marvellous combination of sight and sound, used in a new way, and presented with all the glitter of which Lubitsch, his star Maurice Chevalier and the firm of Paramount are capable. *Atlantic* has the disadvantage of being primarily a stage-piece adapted for the talking screen. There is no hint of the irony of this great ship, man's triumph over ocean, going down, and of man setting out to escape in little lifeboats. There is no sense of ice against steel (it is, or would be, the tragedy of the *Titanic*), and of man against both. There is simply noble speech and hackneyed situation. The German version, made with a different cast by the same director, was far better acted and the language came over well; the characters at least seemed living. But such an opportunity was missed here that I resent the cheap pseudo-dignity directed solely at my emotions; and made, as far as technique goes, very badly.

Hallelujah; Crossways

The Negro film, *Hallelujah*, is emotional, but that is the director's fault and not the actors. They bring with them a plasticity and freedom from convention which is rare on the screen, and, in these days of stage talent, all too refreshing. It is not their fault that the film is not a good film, and it *is* a great pity. There is much that is lovely, much that is interesting, and also much that seems genuinely Negro in the film. But it is badly made, loosely put together in about three opposing methods, and whether black or white, talkie or silent, would not have been good, really good. Still the Negro voices and their wonderful responsiveness, make it a film not to be missed, and certainly to be enjoyed, as long as genuine sustained merit is not expected of it. It is perhaps worth remarking that it is, in theme, a tragedy.

An excellent example of sensitive film-making was given by the Film Society when it showed the Japanese *Crossways*. This was tragedy in the grand manner. Its matter fell a little short of that height, but it was a matter of simple universal significance, outworn as that phrase may be. To Western critics, its continuity was something new, something that seemed so natural and yet so revolutionary. There was no break between a person's actions and his thoughts. The film cut from one to the other; assuming that it was natural for a man's thoughts to be bound up with his actions, there is no need to separate them on the screen. And, indeed, there is not. But how often are they not forced apart, so that each loses meaning?

One Family

The long-awaited film glorifying the British Empire opened tonight at the Palace Theatre, and those who wish to see the most extraordinary picture yet made by a British firm will have to hurry, as *One Family* is only on view for one week. It includes, besides the much publicized scenes in Buckingham Palace, many excellent sequences showing the resources of the Empire and their bearing on the daily life of an ordinary family. But it also includes a story which is so flimsily whimsical that it nearly negates the very understanding use of film made by Walter Creighton, who was responsible for the famous Wembley Tattoo.

This film, made by British Instructional, is meant, in spirit, to be a

Hallelujah; Crossways

tattoo – a review of the Empire's markets. But, because of the theme seeking to unify the scenes, it is actually far nearer a revue in the stage sense. The many ladies of high position impersonating the Dominions add to this impression of a society matinée, and the small boy who is the hero of the film is surely an 'infant prodigy'. He falls asleep over a geography lesson and dreams a dream of Empire. So far so good, although the presence of a Barrie-esque policeman is a sore trial. The boy goes to Buckingham Palace and holds a council of the Dominions. This is as good a way as any other of showing us how vast and varied the lands are that form the commonwealth of nations in the British Empire, but then it appears that the sole purpose of this council is to collect ingredients for the King's Christmas pudding and this pudding is really hard to swallow.

The boy goes to South Africa, New Zealand, India, Scotland for materials, he visits the Irish Free State with Lady Lavery's wolfhound, and he tours Australia to the tones of Phyllis Neilson-Terry's carefully modulated voice. In Australia he sees the dry land being irrigated by the building of giant dams, the forming of reservoirs, and the cutting of canals. All this, as an expression of man's will, is stirring. But all the little boy wants is a bunch of grapes for the King's pudding. There is a magnificent sequence of the Canadian wheat fields. It raised a burst of applause from the audience, being finely cut and photographed. But all the hero of the film made of it was that he could get flour for the King's pudding. Acres of wheat fields are only absorbed in a plum pudding with difficulty, and the film tonight lost its balance in attempting it.

We have waited for a march-past of the British Empire on the screen, and now that we get it we find it allied to a Christmas shopping-tour conducted by a little boy with ungracious manners and a squeaky voice. It is more to be lamented because Walter Creighton's use of his serious material is excellent. The portions of the film dealing with men at work express that work with a force and honesty that has never been seen in British films on a large scale, and has rarely been equalled, even in Soviet productions. But *One Family* should have answered Soviet films on their own ground, and here it fails because it only half succeeds in making us aware of any belief. The Empire should arouse something stronger than sentiment; a director of a British film should achieve something more than an ill-kept balance between grandeur and the grandiose. It has thought behind it and great technical skill, and does something new, but it is all mixed up with something stuffy and trivial – snobbishness.

Dante's Inferno

The band of the Irish Guards introduced the film before a background representing Buckingham Palace, and proved, as the Aldershot Tattoo proves, that there are no actors better than the soldiers of the British Army.

Dante's Inferno

Twelve years ago companies were vying with each other in the production of costly spectacles. Sound, which restricted movement, momentarily arrested these extravagances. But as sound was mastered, spectacle returned. It has received added impetus from colour, which can most strikingly be displayed on lavish scenes and huge crowds, and next month we are therefore promised a film which is 'guaranteed to be the most outstanding example of screen art ever filmed'. Meanwhile, we can this week see at the Capitol a picture described as 'the greatest spectacle ever attempted in screen history'. It is called *Dante's Inferno* and that is the name of a side-show at a fun-fair.

Advantage is, however, taken of the associations of the title, and so we see 'for the first time on the talking screen the mythical journey of Dante through the inferno'. We are told that that 'is not the principal burden of the story'. That is true, and burden is indeed the right word. The inferno (of the side-show) grows until it dominates the whole fun-fair. Then, under the weight of its owner's wickedness, it collapses. The canvas caverns crack, plaster cliffs fall on the crowds and innocent sightseers fall headlong into lakes of manufactured brimstone.

This catastrophe gives rise to a vision of the other Dante's inferno. Hundreds of the damned are seen moaning, among more plaster mountains. They look like a crowd of nudists trapped in Iceland by a storm, and they all appear to be actors, for they have good eurhythmic training and their chanting would do credit to a choir. When the vision fades, they put on modern clothes and become passengers on S.S. *Paradise*. But they soon make an inferno of this, for it is a 'floating gambling-palace', run by the wicked side-show owner. He is trying to recoup his losses over the fun-fair. But the ship catches fire. The time seems ripe for another vision of Hell. The owner's little son is, however, on board. So the owner atones for his misdeeds by safely beaching the burning ship. He then staggers ashore, where he is met by a forgiving wife. And we depart gratefully, having seen papier mâché photographed in more ways than we had thought possible.

Das Maedchen Johanna

There is a different spirit about this German film. The answer, or query, is how many sides can a square have without being a pentagon. Joan, as presented in this film, may have been a saint, may have been inspired. The picture does not categorically deny it. But the Dauphin takes no risks and uses her as a political puppet. This German-French Dauphin is far ahead of his time. His counsellors are self-seeking, almost Ugly Sisters, which of course explains much in modern Germany's in-look and makes Joan a Prince Charming. So far, much better. Neither the nobles nor common people will listen to Charles, who (in furs) seeks only the good of his country. But both will listen to Joan, who comes, wide-eyed and post-Bergner, to worship her earthly prince. Charles therefore sees that he can use her as a mouth-piece by playing upon his subjects' superstition. Through Joan he defeats the English. Through her, he is crowned at Reims. And through her death, which he does nothing to prevent, he is able to establish her as a saint in the opinion of the people who had come to see her, living, as a witch.

However much one may disagree with this materialist interpreta-

Das Maedchen Johanna

tion, it is by no means entirely unpleasant to have one's idea of (what is the right) Joan freed from romanticism, pseudo-simplicity and poetizing anent breezes on the Loire. Joan here is a baffled, by no means 'bright', girl, doing her best for her country without the least idea how that will be used. She is thus the perfect patriot and Angela Salloker, by seeming perpetually surprised that the title-role is not the chief part, plays her well. Gustav Grundgens is a taut, cerebral and perfectly of the period Charles VII. The whole film is, indeed, of the period; with a good feeling for armour and none of that *parvenu* lighting which Korda would have given to the Middle Ages. There is much implication that the Dauphin is a leader in advance of his time. But it may be suspected that there is now less stringency, or perhaps a little more evasion, in the German studios. How else would the final message of the film be that Joan, the girl of the people, who is hailed and followed by the people, is nothing but a figure-head for folk not of the people?

The Passing of the Third Floor Back

It belongs, of course, to Charley's Aunt. She should have come skipping in, a musical Magdalen, and that might have made Veidt less backward, since he'd have liked to have been her, too. Or at least, in the time to which this picture belongs. Nevertheless, I think it was unfairly treated. It fails in aims, of which it is not cognizant. But it sets out to do something more definite and difficult than, say, that hormonized hors-d'œuvre, *The Thirty Nine Steps*, or the fantastically unpsychic *Clairvoyant*. A morality play, of an era which made both vice and virtue a limelit whimsy, it at least has the courage of its inhibitions. The chief interest being Veidt, it is a pity that his make-up is Tussaudian and his hair brushed to resemble a wig. But, as usual, it is evident he enjoys himself thoroughly, playing Santa Claus to us for whom the first rule must be that we don't believe in Christmas. Indeed, the chief thrill of the film is, again as usual, whether he'll drink the blood of those he seems to lay beatific hands on. But that, I speak metaphorically, is Santa Claus all over. It is to be regretted that Gaumont have de-galvanized him so much, but he remains, as the cameraman tries to make us believe he's become, physically striking and he speaks the English language more insinuatingly than ever before. Beatrix Lehmann in a fool-proof part has been overpraised, by way of readjusting the fact that in any other country she would by now be a star.

Housing Problems

Following *The March of Time* method, this film matters *via* its material. At first it seems the old stuff – shots of shored-up slums, cat's-eye view of roofs, commentary intellectually and emotionally detached whilst dramatically insistent. By 'old stuff' I imply no lack of sympathy with 'problems'. Simply after a time, in films as in poetry, effects pall. Coal, steel, automobiles, unless strongly handled, are all one. There's usually the same opening – measured tread going to work; whirr of machinery which, if understood, is rarely expressed or explained; emotive fragment on over-exposed sky-line, then a few feet of blasting siren, with more measured tread. Home next . . . washing on line . . . contrast of pants with pear-blossom and factory chimney with boss's cigar. That's called industrial psychology.

But *Housing Problems* is different. Because after we've been looking at the slums – leaking roofs, cracked and bulging walls – the slum-sufferers speak. 'I've been living 'ere for twenty-four years and I'm fed up. Upstairs is coming downstairs and downstairs is sinking. . . .

The Passing of the Third Floor Back

We 'aven't a cupboard in the 'ouse and we can't leave food on the table because of the rats.' A working man, paying ten shillings a week for two rooms, tells of the difficulties of his wife's housekeeping; one lady (and I mean it) explains that 'it takes the 'ole day to keep the dust out of our mouths, let alone lay it'. Another remarks upon bugs: you can't get rid of them because they're in the walls; but you get blamed if the kids go to school with them. Rats are discussed, racily. Briefly, the worst evils appear to be shortage of water, lack of cupboards, rats and bugs, in that order. The victims are living under conditions which it is startling to remember exist in the capital of a large empire. They may be exceptional, but every exception's a blemish.

The film also shows families in the new blocks of flats. Their gratitude is as poignant as the previous complaints. All the houses shown were picked at random. The speakers provided their own material and were not rehearsed. Lighting was run off car-batteries. The makers of *Housing Problems* are, in short, to be congratulated, not so much for the film, which as film could be better, but for their virility in making it.

Koenigsmark

Koenigsmark

This, on the other hand, is a consistently feminine film. The second of the two Elissian Landi-scapes to grace our screens within a week, it has a villain who snarls, 'There are some things stronger than a woman's caprice', and a heroine who delights us with 'Not good-bye but au revoir'. The events of August 1914 are described in these terms, 'War's been declared' – 'Reallah?' – 'Yahss.' And then the heroine appears as colonel-in-chief of whatever regiment she is colonel-in-chief of, and we realize that had Jeanette MacDonald played, as she should have, the title role, this story of love, life and loyalty in the grand-duchy of Lautenburg would have been just as amusing and far more convincing. The sets, it should be mentioned, are of that elaborate French kind which look as if the cameraman had photographed the property room while the art-director was having his lunch. They represent ducal libraries, lounges, boudoirs, armouries, and ballrooms as long but also as narrow as corridors. One of the nicest things that happens in the film is the fire which overtakes them.

Don Herold

Born Bloomfield, Indiana, 1889. A.B., Indiana University. Joined staff of *Life* in 1916, and later worked for *Scribner's, The Commentator,* and *Judge.* Author of *So Human, Bigger and Better, There Ought to be a Law, Companionate Goldfish, Strange Bedfellows, Doing Europe and Vice Versa.*

Mark of the Vampire: Carol Borland, Elizabeth Allan

2. Don Herold

Judge Priest

I regard Will Rogers and Kin Hubbard as the two best all-American humorists of my time. Kin was perhaps better than Will because he had sense enough not to overproduce. He realized that no humorist should write more than two paragraphs a day, and that even then he would produce some chaff. (The fact is, no real humorist should write *any* paragraphs a day.) And Kin was under no obligations to any string of polo ponies; when I knew him his stable consisted of a ten-year-old Franklin.

Will Rogers has enough ripe, round, sound wisdom to make the human race ashamed of itself (which is perhaps a humorist's prime function), and I reverence him. I say this, thoroughly conscious of his large output of drivel, and deeply sickened by his back-slapping, his mighty-fine-fellowing, his terrible Sunday newspaper articles, his exaggerated hemming and hawing and ain't-ing, his systematic boosting of aviation . . . and most of his movies.

This is all in place here, because it leads up to Will in his latest picture, *Judge Priest*. Most of Will's pictures have been in the department of his overproduction, but I believe *Judge Priest* is worthy of him at his best. *Judge Priest* drags groaningly at times and takes a good half-hour to get wound up, but it has tastes and flavours that make it well worth while.

The Affairs of Cellini

A great lady-killer on stage or screen always seems a little ridiculous to me. The chief attribute of such of these gents as I have known in real life has been their indiscrimination. They could quote impressive statistics, but you ought to see some of their women. But even the weakness of being a story about another great lady-killer doesn't keep *The Affairs of Cellini* from being one of the most rollicking films I've ever seen.

Fredric March is a handsome Cellini and he does a few Tarzan stunts in the Douglas Fairbanks manner, but he impressed me as having little of the inner gaiety I should imagine Cellini to have, or which he would have to have, if I were a duchess, to win my nightkey. Constance Bennett is a stately, nose-uppy duchess who is seeking a little sideplay after duchess hours. But it is Frank (Angostura) Morgan who gallops off with the honours in the film. As that darling old dote, the shilly-shallying Allessandro, Duke of Florence, weak, hen-pecked, and out for a little fun of his own, *he* is the picture.

I am a Thief

I wish they would put identifying sweaters on the villains and heroes in some of these crook plays. In *I am a Thief*, one of the less important pictures which I saw this past month, there were about eleven of each, and I didn't know, for the life of me, for which side to cheer. Ricardo Cortez seemed to be the captain of the baddies who were after the Karenina diamonds, and you had no idea at all which side Mary Astor was on; she seemed to be a sort of water boy who was carrying water on both shoulders. To complicate matters, they put in a dud duplicate set of diamonds, which would be about like playing the Army-Navy game with two footballs. The picture itself (most of the action of which takes place on the Paris–Stamboul Express) is far from dull if you don't mind not knowing which is your team, but I really am not much interested in commenting on the picture one way or the other; the point I want to make is that I think that, in a lot of these complicated mystery pictures, the players should wear different coloured jerseys, so you can tell where to place your sympathy – especially if you have to come in on the second or third quarter of play.

Fay Wray and Fredric March in *The Affairs of Cellini; I am a Thief*

Gary Cooper and Franchot Tone in *The Lives of a Bengal Lancer;* Eddie Cantor in *Kid Millions*

The Lives of a Bengal Lancer
The Lives of a Bengal Lancer is one (and an outstanding one) of those masculine desert pictures of the *Beau Geste* school which come along, fortunately, every few years and leave sand in your teeth for a long time afterwards. There is no fiction with more kick in it than that of brave men on desert outpost duty, contending with slimy Arab meanies, who make all other menaces seem pansy in comparison. (When you're dealing with those babies, bullets come zinging at you from *nowhere.*) *The Lives of a Bengal Lancer* is more fun than having your own sand pile.

The heroes, Gary Cooper and Franchot Tone, do idiotic things in order to bring excitement down on the audience . . . such as trying to rescue Richard Cromwell from the clutches of Mohammed Khan, a job that really calls for about 5,000 men. But if everybody lived as sensibly and cautiously as I do, with my life insurance and umbrellas and overshoes and gargles, there just wouldn't be any movies.

I Give my Love
There is a good deal of grasping of small toys (bunnies and tin soldiers, mostly) in *I Give my Love*. It is one of those don't you know me I am your mother panoramas, with an over the hill to the gutter graph. Paul Lukas wastes on it one of his fine sincere performances. Wynne Gibson plays the part of a wife and mother who is a glutton for sacrifice, who goes to prison for ten years for crocking a worthless husband with a flower-pot, who disappears in order not to interfere with her son's happiness, and who, some twenty years later, now a scraggly old gin-hound, poses for this same son for his great painting, 'Defeat'. Eric Linden is excellent as the son. Everything in this picture is all right except the picture.

Kid Millions
Through *Kid Millions*, Eddie Cantor strains, ogles and grimaces, against a background of the most beautiful chorus in pictures. It seems a little absurd that anybody should achieve distinction for picking pretty girls, but Mr Ziegfeld did and Samuel Goldwyn is rapidly doing so; anybody ought to be able to do it; all you have to do is pick pretty girls.

That's about all I can say for *Kid Millions*. The mounting is luxurious, but it has Eddie Cantor, who is just a bundle of annoying self-assurance as far as I am concerned. Nobody with any humour in him would be so hell-bent for comic effects. Yet millions 'love' Eddie,

Ruggles of Red Gap: Charlie Ruggles, Charles Laughton

perhaps because he uses a sledge-hammer with which to make his humorous touches. I may like him in his old age when he wears down. Example of Cantor comedy: 'Are you alone, Eddie?' 'No.' 'No?' 'Well, *you're* here.' It is of such stuff that million-dollar pictures and billion-dollar radio programmes are made.

3,000,000 Little Pixies
Maybe it would have been better, after all, if Walt Disney hadn't made *Three Little Pigs.* Those three little pigs have brought down on us three million baby-talk coloured cartoon simp-phonies, full of singing birdsies, dancing elvesies, and good fairywairies and bad ogrewogres . . . all oozing treacle and dripping gloom.

Three Little Pigs was, of course, as fortunate a bit of happiness as ever hit the screen, but it certainly led its heavy-handed imitators into difficult ground. You can't shake whimsy off of trees.

Most of these gaudy shorts start off with a moan by the Sickly Sisters about a poor little elf, hungry and cold in the snow, or about poor little pants-maker and his wife or somebody else about to go to the poor little poor-house; sadness seems to be a prime ingredient of these simple-awfulies.

The worst to date was reached recently in the one about a poor little birdie who was learning to fly and who was shot dead by a little boy with a rifle. Half the picture was devoted to the little birdie's funeral. (And why is it that the human characters in these things all have to look like congenital idiots?)

This entire trend is the more regrettable because the cartoon movies have such great inherent entertainment possibilities. Mickey Mouse is perhaps the one highest achievement of the cinema to date. The ingenuity of some of the other cartoon series is amazing. Perhaps the second best of them all is Popeye, whose exaggerated virility is a tremendous and welcome relief from the pansy-wansy sissy symphonies that Hollywood is giving us.

The whole field of movie shorts is open to vast improvement. That's why there is such interest in *The March of Time*. While there are a few good short series like Grantland Rice's *Sportlight*, we are still tortured by a lot of two-day productions, usually of the tabloid musical comedy stuff, built around some orchestra leader or some vaudeville team out of a job. And it seems to me even the newsreels have gone blah lately, trying to doll themselves up with the noise of a lot of name announcers.

Ruggles of Red Gap

I went back to see *Ruggles of Red Gap* again, to see whether the rest of the world or I was wrong about it, and I stick by me. I still rate it red. I rub it in that *Ruggles* was a medicine show. I saw it in Bloomfield, Indiana, thirty years ago, and I have seen it a hundred times since, under various names.

I might have rated it yellow if everybody else around me hadn't been singing its praises. When all the world around you is saying green, and your still small voice says red, give the damn thing red, my boy, and you're a man, says Kipling. And even if they had hired Walter Hampden to take the pratt falls allotted to Charles Laughton, I would still call it red.

Of course, *Ruggles of Red Gap* may have been something I ate.

Becky Sharp

Colour is here!

So what?

The great hullabalooed Whitney million-dollar *Becky Sharp*, with the new Technicolor three-component colour process, is here, and I am not the least bit excited. I don't believe it will revolutionize motion pictures one iota of a revolution.

At least, not until they learn how to keep all the actors from looking like roast turkeys.

There is no sex appeal in a gal who looks as if she were in the last stages of scarlatina.

In the first place, we don't see colour in real life to any such extent as they give it to us in this picture. Things are coloured in the world in which we live, but rather dully and greyly coloured – whereas in *Becky Sharp* they are shriekingly brilliant. The colours are the colours of souvenir postcards (which are certainly zero as an art form) – vivid, livid, disturbing and distracting. You see colours when you should be having emotions. If Technicolor can give us colour without giving us colour, then they'll have something.

Colour is just one more thing to get the producers' minds off their real job. This is proved definitely in *Becky Sharp*, which is, despite the valiant efforts of attractive Miriam Hopkins, a dull, boresome picture, which dullness and boresomeness are only intensified by the gaudy splendour of the colour film. Some shots in which the colour is subdued or simplified are magnificent, but it remains a question as to whether or not colour can be kept in its place in the creation of a full-length film.

Experimentally, *Becky Sharp* may have great significance, but *per se* it is just a chromo.

Torture-Pleasure

Nature must have placed within each of us a certain definite appetite for the horrible, otherwise there wouldn't be tabloid newspapers, and there wouldn't be such crowds around sick horses, and there wouldn't be so many terror movies.

I can't quite figure why we should pay real money at a box-office to have somebody scare us half out of skins and wits or to put us on the verge of a nervous breakdown. Goodness sakes alive, I don't have to hire anybody to drag me to the verge of a nervous breakdown; I *live* there; but I suppose some people live miles back from one all the time and have an actual hunger for the jitters.

An immense number of scream and screech pictures seem to have been batting around, this past month, and I guess I had better hand in a theme about them. I hope I get an 'A'.

Personally, I would never (if I weren't a hired movie sitter) (this

Becky Sharp: Miriam Hopkins

Warner Oland and Henry Hull in *Werewolf of London; Go Into Your Dance*

work is not at all unlike sitting as a decoy in a Coney Island bus at so much per hour) place two bits on a box-office window-sill to see one of these chillers. Yet millions of my fellow men pay dough to get in to see these spoovies. Lon Chaney was always surefire at the box-office, and Bela Lugosi and Boris Karloff are Clark Gable to a lot of people. (Clark Gable is usually Boris Karloff to me.) My own idea of fun is to see Fred Astaire or Charles Butterworth or W.C. Fields or even Stan Laurel, but maybe I'm just a scaredy-cat.

I suppose that the satisfaction lots of people get in watching hair-raising movies is in seeing something going on in the world that is worse than their home life.

But when, as in *Mark of the Vampire*, the visor on the suit of armour in the old castle moves up and down, and the players cringe with fright and the audience shrieks with apprehension, and finally a house cat emerges from the headpiece, I feel as if I had been sold out. I guess you just have to join in on these parties, and let go. In short, you have to take part. And it is my theory that, such being the case, the picture should pay you for coming and helping, instead of asking an admission fee. This might, incidentally, be another good way for the government to throw money away; let them establish a Horror Movie Supernumerary Fund, and pay everybody $5 for going to each shrieker.

The best of the current curdlers is *Werewolf of London*. The worst of them are *Mark of the Vampire*, *The Florentine Dagger* and *Bride of Frankenstein*, on all of which I have exhausted myself in the two to five lines allotted to me in *Life*'s great humanitarian 'Stop and Go' department. With a little more abandon, I could have had authentic nervous indigestion at *Werewolf of London*.

Go Into Your Dance (Casino de Paree)

In *Go Into Your Dance*, they don't take time to change scenery; they just have different scenery. They don't take time to change costumes; they just have different costumes. They start out with you in a supposedly realistic story in a night club, and they cover several city blocks with the camera and you are still in the night club. This is a licence taken by producers of big musicals, which licence I am about ready to say should be revoked. I don't know how they will have big musicals without this licence, but I wish they would think it over. Maybe we won't have any more big musicals. Oh, well.

Al Jolson, like so many members of his race and several other races, has unbelievable vitality rather than any singing or dancing ability, but his vitality eventually interests me to some extent. It is all no doubt a business with Al; if he were manufacturing pants he would be at it just as hard. Ruby Keeler is a sweet, motherly girl, with big eyes and nice knees, rather than with much singing or dancing ability, but she, too, eventually gets me. *Go Into Your Dance* is a big, lavish musical, with more of a plot than most musicals, and it is noteworthy that one of the most effective scenes in it is one in which Ruby just rolls back a rug and dances while Al plays the piano, at a total scenic cost of probably $145.

The Scoundrel

The Scoundrel is about one of those bad men who go through life tossing off women and epigrams. But the bad man gets his, this time. He drowns, or semi-drowns, or something, in an airplane crash, and comes back and finds that he is unmourned, which hurts him terribly. It starts out Oscar Wildey and ends up Eugene O'Neill screwy, with Noel Coward talking to himself over his shoulder. The firm of Hecht and MacArthur produced it.

Noel Coward is a busy and talented young man, but when it comes to acting I believe he belongs in the will-power class. His notion of acting is to hold his body rigid and bite out cutting remarks.

Sample dialogue:

Cora (on the floor, crying): 'You don't love me any more?'

Anthony (Mr Coward, with his hat on): 'That is an ungallant question that women always want answered gallantly.'

This would have impressed me greatly about 1910.

The *New York Times* said: 'The most dazzling writing this column has ever heard on the screen.'

Next Time We Love

Here is Universal, in *Next Time We Love*, trying to turn James Stewart into a Fred MacMurray. They give him an old hat and a messy bedroom and they dress him like a lovable, uncouth tramp – but they don't get MacMurray. The way to get MacMurray is to get MacMurray.

Pictures must be wonderful . . . if you see only three a month.

Things to Come

The finest human soul I've ever known was our coloured maid, Ada Tate, who had fifteen children. When (and if) mankind reaches the millennium, we shall all be Ada Tates (with no Mussolinis to steal our

Anna Demetrio and James Stewart in *Next Time We Love;* Margaretta Scott in *Things to Come*

farms and undershirts), and I don't think it will make much difference whether we have streamlined, air-conditioned lifts or all have to walk six flights up. (It wouldn't make much difference to Ada.) And in that perfect world, there'll be grass to walk on with bare feet, and plenty of time to go fishing on the banks of Richland Creek, back in Greene County, Indiana.

In *Things to Come*, Mr H. G. (Buck) Wells chooses practically to ignore any possible evolution of the human soul and prognosticates almost entirely in terms of so-called technical progress. He envisions a world full of gargantuan, sterile gadgets, a sort of M. I. T. field day. Considering the trouble we have with the mechanical ice-box and vacuum cleaner at our house, it will be a hell of a world – one in which we will spend most of our time phoning for the repair man.

Nevertheless, *Things to Come* (with the emphasis apparently on *things*) is a picture well worth seeing, because of its marvellous trick photography of giant mechanical whatsits. It is an amazingly ingenious technical accomplishment, even if it does hold out small hope for our race. The existence pictured is as juiceless as a squeezed grapefruit, utterly devoid of frolic and warmth. About the only attractive features I see in it are absence from colds and indigestion. I could go for a world in which it is unnecessary to wear overshoes, carry handkerchiefs or resort to bicarbonate of soda.

I am but slightly intrigued by the thought of a world mechanically perfect. We have more machines right now than we know how to manage. I, personally, prefer escape from subways rather than sterilized subways; I yearn for a surcease from radios rather than for bigger and louder radios; I want not improved transportation facilities but, rather, more chances to stay home.

And I'd like to go back to the old swimmin' hole of my boyhood and squish mud through my toes.

One Rainy Afternoon
I ran into Looey Brendel, of Bridgeport, who sells valves, and took him with me to *One Rainy Afternoon*, and he said it started out to be Lubitsch but turned out to be Hal Roach. He said a valveful. Looey and I ought to trade jobs. I kept thinking that Mary Pickford would not know about comedy, judging from some of the comedy she used to try back there in the old America's Sweetheart days.

Francis Lederer gets seat 99 instead of seat 66 in a cinema in Paris and leans over and kisses his companion who isn't his companion. On this incident, a comedy is evolved, not without a great waste of

Francis Lederer and Ida Lupino in *One Rainy Afternoon*; Mae West in *Klondike Annie*

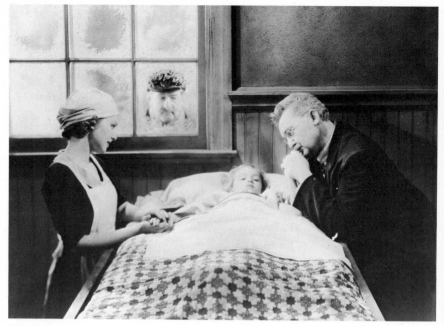

The Country Doctor: Jean Hersholt

hard work by Ida Lupino, Erik Rhodes, Roland Young and other talented and (I suspect) embarrassed people. Hugh Herbert is in it, far too silly to be funny. Mr Lederer is methodically ingratiating and Miss Lupino is excellent, but they are all off on the wrong foot – or I got out of the wrong side of the bed that day – or was born on the wrong side of the bed.

Klondike Annie

Klondike Annie is drearier than most of Mae West's films, and I don't recommend it heartily to tots of any age. Mr Hearst's papers refused advertising on this picture on the grounds, I believe, that it is immoral. I think this is a little over-tidy in Mr Hearst, at this late date. If he had refused the ads on the grounds that the film is dull, he would deserve more sympathy.

I think I would rather let my daughters see Mae West's films regularly than see Hearst newspapers regularly, and I'm sure I'd rather have them see Mae West films than *some* of the films of the more saintly stars. Mae West burlesques sex, kids it, and I prefer that as moral fare for young American junior misses to the over-serious consideration of sex suggested by Garbo, Dietrich, Joan Crawford and others. I'd rather have them take the attitude 'Throw the —— out', when disappointed in some male, than to go into the headache and heartache and 25-pound decline indulged in by some of the slimmer, slinkier queens of the silver screen. A certain amount of 'Beulah, peel me a grape' philosophy is Something That Every Young Girl Should Know.

Klondike Annie is a prisoner in some sort of gorgeous San Francisco Chinese dump and has to stab her way out. On a boat bound for Alaska to escape the law, Annie exchanges clothes and licence plates with a lady missionary who has died. Captain Victor McLaglen connives in the exchange because he has been thataway about Annie since the minute she stepped aboard. Needless to say, Annie is a wow in mission work, and so on. But the Chinese and deathbed and mission backgrounds slow Mae down and dim her glamour, although she still finds plenty of chances to bedeck herself like a circus horse.

The Country Doctor
I've had two babies, practically personally, and I don't see anything funny in childbirth and have always been sickened by barber-shop jests in regard to it. So I was given pretty deep nausea by the slapstick Keystone comedy which the manufacturers of *The Country Doctor* put into the birth of the quintuplets, even to the inclusion of cumulative wisecracks by that old slapstick comedian, Slim Summerville.

Up to that point, Jean Hersholt makes this a most endearing picture, with a soft, gentle, sympathetic impersonation of the kindly Dr Dafoe. Whoever is responsible for the vulgar comedy of the birth episode ought to be taken out behind the 20th C.-Fox barn and spanked, with sound effects.

The latter sequences include a lot of darling shots of the private life of the Dionne quins, which I could watch all night with keen delight.

There is a great deal of diphtheria and similar tragedy in the early footage of this story, a little too strong for your wee ones, in my opinion, and that's why I asterisk you not to take them, as you might naturally suppose you ought.

The Green Pastures
I imagine that God has a sense of humour and I imagine that He is delighted with *The Green Pastures*. We, down here, all get so serious about God, and even go so far as to kill other people in His name, and we are apt to forget that He is probably much more relaxed about

The Green Pastures

religion than we are. He must be, to tolerate so many different religions.

Whatever our various concepts of God, I think we will all be spiritually satisfied and tickled by *The Green Pastures*, and that includes those of us who think of God as a sort of super Owen D. Young with a lot of General Electric push buttons, and those who picture God as an old gentleman with Santa Claus whiskers, and those who think of him as an abstract vapour, and even those who maintain there is No Such Thing. Whatever one's creed or lack of creed, there is something so sincere and sweet and devout in the humour and insight of *The Green Pastures* that he is almost bound to feel elation in it. I suppose there is no need to explain that *The Green Pastures* is a fabular picturization of the story of the scriptures as seen through the eyes of religious southern negroes.

And I feel a depth in *The Green Pastures* which is belied by the fun in it. To me, for example, there is a complete bible in the line spoken by Rex Ingram as de Lawd: 'Even bein' God ain't no bed of roses.' That satisfies the evolutionist in me, and is the best explanation and

It Had to Happen: Rosalind Russell, George Raft

alibi I've ever heard for God's wars and for droughts and for poverty and for politicians and for the backache I have this morning.

Those who feared God might go Hollywood in this movie version of the fine stage production do not know their Marc Connelly. He has touched this movie with the same delicate humour and the same fine feeling he put into the stage *Pastures*, and that must have been one heck of a job among all that machinery and all those mobs on the Warner lot. I'll venture Mr Connelly ignored mountains of advice.

The motion picture, as was the stage play, is replete with delightful lines. I think my favourite bit of dialogue is that between de Lawd and a bed of daisies. 'How you little flowers makin' out?' asks de Lawd. And the daisies answer, 'We's okay, Lawd'.

It Had to Happen
Rosalind Russell will be a good actress if she will quit being a little too smugly twinkly. She is good looking enough to be attractive without turning on the juice. In her more serious moments she can't be beat. Just don't be so damned animated in your nicer moments, Rosy.

It Had to Happen (in which Miss Russell plays opposite George Raft's pick and shovel) is a good movie as long as Leo Carrillo does all the talking, but when George Raft starts to clip everybody on the chin, invariably laying them cold with one clip (even Dempsey couldn't do that so consistently), the picture finds itself out on a Raft.

Mr Raft is soon up out of the ditch and is a big shot in New York politics, clean, honest, tight-lipped and slick-haired, and telling Miss Russell that she loves him. Not very convincing.

The Bride Walks Out
The marital psychologies in *The Bride Walks Out* are about as subtle as a stuffed club, but there are good comedy lines to keep you in the theatre. Gene Raymond is making $35 a week as an engineer and Barbara Stanwyck is making $50 as a dress model. Gene makes Barbara quit work when they marry, because he has old-fashioned notions that woman's place is in the home – the sap. You've seen this a million times on the screen, but they keep on making it, and folks keep writing me asking me why I am so dyspeptic regarding the cinema. Because I have judgment, is the answer.

Gene and Barbara have a swell flat, full of good furniture, and they live well, and Barbara wears gorgeous clothes, and they buy surveying instruments, and have $50 for New Year's Eve parties, but Gene is too

Barbara Stanwyck in *The Bride Walks Out ;* Charles Laughton in *Rembrandt*

Roland Young in *The Man Who Could Work Miracles;* Annabella and Henry Fonda in *Wings of the Morning*

dumb to wonder how this can all be done on $35 a week. The answer is, Barbara is running bills all over the town. Then she sneaks to work, and when Gene learns this he packs his clothes and walks out – the sap. That's how the picture happens to be named *The Bride Walks Out*. God, how can they write them so silly?

But wait. Accompanying this inane mush, is some of the dandiest comedy in a long while – chipped in by Ned Sparks and Helen Broderick (there's a team!) and Robert Young.

I forgot to carry Mrs Herold across the threshold when we were bride and groom, and I'm afraid I haven't the strength now.

Rembrandt
Rembrandt (the life story of the great painter) has Actor Charles Laughton and Director Alexander Korda and other ingredients of sometimes noteworthy films, but it shoots its climax too, too early and then runs down like an eight-day clock. When Rembrandt paints an insulting group portrait of the Civic Guard of Amsterdam, *The Night Watch*, and then derides the town nabobs verbally, he is through. And so is Mr Korda's film. Mr Laughton, having made a great hit with his recitation of Lincoln's Gettysburg address in *Ruggles of Red Gap*, is now evidently going to go in for recitations or readings in a big way: in *Rembrandt* he stops the action, or lack of action, about three times to say pieces, like Little Willie.

This picture certainly could have been much better if it had been three-fourths rise and one-fourth fall. We should have had the climb of Rembrandt to fame, with hints of the independence which were eventually to be his undoing; then the blow-up; then a rapid tobogganing to poverty and oblivion. As it now stands, it is all toboggan and not very good toboggan.

Unblushingly, the foreword to *Rembrandt* speaks of the man as 'the greatest painter that ever lived'. I wonder about that. I doubt that that label can be hung accurately on any artist. I am something of a draughtsman myself, in a fifth-grade sort of way, and when I looked on a lot of Rembrandt paintings in Amsterdam, I was convinced that the fellow sometimes draws terribly. Many of his figures are too short, and much of his foreshortening is exaggerated and awkward. The greatest artist of all time? Where does Walt Disney come in?

The Man Who Could Work Miracles
The Man Who Could Work Miracles is a childish bit of conjecture, despite (or by virtue of) the fact that it was written by Mr H. G. Wells.

For several years, now, I've suspected that Mr Wells was in his second sophomorism, and now the conviction is clinched. Mr Wells asks, as Mr Wells would, what would happen if a man could work miracles in this world here and now, and he gives us a sort of elongated Minsky or medicine-show sketch in which a timid Englishman first pulls rabbits and, finally, epochal social reforms out of hats, and eventually decides he isn't as happy as when he was just an ordinary fellow. Well, well, Mr Wells! I do hope Roland Young, one of my favourite actors, will forgive me for my opinion of this affair, in which he takes the title role.

Wings of the Morning

One of the most interesting new people in pictures is a French girl, labelled Annabella . . . a looker and an actress of the first water. The name is a mistake; it sounds as if it belonged to a muscle dancer in a carnival tent. The girl's real name is Anne Carpentier, and I suggest that she keep that or go to Ann Carpenter. She's too good to be Annabella. She was in *Le Million,* and now she's in *Wings of the Morning.* She's fine.

Wings of the Morning is almost a new high for Technicolor, and surprise, surprise – it's British. The story is only so-so, but it has its gorgeous colour photography (far less postcardy than most of our American colour movies to date), it has Annabella, it has John McCormack stuck in rather abruptly for three songs, and it has Henry Fonda, one of the most personable, sincere, and able of our young leading men. The story spans three generations, which is always tough on a picture, and it concerns gypsies and racehorses, and the Derby. The colour on the jockeys made it possible for me to tell, for the first time, which horse was mine, in a motion-picture horse race.

John Marks

Born Sarawak, 1908, of Swiss-English parentage. Magdalene College, Cambridge. Film critic of *Granta*, 1927–8, editor, 1928–9; worked as free-lance journalist in Madrid; entered London publishing, 1930. Film critic on *New Statesman*, 1935–6. Translator; joint editor of *Night and Day*.

A Midsummer Night's Dream: James Cagney, Joe E. Brown

3. John Marks

The Crusades

Behind the curtain with the spotlit flaming cross on it, twenty-five chaps in armour knelt or blew bugles while a travesty of Peter the Hermit exhorted them to wage the third crusade. He roared that it was 'the will of God!' – but *Paramount Picture* on the screen behind him gave that the lie direct. Thus the Carlton backs up its own poster crusade and 'prepares' De Mille's boy-scout public for his latest and most lavish spectacle. Still, this is a film which has to be seen, if seeing is believing. An impressive object-lesson in the art of unprincipled and profitable waste. So epic, so *kolossal* that it has only room for two dramatic moments: Saladin's rejoinder to the assembled Christian kings, and the head-on collision of the infidel and English hosts. Apart from these salient excitements, the action creeps from one minor climax to the next without getting anywhere at all except along the tangled heart-lines of Loretta (Berengaria) Young and Richard Cœur-de-Lion. Sex and medieval welfare alternate regularly: a sentimental lull, a clamour of sound; both indescribably false. But the history is merely freak, the maudlin modern love-affair is the worse anachronism. Miss Young has always struck us as highly improbable in every film we've seen of hers since *Zoo in Budapest*. She is five feet three inches tall, weighs 105 pounds and has very healthy-looking American teeth. The mincing, starry-eyed silliness of her Berengaria is hard to describe; perhaps because she could not improve on what De Mille wanted. Henry Wilcoxon, on the other hand, gave a spirited performance as Richard Lionheart; he lent the hearty inanity of his lines a pleasing sincerity and gusto. This can't have been easy, as the dialogue was futile, its low-water mark being reached in a conversation between villains playing chess, in which every move was a check, every remark a melodramatic innuendo.

Joyless Street (Die freudlose Gasse)
Twelve years is always a long time; in the young life of the film, it's an age. The precocious art of the cinema progresses swiftly enough for Pabst's *Joyless Street*, made a dozen years ago, to have become, in 1935, a bewildering and jerky shadow of its former self. It has been largely (and mercifully) cut; which would account for the absurd jumpiness of the action. Its make-up, lighting and drama have a long-forgotten crudity, and the tempo is exactly that of an early Chaplin film; the gestures, born of a similar speechlessness, are comically the same. Subsequent technical improvements in photography explain, of course, that scuttling double-time at which its characters jump to conclusions, in and out of doors, and through tragic and emotional scenes. But its night-life – and those short skirts! – complete our sense of vertigo: how did anyone manage to languish in a knee-length sack? Greta Garbo in this, her first star-part, almost accomplishes that feat: blackeyed make-up and all, she looks very beautiful and acts with a restraint which, we now see, must have been startling at that time. Dark-haired, at seventeen she had what today, as a Hollywood star, a blonde, and a glorious gawk, she still preserves: a blessed and unique personality. *Joyless Street* has therefore only a laboratory interest; and probably, of all the quickly perishable arts, the flickering passage of a film into its own peculiar limbo of lost light and faded inspiration is the least to be regretted. We have of late had several of these séances with the ghosts of Ufa's heyday: it is instructive and pathetic to watch them follow the early Westerns and glamorous Griffiths into that antiquity from which Chaplin holds back only on one foot and the great Russians are still, but so narrowly, preserved.

Loretta Young and Henry Wilcoxon in *The Crusades*; Garbo in *The Joyless Street*

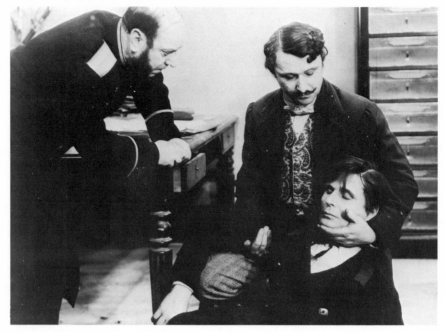

Crime et Châtiment: Pierre Blanchar

Crime et Châtiment

A great novel hardly ever makes even a passable film. Running time is too short for man's proper study in any but its most generalized or merely pointed forms; words under the studio arc-lights glitter but seldom glow – because character can be summarized on the screen, not developed. Unfortunately your big novelist needs elbow-room. . . . Fearful hackings and pommellings ensue when Hollywood's plastic surgeons get to grips with literature: *Les Misérables, Resurrection, Anna Karenina* and even *Monte Cristo* they reduced to wordy pulp. Of *David Copperfield* they made a huge and stiff but passable likeness. *Crime et Châtiment* is altogether different: a direct and masterly French translation of Dostoievsky into cinematic terms. It is long, because *Crime and Punishment* is a long book. It is successful because its director's respect for his subject goes further than a mere ring-a-ring-o'-reverence round a bronze bust in the box-office. Unity of purpose in this film is so complete that Chenal's direction, the acting of Pierre Blanchar as Raskolnikov and Harry Baur as the Magistrate, the penetrating simplicity of Marcel Aymé's dialogue, the intelligence of the 'adaptation', and Honegger's music, are all equally admirable: elements combined and concentrated on scansion. Chenal has made a fine 'literary' film. He imposes an ample tempo with his first long tracking shot and relies throughout, to the last murky fade-out, on a perfect sense of timing. The underlying beat is slow; with all the more effect he can hurry when he needs to. His roving camera masses, deploys, emphasizes the literary argument, so that movements imply emotions, silence harbours thought, and great rushes of words actually convey meanings. . . . The result is not the usual jerky working-model, nor yet an advance which other film-makers might safely follow – but a difficult and drastic achievement of television.

A Midsummer Night's Dream

It should be obvious that the screen is no place for Shakespeare. What's he to Hollywood or Hollywood to him? To cinematize poetry you have to paraphrase it – and so leave out Shakespeare or accept the shadow of an image. Of course, every film-studio is doing it now, or proposing to do it. . . . A gigantic game of noughts and crosses. Still, if you must film Shakespeare, if culture cannot be denied (and you can suddenly disregard box-office), clearly *A Midsummer Night's Dream* is of all his plays the least unlike a scenario, and the one to start on.

So, for a start, his name is writ large among the credit-titles; his lines are scattered over two and a half hours of entertainment; and you 'give him the works'. The works are every pulley, smokescreen, illusion, monkey-wrench and fairy-business that the ingenuity and 'intestinal fortitude' of Messrs Warner Brothers' technical staff can devise. So Herr Dr Reinhardt realizes his 'own dream of doing the play with no restraint on his imagination'. Absolutely none. And no doubt the groundlings at the Globe would have relished the result; but the man in the street is blasé about tricks and shy of Shakespeare. He may well be appalled by this devastating combination of the two. Reinhardt should have learned from Disney's Little Pig that the works and the play 'don't mix'.

Shakespeare's part of the film holds its own all right – because all the other ingredients keep to themselves, too; they none of them mix. The first few shots are lavish décor, just another millennium; the fairyland that follows is bigger and better Drury Lane pantomime (De Mille again, plus a dash of Christmas-card culture); the fooling of Bottom and his cronies is pure Shakespeare; the four lovers, an amateur-theatrical romp (Reinhardt?); and then a splendid staircase (Korda) brings all this 'tragicall mirth' to a blessed end. One hesitates to say, baldly, what has happened – but there it is: they've put the ache in Shakespeare.

In all this hollywood of Arden, a single pirouette of the lissom Mlle Theilade is worth two dozen anxious fairy take-offs; the least gesture of Cagney's expressive hands, twist of Joe E. Brown's surprising face, querulous gasp from Quince, or giggle of Snout's, puts all Reinhardt's slot-machine frolic to shame. Cagney makes a splendid Bottom the Weaver. So sensitive, so dramatic, and so sure in his rendering of the dual part, as man and ass, that it is well worth sitting through the whole ordeal once for the sake of his scene with Titania and the sweet fooling of his fellows (Messrs Brown, Robinson, Herbert, Harlan and McHugh). We would even be willing to face it twice, but for two unforgivable insults: the raucous Puck and that roughnecking quartet of lovers who so amply deserved him for Cupid.

It is comforting to find, however, that even these have been pardoned the 'impertinence' of their American accent by the wise majority of English critics, who seem to have accepted the likely enough theory that Cagney's voice would have rejoiced Will Shakespeare's heart and that no sounds are so purely Elizabethan as ye vowels uttered in the fastness of the Appalachians – or perhaps in the lobby of the Algonquin. Conversely, of course – though nobody says so – it hardly matters how 1594 spoke as long as, like the present Bottom, your modern actor has a 'reasonable good ear in music'. It is realized now that the American tongue has two very great simultaneous advantages over effete British-English: it preserves, unimpaired, the full savour of that Elizabethan speech which we ourselves once warbled in our palmy days and yet, alive and fluid, has the constant facility to invent quite new vivacities and vigour. Peel unctuous layers of sound off a B.B.C. announcer's voice and there, apparently, at the very centre of the artichoke, you find the modulated squeak of Miss Loretta Young; blushing somewhere interleaved, you may perhaps find decent speech. . . .

The Scoundrel
There are, of course, two ways of discovering the humorous in the familiar: either with a bang or a whisper. On the whole, American humorists tend to find it the first way; and at the same time to reverse the process, starting at absurdity and working backwards. British humorists are more conservative, assuming in their publics a greater familiarity with, and liking for, the norm of sanity and convention. Our jokes are made against a background of all good men and true.

The Scoundrel: Noel Coward

Hence, for us, the startling and highly coloured quality of American quips, which are mostly derisive. American humour at its worst degenerates into farce; ours into facetiousness. Alas, poor Coward! For these reflections, as you may have guessed, are suggested by contrasting that vigorous and sure *Passport to Fame* with a pot-pourri of faded epigrams entitled *The Scoundrel*. The authors of this piece, Messrs Hecht and MacArthur, have previously done far better: not only did they make a fine American picture in *Crime Without Passion*, but they did better by (and without) Mr Coward in his *Design for Living*. Before the camera Mr Coward acts quite well, as a publisher equally fabulous dead or alive (handling either seaweed or poems); but presumably it's not more elaborate, this drivel, because you are meant to see through it – and that's the intended joke. But see through it – to what? Curious that Mr Coward should fall so badly out of step with the box-office. He remarks: 'That's the proper place for life – in one's buttonhole.' But it's the very worst place for one's first appearance on the screen. The film was well made, but not worth making – *ter*-ribly jejune . . . like last year's buttonholes, the ones that weren't fashionable even last year.

Three Songs of Lenin

To judge by the volume of applause that greeted the close of the Film Society's eighty-first performance, *Three Songs of Lenin*, as compared with the bursts of enthusiasm punctuating the second half of the picture, about twice as many people were impressed by its cinematographic merits as by its propagandist force. Yet it was fine propaganda and not particularly good art. Still, it had the primary merit of fully achieving its purpose, and this covered a multitude of flaws. Only if one arbitrarily separated the effects from the effect, the method from the message, was it evidently a haphazard and often wearisome film. The first of three Songs, a Ballad, owed much to Shaporin's magnificent music and little to its meaning. The second, a Dirge for Lenin, though largely composed of old newsreel material, relied less on biographical interest than on a deeply religious inspiration of hero-worship to which a *bourgeois* intelligentsia could only partially respond; as to a powerful opiate of the future. The third, a Marching Song, whirled Director Vertov, his photographer comrades, Shaporin, and the whole audience into a very loud and spirited *montage* of ice-floes, parachutes, the ecstasy of production, a rose, gymnastics, and the statue of Lenin. The wistful refrain of this proletarian triumph was: 'If Lenin could see our country now. . . .' If, too, he could have seen this England at one moment fervently acclaiming him, at the next rigidly quiet for 'God Save the King', he would surely have found such dexterity – or stolidity – both puzzling and perfidious.

The Marriage of Corbal

Since Mr Korda discovered his formula for putting a certain sparkle into British films, so that our best could be likened without shame to the ordinary run of American movies, and now that we have all become convinced that British documentaries are the top, we have tended to forget how deplorably bad, on the whole, the films of this country still are. By the easy expedient of hardly ever seeing a British film and of appreciating the ones we do see as wholeheartedly as patriotism checked by conscience will allow, we contrive to suppose that British films really aren't so bad. Anyone who clings to this comforting illusion – which it has taken us some years, after all, to acquire – should carefully avoid the picture under review. It may be objected that to call this 'a typical British' film is unfair – but the profusion of its accents, the uniformity of its dullness, its ridiculous staginess, make it all too typical. Our big films, as opposed to the negligible easy-going farces produced for home consumption, usually achieve their peculiar

Three Songs of Lenin

white-elephantine proportions of incompetence by international means. Too many cooks of any one nationality – even English – could not spoil a well-meant dish so thoroughly as this story by Rafael Sabatini has been spoiled. It needed a babel of incomprehension to produce romanticism so *raté*, sex-appeal so *kitschig*, drama so boring, and dialogue so bum. Messrs Noah Beery and Hugh Sinclair struggled manfully in this welter of misdirection, and Miss Hazel Terry kept a stiff upper-class lip in the face of absurdity; but their united efforts could not alter the issue. This year was bound to give us a British film even worse than *The Tunnel*; and here it is.

Desire

Presumably the title of this film is Paramount's succinct protest against the Hollywood purity campaign – which had become rather *vieux jeu*, anyway. Film-fans don't need that inducement to see their Fräulein Dietrich and Gary Cooper; and patrons of the movie art know that, Russian cinematography aside, Lubitsch is one of the three great names that have appeared on the screen – second only to

Desire: Gary Cooper, Marlene Dietrich

Clair, and third to Chaplin. In this deft and entertaining picture his influence, as producer, is felt behind Frank Borzage's direction in every detail – which means that it's worth taking plenty of trouble to see. It means, moreover, that the haggard German beauty, who (except, perhaps, in *Song of Songs*) has deteriorated in every picture since *The Blue Angel*, and the bony American Apollo *de nos jours*, who has steadily improved since he played his first, flat cowboy parts, have here something to do and are led to make the most of it. In this romantic and witty film Dietrich at last discovers the joke of being *la femme fatale*, while Cooper adds an engaging polish to his habitual humour, charm and unobtrusive male sufficiency. His acting is just a little better than hers – perhaps because on his face the expression of irony is more readily distinguishable from that look of quizzical vacuity which we have learned to consider handsome or, in the case of a vamp, to accept as sex-appeal. But the best of *Desire* is its direction, and it is this, the tricky, smooth handling of a trite story, that will make it rank as one of the best ten films of 1936.

Bonne Chance

Every smart French film contains a shot of a white Renault tourer flashing down a long straight road lined with poplars. In this delightful first film written by, and starring, Sacha Guitry, as we watch the fleeting scenery over the bonnet of a car, his affable voice comments: 'C'est comme au cinéma!' – and one happy moment finds us at the roadside when Claude and Marie (Sacha and Mlle Jeanne Delubac) rush towards us and away into the distance, tossing a snatch of conversation to the wind as they go by. The sound-track and the film are here expertly mated, for we have learned, in one sunny and economical flash, that they are enjoying a gay, platonic holiday together. This information is essential to the plot, and it has been both naturally and prettily conveyed. A careful, cloying emphasis on chastity has been avoided and we are spared the glaring goodness of Hollywood's clean-limbed Erics and their little-by-little seductions. It is only fair to add, of course, that the mature M. Guitry could hardly risk taking that line. He has a lively sense of the ridiculous. But the point is that he also has a lively sense of film. *Bonne Chance* has its duller patches, but it makes up for them by achieving *finesse* in place of slickness – as we had half expected – thanks to Guitry's virtuosity as an actor, his flair for sophisticated clowning; and, by means of neat direction, a grasp of modern film method which was completely unexpected. His short story of a win in the lottery, which gives Claude a holiday with Marie,

The Gay Desperado: Nino Martini, Ida Lupino

and of the holiday which wins him Marie's love, is richly romantic; but it isn't literary, it isn't sickly, it isn't silly, and it is very far from being just an actor-director's plaything and an amateurish film.

The Gay Desperado
The gifted Mr Rouben Mamoulian has made this film for Miss Pickford and Mr Lasky with the obvious intention of striking a gay, Lubitsch note, and keeping it gay. Perhaps because that intention is obvious his film succeeds at any rate in being jolly. And jollity is enough in this instance (the acting throughout being better than the script), because musical films that are truly witty as well as musical may be looked upon as refinements that to some extent defeat their own box-office ends: Lubitsch and Clair aren't quite as popular as Cantor and Moore. Still, all four of them are good, and we can place this Mamoulian picture right up at the top of the nearly first class in its melodious-movie kind. Mexican music would give any such picture a good start; here the singing of Nino Martini is pleasing and plentiful,

and the guitar-playing of the Trovadores Chinacos could only be bettered if there were more of it. We should, I am sure, have had more of them and slightly less of the charming, operatic, italianate hero, if Mamoulian had had things entirely his own way; in fact the film would probably then not have been just a pretty good joke, but a fine and exciting comment on Mexico – better, almost certainly, than what was left of Eisenstein's sombre tract when they'd finished hacking away at it, and therefore far better than the admirable *Viva Villa!* which, we were told, used up a few left-over shots from the Russian director's *Que viva Méjico!* But that, of course, is pure guesswork – based, as it happens, on moonlight: Mexican moonlight haunting whitewashed walls, a church, a road, cactus and clouds; and also on another Eastern European's superb and superbly comic portrait of the Mexican Indian. Mischa Auer, whom we last saw in *My Man Godfrey*, after helping to save *One Rainy Afternoon*, has stepped straight out of the film I am imagining into this funny film about Mexican bandits which Hollywood has made. His part, for him, is an easy one; but I can't think who else could have played it, and he certainly succeeded in being more *americano* (which doesn't mean *yanqui*) than any other *gringo* or greaser in the picture. Leo Carrillo was content to give the joke of the film – Mexican outlaws innocently aping the slang and tactics of U.S. gangsters – a good run for our money; he did it gracefully and well. Harold Huber, as his aide-de-camp, overacted slightly; and Ida Lupino was miscast. She usually is.

Meyer Levin

Born Chicago, 1905. Ph.B., University of Chicago, 1924. Reporter on *Chicago Daily News* while at the university, and for several years following. Studied with Fernand Léger in Paris; became interested in marionettes and conducted experimental marionette theatres in Chicago, New York and Paris. In 1930 attempted film with marionettes, but uncompleted. Film critic for *Esquire* from 1933. Subsequently war correspondent. Prolific novelist: *Reporter, Yehuda, The Golden Mountain, Frankie and Johnny, The New Bridge, The Old Bunch, Citizens, My Father's House, In Search, Compulsion, Eva, The Fanatic, The Stronghold.*

Charge of the Light Brigade: Errol Flynn

4. Meyer Levin

The Wedding Night

While we're on the subject of prizes, note that King Vidor's back-to-the-soil film, *Our Daily Bread*, won some sort of gold medal from the League of Nations. Doubtless the moral sincerity of the film was worth recognition. But a recent article by King Vidor, in the *New York Times*, explains a great deal of the crudity of *Our Daily Bread* and of his new picture, *The Wedding Night*. I think it shows that Vidor is an intelligent person trying to make himself simple, and succeeding only in being old-fashioned. The strongest hint I have seen as to Vidor's sensitivity comes not from his recent pictures but from a short story which appears in this magazine. It is greater proof of his powers of psychological observation, of his ability to create strong dramatic effects through the use of secondary detail, than is *Our Daily Bread*, or *The Wedding Night*. The obvious comeback is that I am literary-minded and can get more out of a story than out of a picture. But my rebuttal is in Vidor's own statement: 'Artistry does not consist of making a film that only a limited group of people can understand. Rather, we must seek a great common denominator, a means of telling a story that is understandable

The Wedding Night: Anna Sten, Ralph Bellamy

to all classes of audiences – the poor, rich, old, young, European and American. One must hold to human emotions to achieve this goal, because emotions are universal and can be understood by every human being. . . . Emotions can be portrayed by a gesture, a facial expression, a step or two, a lifted eyebrow. The complexity of sophisticated people makes such simple expressions impossible. To explain their situations, one must go into long dialogue, movement must stop, each point of the story must be told by the characters in detail. Speed, movement, and reality vanish. In the picture I have just completed, *The Wedding Night,* I have followed the same formula. . . .'

And there is one scene in that entire picture which disproves his theory. When he is dealing with the sophisticated author-character and his super-sophisticated wife. Bags are packed, she is on the point of leaving. Three times she orders the bags out of the car, and back into the car, as she reasons about her duty to him or to herself. The complete story of their married life is told in that very short scene, told by amusing movement and short dialogue, and told in a way that even a backwoodsman will understand. Vidor's scenes concocted for the heightening of emotion are merely the barren melodrama of the Biograph days. Two men fight on the stairs over a woman, dressed in bridal clothes. Accidentally, she is toppled down the stairs.

But both *Our Daily Bread* and *The Wedding Night* show that Vidor, in subject matter, is trying really to get at the American people. The plain people. He is hampered because his attitude is one of superiority. He is building his films down to them. He thinks they can't understand ideas, that ideas have to be symbolized for them by apparitions on the road and such nonsense. But he does stumble on some solid truths. His portrayal of the Polish village customs as they are transplanted to Connecticut and the settlements of tobacco growers is excellent, but alas scant. There are only two extensive scenes in the Polish farmhouse – the breakfast, and the wedding. The breakfast is by far the best; the wedding is like a standard bit of travelogue. The rest of the picture is a straight 'he and she'. But there is vast material there, in the amalgamation of Polish, Italian, Jewish, Russian folk ways with American folk ways. In the home life of first and second generation immigrant families, it has been untouched. I wish that the next person to touch it would do it simply, without the effort at being earthy. And that he would get a better dialogue writer. Poles do not talk like Indians. *The Wedding Night* is full of horrible gruntings: 'You no go', 'She not stay', etc. That may convey a foreign dialect, but it's not Polish.

Annapolis Farewell

One way to brush it off would be to treat the matter with superiority, sarcasm, the light touch, poof! and bye-bye.

Or to say nothing. Beneath contempt.

Why make myself unpopular? Why court the animosity of a powerful studio like Paramount? And who knows, maybe the G-men are thumbing through the magazines and putting little red dots in front of the names of the little lily-livered Levins who write scurrilous reviews about patriotic pictures.

Why not write about the great, important movies that are appearing this fall, instead of about a silly little programmer like *Annapolis Farewell*, which merely represents the efforts of the producers to milk a few bucks out of the patriots?

The great pictures will be reviewed in due time; the silly little programmer may have a deeper effect on our flesh and brains than all the beauties of Shakespeare and all the platitudes of Tolstoi. For ninety minutes as I sat watching that picture, wave upon wave of nausea went through me; the reaction was actually physical. Now, a screening room is a fairly emotionless place; motion-picture distributors, a few critics, a few advertising men sit glumly watching the film. Reactions are rare.

Occasionally someone takes pleasure in spotting and naming a bit player. At the close of the picture, a few remarks will be exchanged as to the sales possibilities of the item. But before *Annapolis Farewell* had been running half an hour, the exhibitor at my left squirmed and grunted, 'Spreading it on pretty thick, huh?' And before the picture was completely run, one could feel an uneasiness in the room; something like the embarrassment that pervades a party where everybody knows that, in the bathroom, someone has made a mess.

Here is the story of *Annapolis Farewell*: Tom Brown and Richard Cromwell are room-mates in the naval academy. Tom is a hard boy who intends to steal his education from the government, and drop the navy as soon as he gets out of school. He tries to prevail upon his brother, who is an upper-classman and a star in the football team (incidentally he looks as much like a football star as Shirley Temple) to give up the navy and cash in by going professional in football. Now, in the town of Annapolis is a retired Commodore, admittedly the town bore, always butting his way into school affairs, bothering the academy heads, waylaying the boys to tell them about his manœuvres at Manila. He spends the rest of his time making a model of the ship he once commanded, and pacing on the little square of flooring, made from the deckboards of the old ship, which he has inserted into the floor of his room. As a portrait of the futility of a military career, the wastefulness of such a life, and the helplessness and stupidity of the characters who can find nothing to do with themselves after having been dismissed from that type of service, this part of the film is thoroughly convincing. The Commodore is a bore that is a bore.

Comes commencement day. The football hero is graduating. For the exercises, some boats are towed into port, among them the Commodore recognizes his old ship of command. Then he learns that it is to be used as a target in the commencement manœuvres. All day he pads from one office to another, getting the royal runaround, trying to save his ship from this ignominious end. He even tries to see the President. All night he paces the deck-flooring in his room. Finally he makes the great decision.

You guessed it.

So when the exercises are on, and the guns go boom boom (how many thousand bucks a shot is that, boys?) the Commodore stands on

Gentlemen of the Navy

the old deck, seeing the phantoms of his officers pass before him, issuing his commands as at Manila, and mean-boy Tom Brown finally makes the hit that sinks the old tub and her old Commodore.

And then? Bugles, Flags. More bugles. Bands. Deep sorrowing voices. Flag-draped casket. And speeches, speeches. What a hero! Greater than Dewey! Greater than Jones! Such is loyalty, such is devotion, such was the great deed of this old man, who knew no greater glory than to go down with his ship, amen!

And the mean boy wipes a tear from his eye, and snaps to attention beside his good-boy room-mate, and their hands clasp, and a patriot is born!

Sure, dismiss it with sarcasm. Pure drivel.

But remember *Flirtation Walk*? Remember *West Point of the Air*? Remember *Devil Dogs of the Air*? Remember the thousand and one drill-shots of Annapolis you have seen in the newsreels, until you think that camera and sound are in constant attendance on that parade ground?

And do you know that our own sweet and lovable Dickie Powell is right now completing another one of those drivelling drooling candy wrappers with an Annapolis background, to be called *Shipmates Forever*?

And were you at the movies that week when the newsreel consisted of (*a*) naval manœuvres in the Pacific for the benefit of schoolchildren, (*b*) a new army bomber, (*c*) a beauty pageant, and that was all? Except for the *March of Time* on the same programme which showed you how the army was built? And the new *March of Time* tells you how disciplined and military-smart are the 600,000 boys of the C.C.C.

And do you know what picture won the grand prize, the gold medal of gold medals, in Italy's recent world-competition for films? None other than that sweet, innocent little picture about children playing war, called *No Greater Glory*.

Yes sir, boys! The army is holding full peace-time manœuvres, limbering up, showing it has the stuff.

But it's not only the guns that are being oiled. The division of propaganda is taking some first-class exercises, proving it is ready to shoot right into war-time gear. There have been no pictures like *Annapolis Farewell* since 1918. What can be the reason for making such a picture?

Most of the footage is devoted to showing how gay, clean, zippy, is life for the student at the naval academy. Remember that sweet scene where the boys all march into the dining-room, mark time behind their chairs, and slam down on to their seats at a barked command, and begin eating at a barked command? I have seen this sequence in several other pictures, only those pictures were located in gaols, and the mark-time eaters were not instructed to grin happily. And then there is the sequence showing what a swell time the boys have at the annual ball.

Can it be that Annapolis is so badly in need of recruits that it is necessary to make a whole sequence of movies glorifying military life, in order to advertise the place? This would seem to be the purpose of these films.

But of course, if a boy can't crowd into Annapolis he can get into the navy, anyway. And don't forget, navies are almost invariably used in defensive wars.

Yes, we have got far away from the domain of the motion-picture reviewers, but alas, pictures of this sort get far away from the domain of motion-picture entertainment.

There were a lot of war pictures after the war, but this is no *What Price Glory*.

Take the argument that war is inevitable, and that pictures of this type will be 'necessary'. Ask any man if he wants to fight and he says, 'No'. But all over the place they are declaring, 'war is inevitable'. We aren't at war yet and we won't be at war until the popular will, numbed, intoxicated, drugged by such poison as *Annapolis Farewell* consents to such a war. Then it will be treason to come out and say what we honestly think of this kind of picture. No sense in saying the picture doesn't mean anything and can't harm us now because we aren't yet at war. The time to stamp out that type of propaganda is now. No war is inevitable. It is just in these innocent-seeming stages that a war is prepared.

It is no accident that such butter-faced boys as Richard Cromwell and Dickie Powell, hitherto singled out with loathing in my writings as among the weakest representations of manhood to be found on the screen, are the heroes of these propagandistic films. I will come right out and say that everyone who had anything to do with this film, from the authors, Stephen Avery, Grover Jones, Wm. McNutt, and Frank Cravens, through the director, Alexander Hall, and the entire cast, to the cameraman, Ted Tetzlaff, should be ashamed for having earned a few hundred dollars at the expense of truth. Some of these people, like Sir Guy Standing, are talented, show sensitivity. To me, they have recorded themselves as traitors to whatever art they possess, large or small. I think, Tom Brown and Richard Cromwell, that you should have refused your parts in this film.

The cinema is indeed a great instrument of propaganda. If there were such a thing as a true cause for war, the cinema would have no difficulty in convincing people of its need. But a sloshy and premeditated attack upon the so-called patriotic emotions is outside the bounds. Films of this type will appear with increasing frequency unless the public makes known its negation of their message.

So far they are being made as private ventures; they must pay their way. There is one effective place to meet them, and that is at the box-office. It is necessary to do more than merely to stay away from such pictures as *Annapolis Farewell*. Keep others away.

Crime and Punishment
Comparison is the life of criticism, and there is one director out in Hollywood who seems bent on giving us fellows a living, although it would appear that most of the critics are trying to do the reverse for him. As the critics are aware that by taking Mr Josef Von Sternberg out of the kitchen they may be depriving themselves of an occasional

meal, their motive, in this instance, cannot be selfish.

Let us hasten to add that Von Sternberg is in no danger of being removed: *Crime and Punishment* has netted him a new contract. And I, for one, am willing to let him keep on grinding because his mistakes are the most intelligent mistakes in cinema.

Last year Mr Von Sternberg came along with *The Scarlet Empress*, which was completed just after a British film on the same subject, *Catherine the Great*, had been released. It is pertinent to the understanding of Von Sternberg's treatment of *Crime and Punishment* to remember that he was booed all over the lots for his over-embroidery of the screen when *The Scarlet Empress* was shown. He sacrificed story, action, characterization, actors, to a passion for ornate atmospheric composition. In comparison, *Catherine the Great* was a direct, speedy picturization of the same theme, built around a virtuoso performance by Elisabeth Bergner.

Now, Mr Von Sternberg seems to have taken to heart the criticism of his lavishly subtle technique. He has literally torn away the veils through which he loved to film the faces of his actors. He seems bent on proving that he can produce a sharply focused, swift film, simply set, that he can brush aside every pictorial distraction to focus attention on his actors, and that he can direct a virtuoso performance for all it's worth.

The only trouble is that Mr Von Sternberg learned his lesson too well, and chose the wrong vehicle.

Curiously enough, the circumstances of the last comparison are repeated. Again, the scene is Russia. Again, Mr Von Sternberg had the advantage of being able to view a completed foreign product before finishing his own work. In this case, the other producers are French; a note on their version of *Crime and Punishment* appeared here last month.

One omission epitomizes Von Sternberg's production. The murder of the pawnbroker's sister does not take place. In fact, Elizaveta is entirely left out of the American film. If you remember your Dostoievsky, it is this second and purposeless murder which tortures the mind of the student Raskolnikov. He can rationalize the killing of the spidery old pawnbroker, but it is his unpremeditated butchering of the mild, innocent sister, necessary when she happens upon the scene of his crime, that confuses his theories of crime and punishment.

This brings up the entire question of faithfulness to source. Reinhardt did Shakespeare a disservice by sticking to the letter of *A Midsummer Night's Dream*. But you can take a job of filming a novel

Crime and Punishment: Peter Lorre

two ways: (1) Translation into the film medium; (2) Adaptation of a film from the novel.

The French version gives a faithful impression not only of the background of time and place, and of Dostoievsky's characters, but of the frenzied tone of Dostoievsky's novel. In the case of work so universally known, this seems to me to be the aesthetically justifiable method. In the recent rash of Dickens films, for instance, the quaint tone that pervades all of Dickens's writings was sought for. Parenthetically, the Christmas release of *Scrooge*, with a miraculous performance in the name role, achieved this tone.

But from the way Von Sternberg went at it, his name might have been plain Joe Stern again. And I would trust a Joe Stern before a Josef Von Sternberg.

The story, in brutal simplicity, is of a brilliant student of crime who, on graduating from the university, finds himself broke. His sister is about to marry for money. 'Money! Money! Money!' his needs scream on every side. So he murders and robs a pawnbroker. The rest is a man-hunt.

Granted that Joe Stern's picture is addressed to the sub-literary

Crime and Punishment: Peter Lorre

mass audience which might have an idea of Dickens, but would be unlikely to have an idea of Dostoievsky, he has an aesthetic right to
adapt rather than translate *Crime and Punishment*. He starts out by
saying 'this might happen any time, anywhere'. He presents his
characters in present-day business suits instead of in the frock coats
and high hats worn by Russian students of the period of the novel.
By showing a Russian newspaper in one scene, and by other minor
touches, he conveys the idea that this has a Russian background, but
the emphasis on time and place is skilfully reduced.

So far, so good.

The early scenes are given to building up the motive. Raskolnikov is
seen graduating, going forth with high hopes and ideals. Then poverty
is developed. Joe Stern is even so daring as to present a chubby actor in
the role of the hungry student; and Peter Lorre more or less gets away
with this stunt. The landlady screams for money, the actor pounds the
table and cries for money! money! money! and this idea is established
much more elementally than in the French film, where a rickety bed
in a barren garret conveys poverty.

Mary Burns, Fugitive: Sylvia Sidney

For the sake of simplicity, then, Joe Stern omits the murder of the innocent sister. No philosophic complications, no atmospheric hair-splitting. This is a story of a man who needs money, kills someone to get it, and is finally caught by the cops.

Well, all right. But, so is *Show Them No Mercy*, so is *Mary Burns, Fugitive*, to cite some of the more excellent treatments of the recent versions of this most prolifically treated of themes. Joe Stern has simplified himself right down to the class of the Hollywood crime story. The only thing that distinguishes his film is the fact that the criminal is an intellectual instead of a mug.

Dostoievsky's novel is so rich that it would, of course, be impossible to simplify all value out of the story. The outline itself, as I have re-marked before, is the perfect cops-and-robber scenario, and the chunks of action that Joe Stern has retained out of this outline serve nobly. But with the over-simplification of the psychological factors, the film tosses away its chances at distinction.

In acting, Peter Lorre runs a fancy second to Pierre Blanchar of the French version. To begin with, Blanchar has all the advantages of appearance. He simply is Raskolnikov, on sight. Lorre gives a thought-out interpretation. To counteract his bulkiness, he introduces sudden, swoopy movements. Instead of suggesting collegiate age, they suggest bogy-man antics. As his is the only characterization allowed to retain any subtlety by the scenario, he had no one to play against, and his scenes with Edward Arnold are a confused series of rushes, during which the men seem to be trying to outshout each other. Arnold plays the detective straight. In the French version, Harry Baur's detective is a wily, tantalizing old fox, and the cat-and-mouse scenes between Baur and Blanchar are beautifully modulated.

One player, in the American version, seems worthy of the story. Tala Birell, as the sister.

My preference is, naturally, the French film. But granting every premise of simplification that Joe Stern took, and looking at the result in the light of what he tried to do, his *Crime and Punishment* is a healthier and more successful film than the products of his atmospheric era.

It does not, however, top such entirely indigenous portraits as *I am A Fugitive From a Chain Gang*, *Little Caesar* and *Public Enemy*, which dealt with the same theme. *The Informer* is a better picture, with the same instruments of suspense.

Mary Burns, Fugitive

In spite of its pretentious presentation, the film is only an even bet against *Mary Burns, Fugitive*, for, while frankly a mere Hollywood picture, the latter contains some really valuable innovations in the cinema interpretation of the American scene. A new interpretation of a gangster, after all these years, is something that had been conceded as well-nigh impossible. Yet along comes a pleasant and handsome youth, Alan Baxter, who presents a sick-souled, small-voiced, love-mad Dillinger so convincingly that, after three weeks, his small tight voice is still drilling into my ears. The picture is deliberately under-played, and derives an excruciating suspense through contrast with the usual machine-gun gang and G-man epic. The scenes in the model gaol for women, distinctly suggestive of New York's Eighth Street emporium, manage to bear down upon the spectator with the same smooth oppression with which such an institution smothers the spirits of its inmates. And for the light American touch there is a swell bit in the hospital, where Mary Burns and her blindfolded suitor hold a discussion as to the comparative character merit of Popeye and Wimpy. That's my notion of what movie characters ought to talk about.

Mary Burns, Fugitive: Sylvia Sidney

Riff-Raff

If it were not for one dishonest touch, this film would be the outstanding product of the year. It's one of the rare films that show ordinary working folk in their own background. The opening sequences in the crowded shacks of the tuna-fishermen, showing the kids' beds made on chairs, Jean Harlow sleeping in her slip, the scramble of getting to work, the zest and wise-cracking knowingness of the fishers and cannery girls, are swell. Like *Black Fury*, this is a picture that is really sympathetic to workers, but whose plot manipulation leaves a slight taste in the mouth. The picture is great as long as it sticks to people and background; Harlow and Spencer Tracy do a bang-up cat and dog love scrap job, and Joseph Calleia is a treat as the sad-eyed cagey Greek who owns the tuna fleet and the cannery; the dance-hall scenes and the scenes on the boats and in the cannery are spirited, punchy, sometimes riotously and innocently funny. As in *BlackFury*, the trouble between boss and workers is laid to an 'agitator'; in this case the agitator is completely unexplained. When he

Jean Harlow and Spencer Tracy in *Riff-Raff;* Jackie Cooper, Mickey Rooney and Freddie Bartholomew in *The Devil is a Sissy*

comes around, at the climax, to toss a bomb and blow up the fleet, his presence is utterly unprepared for and believable only to those who believe everything they read in the Hearst papers. Spencer Tracy, like Paul Muni in *Black Fury*, plays the role of a fine but conceited worker, duped into believing he is a leader, and used as a tool by the agitator. When he sees his error, he smothers the agitator and his bomb. The net message of the plot of such a film is that the worker has no brains and should stay in his place; while *Black Fury* and *Riff-Raff* admitted the injustice of the wage-scales, and were nasty to scabs, both wound up by pointing out that unions were useful only when they called off strikes. The question is whether an audience reacts more strongly to the emotional quality of the film, which in both these cases was pro-labour, or to the plot-devices. I think that the audience simply lives with the people in *Riff-Raff*, and disregards the unreal turns of the plot. But keeping this picture honest might have made it great.

The Devil is a Sissy (The Devil Takes the Count)
Just often enough to keep a man from giving up religion, some small miracle will come along. A lot of us sourpuss commentators who are reputed to look on pictures through the jaundiced eye of intellect, and to pan everything on the principle of preserving superiority, are really soft souls with an anxious love for cinema; we go along protesting that the tripe doesn't really count, and keeping alive that little flame of faith in the possibility of the movie as the art with the largest common denominator. And every once in a while a film quietly made, no drums of *Anthony Adverse*, no bugles of *Romeo and Juliet*, slips through the mill, and we see the thing, and experience a slight sense of strangeness, and after a while we remember, rather than realize, that we've seen a picture that demonstrates that our own theories are quite possible, quite possible.

It's like running across a really good short story in the supposed to be formula fiction appearing in the daily short-story sections of the newspapers. One realizes, again, that material doesn't have to be false, and artificial, to be acceptable to a wide public, nor does it have to be false to conform to the limitations put upon truth by publishing conventions. And in the same way, we find that it is even possible to make a fairly true and a fairly good and a certainly popular movie within the restrictions of the glad-formula of the films. All that it takes is intelligence of approach, plus a bit of true feeling. You can't disguise or fake that feeling; there's no other way to get freshness into any kind of art. And naturally, you can't be lazy about it.

My own idea is that the bulk of Hollywood entertainment is tripe because it is turned out by a lot of lazy folk who take the easiest way of filling in the formula. And when an unpretentious film like *The Devil Is a Sissy* slips into the batch we get the shock of realizing that good stuff can be had.

On the surface, this little film is as banal as a Hoover epigram; it's merely the yarn about the pretty-mannered boy who had to fight his way into the gang by proving he was tougher than their toughest. It works the old onionpeel about the lad who would commit robbery to get the money to buy a tombstone for his old man, a tombstone with angels on it. But in the re-fabrication of this little business there's an almost Shakespearian disregard for the banalities of the plot. What's a plot anyway? If you got it given to you, you got it given to you, accept the thing and forget about it, and let's have some people in this action.

So the producers, directors, scripters or whoever were the conglomerate geniuses responsible for the flavour of this movie get together and say: Slum? Hell, we might as well give them a whiff of the stink of the slum. School? They dish up a Manhattan public schoolhouse with the two lanes of dents on the stairs, made by millions of kids; and the same stony-faced Miss Vinegar, that has been sitting at the upright piano at the head of the stairs for the last sixty years, playing the march-in song, is right there on the job. From that scene forward, this movie has a reality so unpretentious that it has to catch up with you from behind, after the film is over. Which is in about the sixth reel, where it goes into a kidnap chase.

Certainly, one of the artists fundamentally responsible for the unusual honesty of this film is Mickey Rooney, the kid Cagney. His part of the story opens when his pal (Jackie Cooper) alibis Mickey's absence from school because it is the day his old man is going to be electrocuted. The teacher accepts this as a legitimate excuse for absence, and the rest of the boys sort of envy Mickey his day off. But presently he appears and shuffles to his seat. From the moment he opens his trap to explain belligerently that he got lonesome sitting around the house, through the whole first part of the photoplay to the scene where Mickey and Jackie are hanging on to the back of a street car and Mickey is bragging about how many jolts it took to kill his tough old man, the Rooney kid is performing on a level of mature artistry. It's not merely a natural bit of casting, and it's not entirely clever direction by that old master at loosening-them-up, Van Dyke. Mickey Rooney has an artist's objective idea of the character he's portraying, and he does the job with intelligence and control. If this kid doesn't grow up to be a real actor, then a child and a man are truly two completely unrelated individuals.

No director could have taught Mickey Rooney the exactly sensed timing which he gives to the little glum silences that follow his bravado remarks.

There's another aspect to the film which is fully as important as Mickey Rooney's acting. It, too, is achieved by understatement. The film understates the case of the electrocuted father. An ordinary Hollywood story would have gone to some pains to prove that the old man wasn't really guilty of whatever he was electrocuted for, or that Mickey wasn't really his son. *The Devil Is a Sissy* merely suggests that the father was a small-time robber who didn't get away fast enough, and that you couldn't blame the guy anyway, seeing the rotten chance he had in life. There's another part of the story which is treated with the same intelligent understatement. It concerns Mickey's aunt, who is first seen living in a Park Avenue penthouse, with no apparent means of support except the cartwheels she turns for her 'financial advisor'. In the glad-end of the picture, the young lady, who has moved from the penthouse back to a furnished room, is shown to be on terms perhaps more intimate than chummy with the young architect who is Freddie Bartholomew's father. No explanation of their status is offered; the thing is simply presented for what it's worth, and look what can be done through the Hays office, when the producers use a little intelligence.

One more touch reveals the unaccidental source of the film's excellence. The father of Jackie Cooper is a guy who can't open his mouth without referring to the great sacrifices he went through, over there, and look what this country is coming to, after he fought and bled for it! The character is instantly recognized, and yet it is a type which has not been touched in films, to my recollection. A standard producer's attitude would have been that you can't make fun of the vets, though the vets themselves will probably recognize this pal with hilarity. The whole difference between *The Devil Is a Sissy* and the ordinary run of programme pictures is one of alertness, of a true instead of a cock-eyed angle, of interest and belief in the medium.

The film, let me hasten to add, is not a masterpiece. If it were a masterpiece, it would not be as significant as it is. For in that case it would have to be set aside, as one of those freak lofty achievements in the art of the cinema. It would probably be punk box-office. But this is a film of the same stuff that the bulk of films are made of; it is buttered with hokum and honeyed with improbability; but there's bread underneath, and bread is something people will always eat.

The Charge of the Light Brigade

I rarely walk out on a picture, and never want to walk out on a simple programme picture. It is only the more pretentious cinema efforts, the ones that try to be something besides just another movie, that may stimulate me to walking out. Such pictures attain a kind of individuality, and if it happens to be the kind of individuality that rubs me the wrong way, the spell is broken and I want to walk out, But even in the most obnoxious picture, I can feel the basic, physical hypnosis of the medium. I want to sit and let the thing roll on and on, but there is the conflicting desire to get up and out of the room invaded by the personality of some actor, or by some idea I dislike.

Now, I know I'm not alone in feeling this hypnotic, habit-forming need for the movie. Sociologists, through the activity of social service workers, have in the past few years secured a fairly wide acceptance of the idea that the motion picture is a necessity, rather than a luxury, to the population. It is no longer a shock when a relief client confesses that a quarter out of the minimum-standard-food-budget allowance for the week is devoted to the purchase of movie tickets.

We are all familiar with the escape-mechanism theory as an explanation for this strange need. Perhaps it is the complete, and the proper explanation. An escape once a week into the other-world of the films, and the heart is able to go on. I think there is something more involved than simple escape; I think the need for congregation is there, the need to feel one's self in a room with other folks, sharing a common experience; and also a kind of religious experience in confronting the unnatural together with other folks. Something primitive, like what makes a bunch of savages gather together and watch a witch-doctor.

Too, there is the factor which those who have recently looked at Veblen will call conspicuous consumption. The need to show one's self spending money for something that is not as obviously necessary as food. This is a secondary factor, for it cannot be operative in the screening room, to which we are admitted free; so below this spending factor must be some really elemental, sensory effect of the moving picture.

Maybe it is simple hypnotism. The hypnotist holds an object before the eye – some shining object, that flickers, reflecting light. The willing subject keeps his eye fixed in this single focus. And the hypnotist drones out something simple, something familiar. There is no element of surprise. The subject knows exactly what is coming next. The hypnotist is going to repeat the same phrase, over and over – go to sleep, sleep, sleep – or he is going to repeat it in established, progressive variation, as in counting. He is not going to skip any numbers.

And presently, the subject is in a trance state, freed of responsibility, freed of himself, happily guided by an outside force. He is often disappointed when the spell is broken.

Maybe that is why people want to sit in the theatre and see two pictures instead of one. Periodically, this craze for dual programmes returns to plague the theatre exhibitors. And as the dual-craze progresses, more and more pictures are made in the secondary category, fill-time pictures which exemplify the trance factor most perfectly. Pictures like *The Luckiest Girl in the World*, or *Adventure in Manhattan*, or *Without Orders*, or *The Isle of Fury*, or what's that little picture I saw yesterday. They roll along, and you would be really shocked if they should roll out of the routine. It would be like a pulp story turning Faulkner.

Sometimes this trance-factor is distilled with super-perfection, and the result is a picture that isn't really a dualler, but a super-special. It has stars, and mob scenes, and is promoted big, and it is *The Charge of the Light Brigade*.

Here, a confusion is likely to ensue. The confusion is in the group of movie-goers who correspond to the group of people who read the slick magazines. Now, it is well known that presidents and geniuses read pulp fiction for relaxation; but this same type of critical mind will most likely skip the slick fiction field, and go to the literary magazines for edification. Thus, there are people who are choosey about their movies; they can stand punk movies, Westerns, and they can get a sort of critical enjoyment from the higher type of movie, from *Dodsworth*, or *Fury*, or *Romeo and Juliet*. But they don't know how to take the slick movie. Maybe the way to take it is to see it in a second-run theatre, where the expectant mood raised by the advance promotion is no longer in effect.

For instance, in what is perhaps the most highly intellectualized precinct in New York, Greenwich Village, there is a neighbourhood movie called the Sheridan Square. On almost any evening, you can run into some of the nation's highest thinkers, standing in line at the box-office, to get their weekly, or bi-weekly dosage. I know some writers who, when they are in the heat of creation, go almost daily.

That's the proper atmosphere for a picture like *The Charge of the Light Brigade*. The hypnotic effect is perfect. You find yourself saying each character's speeches just before he opens his mouth. 'We must tell him', the girl will say, when she falls in love with the hero's brother. The next shot will be a close-up of the brother's woodenly agonized face saying, 'I can't tell him'. The next shot will be of this brother trying to tell the hero that he has stolen his girl away, while the hero doesn't give him a chance to finish his speech, because he's impatient to go to his girl. And later, when the messenger creeps out of the besieged guardhouse, sneaking over the walls, to get aid, you know that the next shot will show him killed, and you know that the following shot will show the people in the guard-house, hopeful of relief, unaware of their messenger's death. It all follows and leads as beautifully, and comforting, as secure as logic, as certain as, 1, 2, 3, 4, 5. It is as satisfying as *Bengal Lancer*, as faithful as *Under Two Flags*. You are willingly hypnotized, and each time the trance is deeper, because you have comfortably given up suspicion, you know the litany, you know the ritual will never be betrayed. That's the movie in its most essential form; it's just a punk picture and I like it.

Winterset

Now that the wild flurry of immediate acclaim has subsided, I think we may evaluate *Winterset*. Usually a rear-view is necessary to correct the exaggerations of preview enthusiasm. A few months after the appearance of the greatest picture of all time, a new greatest picture of all time has arrived, and the predecessor is discreetly deflated to the ranks of 'oh yes, that wasn't a bad little picture'. The term 'masterpiece' comes to be used only in the sense of 'current masterpiece'.

But in this case a deliberately considered criticism is necessary to make clear that superlatives, when applied to *Winterset*, should be understood in their literal, rather than in their movie blow-up sense. To call *Winterset* a classic does not mean to rank it with *Anthony Adverse*, *The Charge of the Light Brigade*, or even with *Mr Deeds Goes to Town*. We shall have to shell off the superficial usage and return true meaning to the word 'classic'.

Some Hollywood genius, upon the completion of *Winterset*, shook his head sadly and said, 'This is a critic's picture. The only way we can sell it to the public is through the critics.' So a cinema-stupendous sum was spent to bring America's One Thousand leading film critics by plane, train, and taxi to an all-day festival in New York; they saw the latest red hot and blue musical show in six-dollar seats, they feasted in a rainbow room, they cocktailed, they night-clubbed, and somewhere in between they took in a movie called *Winterset*. Since it was 'a critic's picture' to begin with, I guess the Thousand Best must have been happy that no conscience-problems confronted them, they could take planes and taxis back to New Orleans and Seattle, give the picture any number of stars, and give the same number of stars to *Three Men on a Horse*, next week.

As a sensitive member of the Thousand Second-Best, I am therefore in complete and unbribed freedom to say that *Winterset* is in my opinion the first American photoplay classic. Each of those three words describes a ponderable quality.

By 'American', I do not mean merely American-made. I mean a play whose matter is of the flesh and bone of this country. True, that might be claimed for everything from *Daniel Boone* to *Theodora Goes Wild*. Gangster films and crazy-reporter films are distinctly American, and so are Joan Crawford stories. The historical subjects, from *The Covered Wagon* to *The Plainsman*, had some of the flesh and bone content, the gangster stuff had legitimate blood, but it is only recently that films have begun to admit the mental and social patterns of America into their making. The contrast of the Swede and the big boss lumberman in *Come And Get It* was such a pattern; the whole forepart of *Fury* was such a pattern, and the entirety of *Winterset* is American. Here is a film that involves an adult consideration of our ways of life, our ideas of justice, of life and death, of human worth. It considers these things in a peculiarly American way; all of our backgrounds of thought are taken into the problem, so that the film's utterance is one that could not have been made through any other nation's psychology. Few works of the cinema can stand with *Winterset* as thus wholly expressive of our temper.

Secondly, I have put emphasis upon the word 'photoplay'. I have repeatedly pointed out here that most films cannot even be considered as photoplays, having no integral relationship to the camera-story. Some, like *Anthony Adverse*, and *Valiant Is the Word for Carrie*, are episodes strung together out of novels. Some, like to *Go West Young Man*, are feeble transmutations from the stage. But while *Winterset*, too, stems from a stage play, it has been transformed into a camera-story far superior to the source play. Now as to what is meant by 'classic'. Next to the word 'love', this is probably the most tortured symbol in our language. Narrowly, the word refers to a certain period or style in art which has come to be designated as 'classic', the fuller use of the word is in reference to those works of art which are so purely the product of their day and age that they become timeless. We have classics of Greece, classics of the Renaissance, classics of English literature, and we have had a few classic films, such as *Caligari*, *Joan of Arc*. But I can think of no previous American film of a dignity and scope which might permit it to be placed in this high category. *The Informer* may in time come to be considered as a classic, but even though American-made, it is a film of Irish life, and outside the present definition.

I have used the term 'pure'. This is to emphasize the quality of the classic sometimes described as vast simplicity, sometimes as a loftiness of viewpoint. Technically, I think it could be seen that classicism also involves a wholeness and an insularity of viewpoint. Every detail of a classic style is part of the same time and place, there can be no borrowing, no conscious adaptation of elements from other styles and periods, for then we have the work of a conscious artisan rather than the natural expression of an artist.

There may, however, be authentic roots, vital relationships to the whole cultural heritage of mankind, and I think it is legitimate in an American dramatist, since our language is the English, to show derivation from Shakespeare. I would say that Maxwell Anderson's transference of *Hamlet* to *Winterset* is the instinctive and legitimate continuation of a folk-idea, contrasted to O'Neill's merely cerebral exercise in making the story of Electra into a modern psycho-analytical analysis of a Civil War family.

But these distinctions become delicate and, at last, only matters of literary dispute. Mr Anderson is admittedly soaked in Shakespeare; and he alone of our prominent dramatists retains the use of blank verse. The legend that *Winterset* shares with *Hamlet* is of a youth haunted by the unquiet spirit of a murdered father; and in both instances the murder was an expression of mankind's lust for power. Hamlet and Mio are thought-plagued lads, goaded to ineffectuality by their over-sensitivity, their passion for proof, for justice. Each, at some moment, holds the instrument of destruction in his hand, confronts his villain with sword or pistol, but cannot kill, because of the ingrown futility of doubt. It could be said, too, that Mio has the same struggle as Hamlet against an instinct toward romantic love; the intellectual tries to be cynical toward his heart. Curiously, there is a resemblance between Esdras and Polonius, even a fatal plot involvement between Mio and Miriamne's brother, as between Hamlet and the brother of Ophelia.

But the relationship between the two works is only this partnership in the telling of a universal truth. I do not mean to infer that Anderson had the quality of Shakespeare; his word-use is inferior; his play is

Winterset

bereft of the lightning perceptions that constantly explode the Shakespeare text into immeasurable circles of implication; but his story is as warmly felt, and as socially true as was the story of Hamlet.

There, the transference is complete; the umbilical is cut, and *Winterset* is valid in itself. By drawing his story from the Sacco-Vanzetti case, Anderson has wedded his Hamlet entirely to the American scene; he has told his tale entirely in the terms of an American mind.

Hamlet's theme of justice was confined to palace intrigue; in our time and place there is less social insularity, and the theme receives its fullest explanation in an intrigue that involves payroll theft, gangsters, the frame-up use of the courts by reactionary money-forces, the railroading of a radical for a gangster's crime; in Hamlet's time it was a question of whether a gentle person or an evil should rule a kingdom, in our time it is a question of whether the evil nature of mankind shall thwart the persistent social reforms of the good.

If a work of art is supposed to contain an author's personal conclusions upon his theme, then we may read into *Hamlet* Shakespeare's grey feeling that the best that may be hoped for in the struggle between good and evil is the death of the evil with the good. *Hamlet* ends in a bath of blood. By the same measure, the stage version of *Winterset* could be taken to say that justice cannot triumph in the world, for Mio was killed, and Trock, the gangster, lived, even though he carried the germs of a fatal disease within his body. And by this measure, some might be shocked to find the position of the characters reversed at the ending of the film, with Mio alive, ascendant, and the gangster dead. Does this pervert the message of the artist?

My own feeling has always been one of indifference toward any dead ending. What an artist has to say is given throughout his entire work, and cannot be told or substantially altered with the twisting around of a bit of action at the final curtain. If his story has been one of a long and almost even battle between two forces, then the choice of the victor is in any case arbitrary.

When we begin in the arts, we conceive a great respect for the 'tragic ending' and we sneer at those who ask for concessions toward the public that does not 'like things to come out so sadly'. I feel that this attitude on the part of the mass public is not an expression of lack of taste, or of stupidity, but is rather in itself a superb demonstration of humanity's life-lust, humanity's positivism. I think the artist must consider that when the whole impulse of his people is toward an affirmative life, there must be something wrong when he can tell them only a message of death.

To me, there is nothing so flat as a conclusion in which the characters are killed. Death is the evasion of an artist when he can find nothing significant to say.

I do not say that the photoplay conclusion of *Winterset* is superior as art, though it may be superior in the giving of human satisfaction. To my mind, the story loses itself in plot, toward the close, just as *Hamlet* goes askew in its last act.

Once the characters have all confronted one another, the drama is completed. What follows, in the last act of *Winterset* on the stage, is a chase around corners, with pauses for pompous philosophical speeches. I remember that when I saw the stage version I was progressively enraged, throughout the third act; I could not understand how any writer could permit himself to let a fine work so crumble. The film suffers less, for the simple reason that most of the solemn valedictories have been omitted, and for the added reason that the elements of the chase are an integral part of the photoplay medium, and therefore do not break into the theme, as they did in the stage version.

And as to the film conclusion, I have already pointed out that it is preferable to me. I should like to add that from a purely technical sense it is valid, since the hand-organ and the cigarette-sniper are utilized as a part of the plot, and therefore give the photoplay a rounded completion that can be achieved in a story only when every dropped hint has been picked up and knit into the fabric. This is the principle of economy wedded to the simplicity of classic art: no move is wasted, no detail is without meaning.

There is one more important factor in the recognition of this classic: the factor of production. From the direction of Alfred Santell to the acting of every member of the cast, there is a sense of infallibility, and of permanence. The nervous and fatal mood is established in the entire forepart of the picture, which gives the history of the Romagna frame-up, and which was so badly missing in the stage-play; this mood is sustained with a beautiful sense of tempo throughout the film.

The most banal scenes are treated with remarkably fresh vision. For instance, when the crowd gathers around the organ-grinder there is a sequence of street dancing. The dancers move with a monotonous gracelessness that is at once imaginative, realistic, and within the mood of the scene. A kid dances, one leg of his knickers loosened, dangling, bagging. That simple and real touch is nevertheless a subtle piece of choreography; it gives his instant dance a lopsided movement in character with the twisted motivation of the story. This is in the classic tradition: no detail is out of harmony; even the song has ironic meaning, for the song, given wordlessly, is 'I'll be glad when you're dead you rascal you'.

It has been pointed out that the use of actors not well-known to the movie audience gives the action a greater reality. Another touch in the casting is worth noticing. John Carradine, hitherto associated with sadistic, villainous roles, is presented as the idealistic Romagna. He acts the part with extreme effectiveness; there is subtle understanding in this bit of casting, for it is Carradine's air of idealism, his projection of character-integrity, of whole-souledness that makes him convincing in his villain parts. The character of Esdras, played on the stage as a long-bearded Talmud-mumbling Jew, a Fannie Hurst stock character that has lost all meaning, is improved in the screen performance; Maurice Moscovitch's seamy-faced, worriedly philosophical old Jew is closer to reality.

The classic nature of the photoplay is further enhanced by the fact that, in its cinema essentials, *Winterset* is simply the traditional gangster movie, deepened to philosophical and social meaning. The ordinary gangster movie came closest to being a native American folk-story, and it is altogether fitting that the first poetically expressive American film should make use of the gangster legend. How even the worn-out devices of the gang movie can be employed with fresh effect is shown in this film; the guns with silencers produce a sinister quality unused in, and yet related to, the hundreds of bang-bang killing films that we have had. Perhaps this hushed and controlled effect is symbolic of the difference between art and mere entertainment.

In final definition, classic art usually deals with grand subjects, with the verities, the fates. The photoplay never loses this view of man as a struggling element in the complex of outer forces. There is almost a physical thrill for the spectator in the perfect art with which the camera follows the various characters, gradually converging their paths until they are all brought together by the dirge-like song of the hand-organ, in that gloomy square where the children dance. In this, the film again proves itself a true medium of the major arts.

Alistair Cooke

Born Manchester, 1908. Jesus College, Cambridge, 1930. Research in dramatic criticism, Cambridge, 1930–2; Commonwealth Fellowship at Yale, 1932–3; work on American language, Harvard, 1933–4. Film critic, BBC, 1934–7; London commentator, NBC, 1936–7; emigrated to United States 1937. BBC and *Manchester Guardian* American correspondent and commentator since 1938.

Top Hat: Fred Astaire, Ginger Rogers

5. Alistair Cooke

Top Hat

John Grierson has just put out a new article. I don't mean a new documentary film for the General Post Office to be lucky enough to sponsor. I mean an article written with pen on paper, or possibly, if I know Mr Grierson, with pencil on pillow, but proving again that of all writers on cinema he is the only one who manages to make film jargon sound like a special clue to ordinary human wisdom. In the course of this essay, Mr Grierson starts to praise a new book, which tries to set down in cold print the emotional effects of fade-outs, close-ups, dissolves, wipes, and the rest, a book which is trying therefore to write an anatomy of the cinema. Sighs Mr G. – 'the curse of anatomy is that you must first kill the body you are going to work on. Cinema is no longer on the wing or caught in the bright flashes of occasional inspiration. It is on the cold and horrid slab in process of dissection as to viscera and nerve fibres, but the real factor in the situation is that the subject is stone dead.'

Well, now and then a critic escapes from his surgery and wants to chase his butterflies, or catch cinema on the wing, as Mr Grierson puts it, along with the rest of the world. There are films, and some of the greatest – especially in comedy – which release chiefly those energies that spring from benevolence. This is fine for families but bad for criticism. They seem too good to talk about. Whatever piece of life they take a look at they deal with so authentically and surely that it seems a clumsy retreading of the good ground to talk about them at all. You have to imagine the whole thing done badly in order to praise the way it was done well. Of such was *Alice Adams*. And so, I think, is *Top Hat*. There's no call at this time of day to pin Fred Astaire down to the mortuary table and start dissecting him. And I'm afraid *Top Hat* is the sort of film nobody wants to have analysed. It's not so much a film that, as we say in our lazy moments, *defies* criticism. It's a film that doesn't encourage it, though. It says, Go on, you criticize me and just see all the people you're going to pain. I defy Mr Grierson or anybody else to catch hold of Fred Astaire once *he's* on the wing. Fred Astaire soaring up and down rooms is good enough for most of us, without making him unscrew his legs to see how they work. The only assurance you need in a musical is that those legs do work. In fact, Mr Astaire probably wouldn't mind giving the rest of his body to the slab for dissection. For his legs can do most of the things you and I will need a harp and a fancy dress for. The dialogue is witty enough, but those legs are wittier. The new and funny Helen Broderick winks wickedly, but those legs wink wickeder. And so it goes. Looking back on it, I have just one grouch. I wish musical comedies didn't have to take quite so prosperous and Rotary a view of life. It hurts after *Alice Adams*. I for one shall enjoy watching Mr Astaire and Miss Rogers as a mere sailor and his girl in their next film. Even then, I suppose the battleship will have a scrumptious ballroom where all the real killing is done, and I expect the port-holes serve chocolate milk-shakes at the drop of a hat. But there it is, you take what you get, especially as Mr Astaire and Miss Rogers are, from all accounts, not to be together again. I don't know why I'm calling them Mr and Miss. But Fred sounds all wrong. Let's hope when his present partner deserts him he'll call himself by his real name and make a new series of musicals, partnered as God meant he should be, by his first and oldest flame, Miss Minnie Mouse.

Anna Karenina

When you start to write about Garbo, you are reminded more forcibly than ever that practically all the criticism of emotional acting we have reads like a fourth-form essay on the character of Napoleon.

One of the reasons, I suppose, why there is no aesthetic of acting that has got beyond the age of puberty is that very few of us are ever watching acting at anything but that age. Acting doesn't often go to the head. It hits you in the pit of your stomach. And when a woman is acting it strikes most of us, heaven help us, hard on the left side of the chest. So if these notes seem over-ponderous, and stress with suspicious high-mindedness the maturity of Garbo's new performance, you can comfort yourself with the reflection that they are just professional periphrasis for a yen.

An actress is usually said to be mature at the time when her daughters threaten to take over the parts she made her name in. But Garbo's maturity is not the maturity of her career, it's a wise ageing of her outlook. The old, bold, slick disdain has given way to a sort of amused grandeur. Physically, this means simply a new balance between two features – a softening of the eyes, a hardening of the mouth. Garbo's 'appeal' was always the commonest of romantic conventions – the world-wide convention of the come-hither look. She managed, because she is a supremely beautiful woman, to make it look like a mark of religion. In *Anna Karenina* she moves a plane higher, she makes it the token of a philosophy. For the most modest claim of a philosopher is to guess about the last step soon after you've taken the first. And in the first five minutes of the film, when the smoke artfully provided by the train clears away and reveals the Garbo's face, you might just as well pick up your hat and go home if you too can't guess the end. Before she has even chosen her lover, her look tells you it doesn't much matter who he is, they all go the same way home. From our point of view it could very well have been almost anybody but Fredric March. He brings to this very pre-War, elaborated Russia the manner of a West Point cadet entraining for a Junior prom, a manner that singles him out for more than his share of protection. And he gets it. They all get it. For the new Garbo grandeur, this tolerant goddess, wraps everybody in the film round in a protective tenderness. She sees not only her own life, but everybody else's, before it has been lived. This fatalism has happily passed over into her technique. And since the plot is now high hokum, the chief excitement is to watch how perfectly she now sees backwards, like a perpetually drowning woman, not only her life but her part: the way, at one point, she takes Fredric March's arm in the box, the way she looks down at the baby of a young friend, the way she picks up the field-glasses to watch March fall from his horse, the way – years ahead of the acting text-books – she hides a broken moment not with a cute nose-dive into

121

Anna Karenina: Garbo, Fredric March

cupped palms, but with the five inadequate fingers of one bony hand – her gestures, too, therefore have the same tender calculation, the same anxiety to treat people with perhaps too much care at the moment, because she knows what's going to happen to them in a year or two. Tenderness is a prickly word, but it's nothing short of tenderness that has happened to the Garbo. She has suddenly and decisively passed out of her twenties. She no longer brightens to exciting, or handsome, or new people. And this quality of gentleness, a gift usually of women over fifty, is an overwhelming thing when it goes with the appearance of a beautiful woman of thirty.

It's no use to talk about the others or even much about the direction, which like most of Clarence Brown's work is very conscientious and crassly unobservant. It provides mouth-watering, classic Metro backgrounds for Garbo to move against, and when any one of a dozen people threatens to get in the way he is briskly and reverently swept into the nearest convenient corner. Basil Rathbone keeps up a steady electric hum as a refrigerator, chilling us all with his clockwork unconcern for other people's moods. But when anybody else looks up or down, laughs, asserts, boasts, or begs a favour, their well-meaning acting gets referred back to the way Garbo looks at people these days, the way she implies that the least you can do for people in this stupid, brawling world is to keep them warm and give them a share of comfort before the end comes.

La Bandera

In *La Bandera* the title and the dialogue may be foreign but the story is as homely as the screen itself. There's no need to ask why it's always three men who join the Foreign Legion, except that it allows more variations in the dumb partner. In *Beau Geste*, if I can lean back so far, there was one silent partner; in *Bengal Lancer*, one small baby for the other two to get noble about; in *La Bandera* the stooge cleverly pretends not to belong to the other two at all, skulking around as the villain instead, until the last few feet of film are giving out and he dashes in just in time to look down over his left shoulder as he shakes with his right hand.

But suddenly, adroitly, there comes a film of the Foreign Legion printed indelibly not on celluloid but on the lives of a half-dozen people; taken not against Hollywood canvas but against the firm, credible background of Spain itself. The story is trite enough, the acting is distinguished only as a comparative relief in understatement, all except Annabella, who is overstated to a degree, so that sooner or

La Bandera; Raymond Massey, Ralph Richardson and Margaretta Scott in *Things to Come*

later even Gracie Allen would catch on to the idea that she is there to provide the love interest; so I take it that the positive merits of the film are in the watchful but undallying direction of Julien Duvivier. When the French cinema dies it might do worse than find his name written across its retina. Since René Clair bowed himself out of distinction with increasingly obvious gestures, there has been no one in France who could be graceful without taking on the aspect of a daffodil. *Lac aux Dames* was a film to preserve because it showed the most characteristic weaknesses of French direction. They needn't keep even all of it; there was one sequence that would do, what they tactfully call a 'sensitive' boy set alongside a plump, perky little girl, real enough; the progress of their emotional scrambling, their holding off with what Robert Benchley calls 'cricket trouble' against a background of coyly draped – believe it or not – fishing nets. If the film failed it could only have been because the fishing nets failed to cause the spring stir in interior decoration that was expected of them.

M. Duvivier is sensitive, too. And he's also a male with a gift of tenderness which he seems to accept in himself as something not to melt over. But if he has one thing more than another it is the practically unique power today of looking generously at beautiful scenery without bursting into sobs. There's a lot of filtering in this film, but it's not beauty seen through a Hollywood veil of tears; it's not an album of postcards, like Dreyer's in *The Passion of Joan of Arc*; it's not M.-G.-M.'s telescope; not Mr Korda's spectroscope: it looks like an exquisite newsreel taken away and baked brown to give you the feel of the air. And in dialogue scenes in the open air Duvivier has managed to improve on an inevitable alternative – that of taking no-nonsense pictures with the light behind you; or taking fantasy pictures, like Murnau's in *Tabu*, into the sun with a shaded lens. Duvivier shoots across the light with the sun just striking his lens. It is typical of his sensible realism that he doesn't bother to use Flaherty's effective refinement, that trick of taking all your pictures before ten in the morning or after five in the evening, which gives to trees and people in a single plane a lovely, unreal stereoscopy. Up to the arrival of Annabella the film is a masterpiece. After that it's just another movie. But it has scenes – the arrival in the dormitory, the cabaret scene in Barcelona, where a mobile camera gives you the strange feeling that a delicate, alert mind is behind the camera easing you into every detail of behaviour; not, like the usual mobile camera, giving you the increasing fear that a hypochondriac is in full control.

Things to Come

To put a Frenchman and an American together in real life may mean a fight. But putting them together on English soil and having a Hungarian as a go-between seems to be a perfect set-up for a good British film. It worked pretty well with *The Ghost Goes West*. It has worked again with *Things to Come*, as visually exciting a film as ever came out of a British or any other studio. For this epic, the combatants merely changed corners while Mr Korda (Alexander, that is) again acted as promoter and referee. This time the American, William Cameron Menzies, is the director; the Frenchman, Georges Périnal, is the cameraman; and another Hungarian, Vincent Korda, came to from a bout of inspired nightmares and designed the sets. Mr H. G. Wells wrote the story and script, and we might have been able to forgive and forget if the piece were not already being tipped for the prize exhibit in a career of prophecy.

It travels the grim years between 1940 and 2036 in everything, it should be said, but its dialogue and psychology. Not since that woeful effort, *The Dictator*, has there been dialogue in the movies that would have sounded so commanding on the stage of Drury Lane some time, say, around the eighteen-eighties. However clean and tidy they made the world to live in, these Cabals and Passworthys were still talking in 1970 and 2030 like *If* and last winter's golf club dinner. The acting doesn't help at all, being performed by three actors who on the stage have grace and power and possibly even delicacy, but who here look and move like the latest additions to Madame Tussaud's. Perhaps the theme overawed them. Perhaps, but whenever there was some undertone of feeling to express, their faces did not show it, the camera had to crouch away and let them fling up an arm. Raymond Massey, Sir Cedric Hardwicke, and even Ralph Richardson should not misuse their powers in films until they can forget all about their golden voices and learn that the film microphone will take kindly to tiny inflections of humour (*cf.* W. C. Fields), pathos (*cf.* Zasu Pitts), and commentary (*cf.* Popeye); that the movie camera will not overlook infinite subtlety of facial play (*vide* Chaplin, Aline MacMahon, Jean Gabin, Victor McLaglen, Myrna Loy, Claudette Colbert, Otto Tressler, Charles Butterworth, Raimu, Hepburn, Lionel Atwill, Raymond Walburn, *et al.*). But the microphone hates being preached at, and the camera hates being glared at or flirted with. In this film there is hardly a glimpse of a 1936 face or talent. They are all back in 1900 with Lewis Waller and Ada Rehan. All except Margaretta Scott, who looks the image of Theda Bara even down to the vamping costume.

Things to Come

To have had the acting and dialogue sound like this year would have helped a lot, but it wouldn't have made the thing profound or even satisfactory as prophecy. To look like Greta Garbo or talk like Groucho Marx may be a part of glory, but they are also a part of our present lively Inferno, whether you look on them as Dante and Virgil or just as inhabitants along with the rest of us. Armageddon will hardly respect the difference. And though he would be a great man indeed who showed in human faces and behaviour the development of human psychology over the next hundred years, I'm afraid that unless the thing's attempted, unless we hear people using language and see them using gesture differently from us, it's no good telling us that we are in 2036: it's just a fancy dress ball, here and now, at the R.I.B.A.

Even as propaganda, and that would be the most charitable view of this film, *Things to Come* is well meant but not very shrewd. For it leaves out humour, thereby offering a strong debating point to stupid people, who may not know that man can still be funny, though wrong for centuries.

If you haven't seen *Things to Come* and have read so far, you're probably disgruntled. And if you have seen it, angry. For when a film has bad acting, dialogue, psychology, what has it? Luckily, even when it has all these, it still needs the things by virtue of which it becomes a film and not a play in three acts with two intervals to drown its sorrows in. In a film showing the death of a nation and its rebirth in a new age of sight and sound, the only people who must have imagination are the scene-designer, the director, and the cameraman. And the achievement of *Things to Come* is no more and certainly no less than the ingenious hours spent around little white models by William Menzies, Vincent Korda, and Georges Périnal. Without tossing a penny, I should say that Vincent Korda is the hero of the piece. For he has to start designing in 1970. When it comes to considering what sort of rooms we shall be living in in forty years (mine's in oak, just six feet by three) your guess is as good as mine. But it could hardly be as good as Vincent Korda's. By a few imaginative strokes on his drawing board he has made the piece a lovely thing to look at. At the same time, with the same stroke, he has been guilty of a rousing act of insubordination. For his drawing board and his models, come to life in the film, dispose of an argument that wastes a lot of words and all of Sir Cedric Hardwicke's part. It is the gayest mockery of the whole piece that Mr Korda's sets relegate Mr Wells's dialectic to the last and not the next century. According to Mr Wells, in another hundred years, after the intervening holocaust, the relation of artist and scientist will still be at the stage it has now got to in our country in the sixth form of schools; it's that charming superstition which the nineteenth century still leaves us groping through – the idea of a scientist as a man brewing smells and destruction in a test-tube, and the artist as a long-haired youth with the first claim on beauty. Mr Korda's imagination has left this piece of ancient pottery in the gutter, but it's a pity that it tinkles there in the intervals of Mr Bliss's music. Mr Wells as applied scientist probably gave a lot of help with the detail of the sets. But Mr Wells as sociologist should surely have called in Mr Lewis Mumford, who would have told him, what Mr Korda's settings visibly demonstrate, that the artist as beauty specialist will be a vulgar survival; and that if the progress of technics does nothing else it will destroy the necessity for a protest against elaborate gadgets designed to simplify needless activities (there will be no need of vacuum cleaners when carpets are a dirty anachronism); that it will, in Mr Mumford's phrase, 'devaluate caste and purify æsthetics'.

Mr Wells's conception is as severe and serious as any he has made. As serious as, for example, *The Time Machine*. But no newer. Not only in dialectic does Mr Wells's conception falter. But also in the detail of applied design. Of course, it's a thankless job being a prophet, for the more brilliant you are, the sooner somebody will take your hint and make your foresight look, in retrospect, like myopia. It must be heartbreaking for Mr Wells to be told that the costumes he predicted they'd be wearing in 2030 are to be the very thing in beach-wear this summer. But there is a category of less inevitable error: the aeroplanes drone away from exhaust trouble just like the dear old *Hindenburg* of 1936 (remember?); the chairs are any modern chair done in glass; they have glass elevators, but the point is – they still have elevators. By abundance of such basic details, *Things to Come* shares with most Utopias the primary error of making Today the premiss, of pretending that new civilizations do not differ in kind but only in the degree of decoration, luxury, leisure, and so on. I wouldn't have minded being asked to swallow a civilization in which the main idea of living was to stand on your head or worship domestic animals, anything so long as the idealism of Mayfair and Beverly Hills, 1936, was not going on as the regular thing in the next century. They might have spoken some new language – say Basic done in American with a sprinkling of Chinese, which is what they are as likely to talk as anything else, if they still have roofs to their mouths after that final air-raid. But anything rather than 'How frightful!' and 'My God, why must we murder each other?' But no. After the most accomplished, the most pestilential clean-up in history, the new civilization offers a trim-looking girl from Roedean, pretty but still straight from Roedean, asking Daddy's permission to go off with the good-looking juvenile, not for a week-end in Devon, to be sure, but I expect there's nothing against necking in a space-gun.

There is this to say, that if you can bear to think of the future as another hundred years of prosperity, without rebirth, revolution or misgiving, then M. Périnal and Mr Korda will make you think you've been there. When the lights go up and you look around everybody looks as dowdy and fussy as may be. And when you get outside the theatre, London is back in the Middle Ages.

They may say that they were only making entertainment, always a useful get-out for the movies when a pretentious undertaking turns out badly. But I hope for their sakes this wrangle has shown that almost for the first time in the movies a film of a sort has been made out of a social experiment. If this idea of the future rates less as a prophecy than as a materialist's dream of paradise, well, there will be time for others. Unless the coming peace overwhelms us before 1940. Perhaps, while there's still time, J. A. Hobson, Gerald Heard, Harold Laski, and the Webbs in our country will now be invited to come into a world that sadly needs them, the world of the cinema. And let us hope that Mr Mumford will be brought from America to work on a more ambitious film with M. Périnal. Maybe that would be the best of all. If they can get Alexander Korda to act as referee, the first British masterpiece is practically assured.

A Tale of Two Cities
The best thing about *A Tale of Two Cities* is the naked, whiskerless face of Ronald Colman . . . it's the first time we've seen it and it has fine eyes, a long humorous upper-lip and a tautness and intelligence you would never have suspected from the evidence of that moustache and those sideburns. There's not much else to praise. In the midst of preposterous aristocrats and Hollywood peasants, I found myself coming back to meditations about that face . . . and other faces. It may have been because earlier in the day I had just seen again a Russian classic, *Potemkin*.

As I watched the heads being cut off that evening I couldn't help thinking that Hollywood has here given us a sadly truthful symbol of what may happen to our movies in the day of social rebirth. Of what in fact has already happened to the movies once in their history. Before the sharp knife falls on, Heaven help us, Ronald Colman's neck, you don't see his face any more, you only hear a voice whispering intensely on the sound-track those celebrated words from the Christmas almanacs.

Until the Russians started to make movies most of us thought of a silver screen as just about the right size for two heads. Without much effort we learned to know the state of Ben Turpin's eyesight, we got to know the number of Mary Pickford's curls without even counting, our heart beat a little faster at the sight of Alma Taylor's nearly perfect mouth. The Russians must have known this was a bad thing. And because, I suppose, the face is the most bourgeois member of the body, they cut it off. We could no longer warm to a picture at the way the heroine winked. Because Russian heroines, if I remember rightly, don't have faces to wink with. I'm not saying this hasn't been a very fine thing. I would gladly sacrifice all the Wheelers and Wolseys and Laurels and Hardys in the world if Eisenstein wants to show me the flexing of somebody's bicep, the gleam of a Russian shoulder-blade. But even a Russian ankle is no compensation for Myrna Loy, for her face, I mean, and the other evening I would gladly have swapped a dozen of M.-G.-M.'s tramping feet for a few more glimpses of Ronald Colman. Me, I like faces, and I've never been able to work out why it's fine and fancy for a novelist to describe the effect of a piece of dialogue on somebody's face and why it's vulgar for the movies to show it to you.

The latest news from Russia is that a halt is being called on the Soviet epic. They feel that we know by this time whereabouts they stand, and that the new regime can be better advertised for some time to come by light pieces showing what a joyous, rib-tickling affair life has become in the U.S.S.R. I wish I could believe that the Russians embarked on this new age in cinema with a merry heart and a twinkling eye. Or even that they are doing it from shrewd motives of policy. But I suspect that the Western World was tiring of all those limbs and bodies, acting though they were from the most noble ideals. And that the patrons of foreign cinemas, debauched as we are, got rather more pleasure and interest simply from watching the faces of the minor characters in the commercial, and probably quite grossly inspired, works of Hollywood and Elstree. Whatever your political opinions may be, it takes an awful lot of Russian sinew to make up for losing W. C. Fields's face. And though it seems to me he would be a madman who needed to think twice about the social honesty of the world of Hollywood or the world of Moscow, I hope the Russians' new move is done for purely business reasons. Then we can go back to our faces without feeling we've turned our backs on a great experiment. We're still here, Russia, when you want us, but we want to know what your women look like and whether you have anything to offer in exchange for the Garbo's mouth, Lee Tracy's hands, and the cheekbones of Katharine Hepburn.

Fury

When the exiled Fritz Lang arrived two years ago in Hollywood, it seemed unlikely that his morbid talent could take a permanent sun tan. California is balm to the folksy virtues, and it was right that Will Rogers should be the sage of the Sunny State. It was right, too, that when he died Irvin Cobb should take over those reassurances and keep alive the practical irony that the local dollar diplomacy encourages. But California is no place for de Maupassant. It will cure all sorts of things, a neurosis, precocity, the curious English snobbery against having a good body. But a million-dollar smile is no gain to literature. And the light of day that hampered Feyder, Pommer, Freund, and Pabst could be expected to drive Lang out of his psychological laboratory on to the cheerful thrills of a roller-coaster.

In those two years he must have put down his test-tube many times. But he went back, though the colony suspects black magic and said one time they couldn't pay for it. When Lang was finally assigned to this picture, a general gloom settled over the production. A production manager told him at the beginning, without any hope of convincing him, to remember the slogan, 'Eight million dollars can't be wrong'. Lang pledged himself to this maxim and has turned out a picture sociologically more profound, technically more competent, than any he made in the days when cardboard sets and a dozen extras were bound to be right.

The story so vividly resembles the San Jose lynching that Metro pointed the reminder, as United Artists did with *The Front Page*, by stating in an opening caption something to the effect that this was all going on in a mythical kingdom. Somehow, I kept thinking of the United States all the way through.

Lang swears he thought of nothing but a story about a mob. 'Lynching happened to be the result', he said. 'I've been through four revolutions and I've made an intimate study of how people act. They often start out in the best of spirits.' The studio officials, on the other hand, thought they were making a picture about a lynching. And they were scared. They didn't want to make it. They must have winced while

Ronald Colman in *A Tale of Two Cities; Fury*

Norman Krasna was writing his fine script. And they warned odd people that hardly a foot of it would be likely to get shown. In the end, the picture was made. But Metro were unperturbed. They thought it mediocre and considered running it as a second feature in a double-bill programme. *Wife v. Secretary* they thought would take it nicely. Jean Harlow supported by Fritz Lang!

It is worth letting both parties stick to their stories. Somewhere between Lang's psychological absorption and Metro's disappointment over an unentertaining lynching, there slipped in the best film of this and maybe of any other coming year.

Perhaps *M* was not about the Düsseldorf murders; it was about the browbeaten sadism of a kindly man. *The Testament of Dr Mabuse* again may be no case-history, but the merest fantasy cooked up on a dark night by Lang and Thea von Harbou, his wife blessed with the same pathological hobbies. But Lang's insistence on form seems, after *The March of Time* and a new technique of reporting in other forms of journalism, a little queasy to claim any more for the cinema. Either the cinema makes films about living nowadays or it should be put back in the old Cambridge era that was known as the Passing The Love of Women Days (1926–30). And though Lang is perhaps right to see a pitiful social problem, as Hindenburg saw an equally horrible one, as mainly a technical puzzle of manipulating units of men, we have to insist on the privilege of an audience to be seeing a film about a man who lost his girl and who in the end won her back again, as Hollywood allows that he should.

What has happened in *Fury* is a crazy and blessed coincidence of two points of view, neither of which could alone make the movie half as good as it is. Like a mother who sentimentally wants to see a lithe body that's part of her own. And a father who wants a son to carry on the business. Somehow they produce a child with character. Lang wanted to see a mob behaving as accurately as he could make it. And Metro sensibly knows that the movies are a business and not a crusade. So they together spawn a film of fundamental social significance. They produce a social document that if it had been seen on paper first no Censor would allow. And Eight Million Dollars begins to tell nothing less than the truth.

It's superficial (and I think dead wrong) to think of Hollywood as a cynical check on brave artistic impulses. Hollywood puts out less nonsense than most art-theatres. And in its ordinary product shows a sense of life that would galvanize any repertory theatre movement. But these are incidental artistic ideas. Hollywood's first notion is to sell a product. And *Fury* has made it important to see that that standard can have remarkable integrity. Whatever will sell is allowed. Our own industry is not so clear-minded. If this film had been about South Wales – about, say, a Chinese riot in Cardiff, I doubt if it would ever have seen the screen. Whereas, whatever the causes, to Metro and the Will Hays Organization must go enormous admiration and credit for putting out a film about their own country which no other country would have dared do.

So *Fury* becomes, both as propaganda and entertainment, no dialectical protest against the immorality of lynching. Lynching has been, indeed, in American history just as often theoretically a moral act undertaken by clans and vigilantes rising up from the people against lawless minorities. But where *Fury* passes superbly beyond the apt melodrama of *Barbary Coast* and *Frisco Kid* and even *The Birth of a Nation* is in exhibiting (through Fritz Lang's direction) and diagnosing (through Krasna's dogging script) the kind of emotion that unites nice middle-class people in obscene hysteria. It fails to show the *sequence* of that emotion. And the real dénouement of the picture, the kinds of reaction that the lynchers feel between the fire and when they appear in court – this is not there.

But *Fury* is a tremendous beginning. The end for the cinema will be in a Dostoievsky, who knows the tragedy of these emotions. Or in a Fascism, which merely likes to feel them.

Mr Deeds Goes to Town

It has become almost a reflex with this critic when the word Capra is mentioned to drop the job in hand, rush for a pen, and scribble the phrase, 'engrossing affection for small American types'. Well, after Mr Deeds, I'm not so sure. It has nothing as affectionate or authentic as the eve of the Derby in *Broadway Bill*, or the Southampton wedding in *It Happened One Night*. And the judge in this new picture, and the two old ladies from Maine and any amount of other characters are all grand ideas but they are not like Happy, and Louis the Lug, and the feed-man, and Raymond Walburn's colonel, and the man who wanted to swap a cane for a hot-dog ('What d'yer want for a hamburger, a telegraph pole?'). They are more like Capra-characters than Americans. Whereas those others were both.

As an idea-movie it's irresistible and apparently means more to more people than his previous Tarkington-cum-Clarence Buddington Kelland comedies. This is just Kelland injected with the Capra drive. Capra's is a great talent all right, but I have the uneasy feeling he's on

Gary Cooper in *Mr Deeds Goes to Town*; Eleanor Powell in *Born to Dance*

his way out. He's starting to make movies about themes instead of about people – *Mr Deeds* is tremendous because the idea is taken charge of wholly by one person and one glorious part, Mr Deeds himself. But the dramatization tends to get tense by night and inside rooms, and to mist up when it gets outside in the street. In the earlier films, the best scenes were cheerful sequences in an unambiguous sun – going to see Gallant Lady arrive (*Broadway Bill*), the crazy drive with the rascal baritone (*It Happened One Night*). Capra has been used to seeing Americans briskly and comically by the dawn's early light. Perhaps only when he has finished his next film (which gloomy rumour has it is to be a literary morsel of James Hilton) will he know which is his lost horizon.

Born to Dance

I found myself the other night at a musical comedy (I mean with real people on a real stage and curtains going up and down, and everything). The lights went down, out came the purple spot, the conductor signalled to the man with the triangle, and the leading lady – a feat of preservation but no hoofer – started to dance. She has, I was told, a considerable West End reputation, but though her legs moved freely enough her trunk never seemed to belong with them, she looked untrained, her head was a marvel of bad pointing and her arms were just comic relief. She seemed in fact to be one with the majority of English musical comedy stars in insisting on the essential refinement of thistledown. She can't dance, so watch her be a snowflake. When she had finished, my companion, a dancer, left the theatre quietly in a hearse while a large audience flicked the dewy tears away and applauded roundly, no more and no less roundly than they will next week, next month, at Eleanor Powell, who has a figure, exquisite balance (remarkable in a tap dancer), a pair of heels unique in Christendom, and the retrospective record of thousands of patient working hours, at least one sweating year spent at the magical black feet of Bojangles Robinson, the master himself. She has also a grin pinned from ear to ear which dismally insists she's just a nice, fresh girl in there trying to please. But that's neither here nor there, it's the heel you're watching, and failing to follow with hearing that is, alas, no more than human.

And where does it get her, this training, this astonishing if monotonous talent? Who really feels the thrill of the thing and can offer the sincerest applause? The film audience? They'll be reacting next week with similar gasps to the Three Pippins performing in pantomime or somewhere along the Edgware Road. The film critics? There's not one of them even knows the difference between soft-shoe and tap. So it must be the half-trained regiments of vaudeville itself that packed the Empire this week and took a lovely revenge they have had coming to them ever since they knew they were too low to appreciate the brooding epics of Flugenspiel, the superb *montage* reserved for patrons of the Academy and Studio One. It's sad to think how conscientiously the critics, the Cambridge School for instance, with their alpha minuses, distribute the 'levels' of appreciation, assigning *Born to Dance* to somewhere pretty low, whereas the *Alcestis* is admittedly high, but no higher than even you may aspire by the grace of education. And then you go into the Empire, and here is the East End and an odd darkie knowing what it's all about, and the film critics nowhere at all. Thus does life get its own back on I. A. Richards. So God having created Aristotle, creates for spite – a darkie.

And what is left for the film critic to understand? Well, there is Buddy Ebsen, nearer our ken because his gift is expressed not only in dance but in the human terms we know something about, his grotesque gravity turns to kidding not only in his steps but in the curling of a lip, in the slow spreading of a gawky thumb. There is Raymond Walburn, alertly absent-minded. There is James Stewart, trying to be ingenuous and charming like Gary Cooper but many tricks and years behind. There are several Cole Porter lyrics, a couple of good tunes and more than a hint of his genuine musical wit. There's Reginald Gardiner conducting an invisible orchestra, by the precision and mock ecstasy of his gesture recalling another clown's name, and that the greatest. There is a sequence when the U.S. Navy dives overboard in a body, funny in itself but suggesting suddenly what a movie *Zuleika Dobson* would make, the mass suicide the high spot, the beads of perspiration on the Roman Emperors' statues as funny and more credible than the book. There is Frances Langford – but there again we are back where we started. For though she's just another crooner to us critics, it's the swing fans this time who will know her voice is a rare one and her jazz phrasing a gift from those wise and cynical gods.

Ramona; Fifteen Maiden Lane

It is *Ramona* in Technicolor which is meant to attract passers-by into the Tivoli this week, but it's *Fifteen Maiden Lane*, a simple monochrome, that should keep them there. *Fifteen Maiden Lane* is about a particular New York jewel robbery. *Ramona* is the California heroine of the eighties generalized into a tinkling symbol of Womanhood.

So far it has been impossible to copy in the movies the quality that makes the Hulls and the Hichenses and the Stratton Porters, the mental unity, the single-mindedness denied to any author higher than the fourth-rate, to possess which all better writers would gladly sell their 'discriminating' public and their old grey flannels. We sensitive hacks stammer at a subtlety, express pity in many a pondered adjective, but the most we achieve, by way of circulation, is the swapping of curious anecdotes, the exchange of private snifflings, while the tears of a Hichens drench the lending libraries of the world. Black-and-white film is too kind to character, to the undramatic details of an etching. However brilliantly they light the Sheik and Freckles, the shadows that set them off are nothing short of black, they are dark, confused and may hide real people, small men in drab clothes as well as cloaks and daggers. But in colour even the shadows are a succulent and penetrable blue. Any single still, however tragic its title, could be made into a postcard and mailed confidently to old men and maiden aunts, for the tone of the suffering is as comfortable as the groups of G. F. Watts. Just as you notice with him that a stricken angel is as nicely posed as the next unlucky spirit, so in *Ramona*, when Don Filipo is dying – I think it was Don Filipo – the two visible walls of his rooms are differently lit though equally pleasing. And it's clear there's no sense in worrying for his health, he's pretty certain to pull through when even the director is *that* interested in the décor. *Ramona* is unlucky, too, in its locale, that is if it was meaning to move and depress us. Since southern California is itself not unlike a colour film, it is here able without any strain to reflect the rich cloudless complacency of the novel. In monochrome it would have been cheerful enough. But colour adds to it the last platitude, the encircling halo that best-selling epics are always straining for.

But poor *Fifteen Maiden Lane* by comparison is merely competent, smooth as a billiard ball, amusing, and ninety times more exciting and intelligent. It has nothing at all to say about Devotion, Self-Sacrifice, Man's Inhumanity to Honest Injuns – it's just there to explain as neatly as a supporting film dare how a jewel robbery was solved and how the 'fences', or receivers of stolen goods to you, were tricked and exposed. *Ramona* is all about mixed blood and that old knotty cosmic problem of the difference – remember? – between 'love' and 'being *in* love'. Whereas Claire Trevor asking Lloyd Nolan, in the last three feet of film, to take her out to luncheon is the nearest *Fifteen Maiden Lane* comes to a carnal statement. Not that it's a mere hygienic thriller, with the characters as human as chessmen. Claire Trevor, a hard and humorous talent, never forgets that she is meant as the

Love From a Stranger: Basil Rathbone, Ann Harding

sustaining overtone of Sex, making even Cesar Romero lose his well-oiled head, throwing tough guys and gangsters' henchmen off their job with the bewildering variety of her Bonwit Teller clothes, the clean groomed limbs of her. But that's the only note that spells box-office for this sharp, delightful little picture, which two years ago might have called itself *The Thin Man*, and nobody would have known much difference.

Ernte; Manhattan Madness; Love From a Stranger

It's always supposed to indicate a keener sensibility to be sniffy about the beauty conventions of one's own day and age. When Dr Johnson was asked what he thought about the London beauties of the time and their habit of making up their faces, he replied: 'I don't like to see an Englishwoman sailing under French colours.' Me, I've tried to keep up with the movement and I get along all right just so long as they keep Carole Lombard in long-shot. But the moment she's in close-up, I can't swing it. One glimpse of the impudent nostrils, the swelling bosom, and I'm a stricken man. This may be 'conventional beauty' to the intelligentsia, but I never yet minded being in a house with a beauty, however conventional. Yet this fault has its compensations. I can look on, for instance, with comparative calm, at practically any Central European with frizzy hair, thighs like market day, and a silk ribbon tied in a bow round the middle of her evening gown. My appetite may be low and panting, being content merely to watch Myrna Loy and Ginger Rogers moving about up there, but I feel no restless urge, like more intelligent critics, for a Viennese actress with a thirty-five waist and eyebrows that meet in the middle. Anybody with my gross standards cannot hope, therefore, to judge Paula Wessely. Of course, she's a good actress, she's sincere and calculates her naïvety very cleverly, and is downright and plucky through her peasant tears. On paper, she's fine. But she's not acting on paper. She's acting in a dark room on a dark night with a lot of people sneezing and at least one film critic risking flu, on her behalf. And sincerity is not enough. Neither is clever acting, and cute horseplay, and stirring feudal devotion to the Rittmeister, and brave tears. Any other time she'd be given marks for all these things. But they were nothing short of a stab in the back, the night she gave me influenza.

Manhattan Madness is kinder to the rheum and its conventions are less nostalgic. It doesn't madden a blear-eyed audience with shots of swaying corn and a spring that will never, never come. On the contrary, it's a crisp, incredible newspaper story in the credible fairyland which

Hollywood so cunningly represents as Manhattan. But for all it's only a convention, along with the balloons and the gaiety in Viennese films, the policemen and Cockney moustaches in Hitchcock films, it's more plausible than most and has a life of its own. Joel McCrea works in a newspaper office that looks like one, his Press Club might be a press club, he takes recognizable taxis and blows steaming coffee, sitting up at two in the morning on a stool at quick-lunch bars with Jean Arthur, who's as husky and friendly as any New Yorker we know. Though the story is nothing, and the pace seemed slowed the night I was there, because the sound-track was being played too low, it was this Hollywood convention that made the evening, the visual convention of a New York that is nearer the New York of Ed Sullivan than *Ernte* is anywhere near Vienna or Hungary, than *Love From a Stranger* is near the Bayswater it supposedly starts out from. It's the background of *Manhattan Madness* that cheers and stimulates, whereas it's the background of *Love From a Stranger* that for more than half the film gets in the way of a first-rate melodrama. Trafalgar Films, Ltd., do their part to scotch these nasty rumours about the local film industry by introducing us to Ann Harding as an object of pity, a poor working girl living in a flat that would cost, at a modest guess, about six hundred a year. Our hopes pick up when she wins a sweepstake and when Basil Rathbone, his cultivated brow pained at the mention of 'guide-books', offers to show her a strange, lovely Europe, personal 'out-of-the-way' places. Mr Rathbone's untrodden ways take in the Champs Elysées, the Folies Bergère, Rome, Cannes, a suite at the Dorchester, and – believe it or not – a 'place' in Kent. It's only when Miss Harding is finally locked in that cottage in Kent, with no hope of escaping to Stratford-on-Avon, the Taj Mahal, or Lake Killarney that the movie can settle into a single episode of beautifully developed and well-written masochism.

Robert Forsythe

Robert Forsythe (real name, Kyle Crichton), the son of Scottish parents, was born in 1896 in the coal-mining district of Pennsylvania, worked in the mines and in the steel works there, managed to get a college education. Contributor to the radical weekly, *New Masses*. Associate editor of *Scribner's Magazine*; staff writer on *Collier's Weekly*. Author of *Reading from Left to Right* and *The Marx Brothers*. Died 1960.

Belle of the Nineties: Mae West

6. Robert Forsythe

The Fountain

I have thought the matter over and have come to the conclusion that
something drastic will have to be done about the English. Treating
them with kindness is all very well but the results are not worth the
effort. Being tart with them has its points but they have been petted
by the fates so long that the mildest word of reproof causes them to
sulk and there is nothing quite so depressing on earth as an Englishman
feeling inferior. Naturally I refer to the upper clawss English, those
monstrous people who cry 'played!' in an ecstatic voice during the
course of a tennis match and who depart with a 'toodle-oo' and a
'cheeri-o'.

For a time I felt that something might be done but that was before
Hollywood made *Cavalcade*. The effect of this was so profound in
the Brown Derby and the Cocoanut Grove that actors sat through
entire meals without being able to understand their companions who
were speaking in a combination of Chaucer and early Okmulgee,
Okla. The fact that the English themselves made *Henry the Eighth* in
which the King was shown to be an uncouth gentleman was set down

145

as a historical incident. The further fact that Henry's descendants ate at the London Kit Kat and went insane over Sophie Tucker was regarded as a complete confirmation of the fact that the British were a race of such culture they could afford to be democratic.

Several weeks ago I felt that I had done my homage toward English gentility by my presence at *One More River* but the strange fascination of these unbelievable people brought me again to the Music Hall last week to see *The Fountain*. The tabloids have been built upon this pandering to morbid curiosity. The first words of the English officers in the Dutch internment camp made me realize that I was doing myself no good by this surrender to my lower emotions but I could do nothing but sit and writhe, entranced by the amazing spectacle.

The picture as usual has to do with a noble English lady who is caught. From what I can learn the British have a difficult time being married and a terrible time getting out of it. In this case the lady is torn between the young Englishman she formerly loved (now conveniently present in her uncle's home in Holland) and the German officer to whom she is unfortunately wed. I was anxious to see the picture because I had read the book by Charles Morgan, which was a great success in politer circles several years ago. Mr Morgan is the dramatic reviewer of the London *Times* and is definitely of the opinion that there is nothing more precious than the human soul provided it is resting within an English bosom. He is considerable of a mystic, too, is Mr Morgan and he has acquired the knack of combining a trace of lust with an abundance of spirituality in quantities calculated to provide the maximum of titillation with the minimum of self-reproach. Mr Cecil de Mille has produced the same effects in a more vulgar manner by utilizing the naked bodies of a Broadway night club in a great biblical romance.

The clearest indication that the British Empire is coasting toward the foot of the hill is the nature of its literary product. Without reading the book it is possible to tell what it is about by the way it has impressed William Lyon Phelps and by the way it is moving in the lending libraries of this country. If it is doing well, you may set it down as an axiom that the subject matter of the volume has to do with punting on the Thames or jaunting about with a travelling circus or living in a street with the most interesting people or of travelling the highways with Robin Hood. The point is that the English are living almost entirely in the past. They hate the present, which sees their decay become more evident with the months, and they cannot bear the thought of the future. This is what a British critic means when he

The Fountain: Paul Lukas

inveighs so ferociously against the prospect of collectivization and pleads so fervently for the individuality of the soul. He means the white flannelled soul of the gentleman living in Surrey; in no possible case does he refer to the individual soul of the man living in the slums of Glasgow.

Quite recently J. B. Priestley started out on a tour of the tight little isle. At first we have nothing but the thatched roofs and the verdant green lanes and the softness of the landscape. Then Mr Priestley begins to see another England, one which he obviously had not dreamed of before. He sees the ruined textile mills of Lancashire; he sees the mines of the Midlands; he sees the drab streets of the mill towns with their hopeless humanity on dole sitting in the doorways as if waiting for death. England, my England! Is this just something of the depression years, is this just a new blight sent by God to punish the proud Britons? For hundreds of years the slums of England have been the most hideous in the world; since the days of the Industrial Revolution there has been no misery like the misery of the English working-class. The finest book by an American on the latter subject is *Irish Slummy* by Tim Mara, which tells of his boyhood in Liverpool. It is an amazing picture of the degradation which can come to a group of people by the conditions under which they live. I remember reading this book at the same time I read an article by the English Fascist, F. Yeats-Brown, he who wrote *Bengal Lancer* and other books telling of the brave stand of the British against the 'fanatical' tribesmen of India. (Nobody but a fanatic, of course, would think of protesting against the beneficent rule of the British.) Yeats-Brown has just returned from a trip to 'hideous' Russia and is coming down from London to Sussex just at that time of dusk when the smoke twines up in little spirals from the thatched cottages sitting in their verdant lanes. England, my England! cries Yeats-Brown. Yes, his England, the England of peace and quiet and comfort built upon the labour of children of ten working in the mines of Scotland, built upon the poverty of Egypt and the hell of India.

Everything depends upon the point of view. Stark Young in *So Red the Rose* has just shown how gracious, soft and beautiful the slave-owning civilization of the Old South could be. Of those who made it possible, little is said. At the moment the yachts are off Newport preparing for the Cup Races. America will be represented by the Resolute, built and raced at a cost of $500,000. Mrs McLean has just returned from Moscow where she gave the natives a 'thrill' with her exhibition of the Hope diamond. According to *The Times*, she landed 'literally glittering with jewels hung in a loop over her arm and forming a chain for her diamond-studded purse, which contained a cigarette case decorated with the jewels'.

But pity, my dear children, pity is the supreme virtue. As I sat watching *The Fountain* I had nothing but sorrow for the pallid emotions of the poor pallid people. It was difficult to keep from laughing at the heroic passages of Samuel Hoffenstein, who once wrote publicity for Al Woods and was now so British that one expected the audience to break out in cries of 'hear! hear!' Or at least 'pip! pip!'

The main theme of *The Fountain* is as I have outlined it but there were slight elaborations of its general contour. Ann Harding is the heroine who begins sobbing at the first sight of her former English sweetheart and ends in a torrent of tears at the deathbed of her German spouse. The latter gentleman, well played by Paul Lukas, had returned from the wars minus an arm and an ambition to live. Julie, entangled with Lewis (who is as soft a gentleman as even the Empire has ever turned out), sacrifices him for her greater duty to Rupert. Jealous members of the household allow Rupert to know that Lewis has been ascending to the bedroom of Julie in those trying days when Rupert was holding the Hindenburg Line. He hears this at the same time the news arrives that the sailors have mutinied at Kiel (hooray! from our side) and the Kaiser has fled (boo!). He collapses for keeps this time and finally, after a prolonged death scene, passes on. The mistake I made, says Rupert, nobly brave, was in loving you when you didn't love me. But I have learned to love you since, cries Julie frantically pulling him back from the Gates of Heaven. No, replies Rupert gently, you only feel sorry for me because I am injured; you really love Lewis. I can die happy that I have loved you. He does same.

This is what Mr Morgan would call treating of the fundamental human emotions. To understand this you must realize that the afore-mentioned English upper-clawss are a singularly childish and un-original breed, at least in their present incarnation. The original manuscript of Carlyle's *French Revolution* was thrown into the fire by John Stuart Mill's maid. When T. E. Lawrence, the Sheik of Arabia, wrote the book of his war experiences, he lost the original manuscript in a taxicab. Major N. N. E. Bray has now written a book saying that Colonel Lawrence was very small potatoes in Mesopotamia. And what do you think happened to Major Bray's book? *The Times* was telling about it Sunday. 'Once the manuscript was lost while the author was en route to visit Ibn Saud. Recently a housemaid threw the second half into the fire and, like Carlyle's *The French Revolution*, it had to be entirely rewritten.'

I have a little plan worked out in case Colonel Lawrence wishes to answer Major Bray. The Colonel will take half the manuscript and place himself in a taxicab sitting before the house. When properly settled he will light a match and drop it in the petrol tank. This will dispose of the first half of the manuscript. Within the house the usual housemaid will be sitting before the fire with the other half of the manuscript in her lap and waiting for the signal. As she waits she reads a copy of *The Sheik* by Ethel M. Dell. Upon hearing the explosion without she will take the manuscript and carefully drop it in the grate. The original part comes in what happens to the Colonel. When the cab explodes, disposing of the first half of the manuscript, it also disposes of the Colonel. This inaugurates my campaign against the English.

Belle of the Nineties
When you consider Madame du Barry and Nell Gwyn, it is evident that Mae West has made a mistake in confining her immorality to

stage and screen. Granted that a woman of her intelligence could be prevailed upon to favour a Congressman or a Secretary of War, the spectacle of Miss West affecting state policy as well as private temperatures is something which no future historian could afford to overlook. It is plain that on any basis of comparison she belongs to the great line.

There are so many indications of the breakdown of capitalistic civilization that we are inclined to become tender and sympathetic in the midst of the débâcle, much in the manner of 'don't cheer, boys; the poor devils are dying', but it is obvious that Miss West, more than any of her associates, symbolizes the end of an epoch. Her stage plays, *Sex* and *The Drag*, uncovered such a horrifying picture of homosexuals, Lesbians and ordinary degenerates that Miss West was sentenced to the workhouse for ten days as a way of restoring the faith of the populace in the great city. Her motives in presenting the plays were undoubtedly mercenary, but her attorneys overlooked a great opportunity of establishing her as a sociologist and humanitarian, moved solely by her concern for reform.

The movies were more astute in their management of her films. They retained the spiciness, the lustiness and bawdiness, but they carefully confined them to the past. In a sense it may be said that the golden era of Chuck Connors and the Bowery was bourgeois vigour as its peak. With all its dirt and squalor the Bowery managed to maintain an Elizabethan rowdiness and crudity which could pass as strength. The Puritan was at last defeated; men were again honest animals. They killed, they whored and they flaunted the broken bits of Methodist morality in the faces of the nice people who came down to look with fascinated horror at these mad barbarians.

The Christian fathers are quite correct in worrying about Miss West. Whether the success of her bawdiness is a sign that we have conquered Puritanism and are a mature people at last, or whether it represents a complete collapse of morality, it is evident that it reveals the lack of authority of religion. The Catholic campaign for clean films succeeded in changing the title of the latest West film from *It Ain't No Sin* to *Belle of the Nineties*, but it is still Mae West in *It Ain't No Sin*.

But it is in her stage plays that her significance lies. If we judged alone from her screen comedies we should be tempted to say that she represented sexual honesty in a world given over much too completely to the antics of the fairy. I refer to the world of the theatre and to the race of people known as perverts. Without seeking to alarm you with a sensational exposure of vice conditions in the green room, I may say merely that the condition within the profession is notorious. The facts of the matter are plain enough, but I may not be able to convince you that they have historical importance, and I am not even going to attempt to prove that the bitterly reactionary character of the stage, with the few exceptions you recognize so well, are the result in some small part of this same disease. We know quite well that the reasons for reaction are class reactions and if I make any point at all in this respect it would be to indicate that introversion is essentially a class ailment and the direct result of a sybaritic life which finally results in profound boredom for lack of any further possible stimulation or titillation. It is invariably associated with those twin elements of perversion, sadism and masochism, and generally reveals itself among the thinned-out representatives of a decaying class. The sadistic cruelty of Hitlerism is no accident. It is the unmistakable symptom of an incurable malady.

I am not a psychologist and what I have to say about the coincidences of history in this regard are not to be taken as gospel from the scientific archangels, but three widely separated incidents prior to the World War have always struck me as being significant. There was first the Oscar Wilde case in England. The divorce suit of Sir Charles Dilke with its resultant exposure of the hypocrisy and moral laxness of the aristocracy had been the first break in the dyke of British class superiority. It showed that not only were the nobles human but they were something less than admirably human. Even this, however, was outshadowed by the revelations of the Wilde affair. The wave of indignation swept Wilde to jail, but it also revealed the fact that sexual debauchery was so common among the nobility that Frank Harris could report, without legal action being taken against him, that seventy-five members of the House of Lords were notorious perverts.

Not long after, Germany was stirred by the revelations that Prince Philip Eulenberg, intimate friend of the Kaiser, had been accused by Maximilian Harden of indulging in unnatural vice. Harden had attacked Eulenberg publicly in his paper *Zukunft*, trying to force a charge of libel. Eulenberg refused and was disgraced. Evidence later produced in another trial at Munich proved conclusively that he was guilty. What was even more damning was the knowledge that others besides Eulenberg of the Imperial court were involved and that conditions were generally bad in high circles. The War came along several years later to place the world's attention on other forms of perversion such as mass slaughter, and it was only with the advent of the *Fuehrer* that homosexuality was raised to the rank of statesmanship.

There was a third case in Russia which practically coincided with the outbreak of the war. By a coincidence France at the same time was so stirred by the sensational trial arising out of the killing of Calmette, editor of *Figaro*, by Madame Caillaux that the death of the Archduke at Sarajevo was almost overlooked by the smartly gowned crowds who gathered in court each day for the details. In the same way the nobility of Russia could scarcely take their fascinated gazes away from the St Petersburg scandal long enough to watch the troops marching to the front.

What Mae West did in the plays I have mentioned and what she does in her motion pictures is to show in her frank cynical way the depths to which capitalistic morality has come. There is an honesty in her playing which is even more devastating. It is not the bouncing lechery of Ben Jonson but the mean piddling lewdness of the middle classes getting their little hour of sin before the end. Miss West has a marvellous capacity for the theatre and she acts in what might be termed the grand manner, but I can never hear her 'C'm up an see me some time' without thinking of Ruth Snyder carrying on her cheap pathetic romance with Judd Gray. Because she epitomizes so completely the middle-class matron in her hour of licence I feel that Miss West has never been properly appreciated as the First Artist of the Republic. It is palpable nonsense to be concerned about such children as Katharine Hepburn, who will be as forgotten as Mary Miles Minter in a few years' time, when we possess a lady who could assume her position now as the Statue of Liberty and who so obviously represents bourgeois culture at its apex that she will enter history as a complete treatise on decay.

Chapayev

Let there be fireworks and dancing in the streets! Enough of restraint, enough of fine cinematic hair-splittings, enough of everything but elation. *Chapayev* is in town! Not since the great days of the Soviet silent films has there been anything like it.

The picture was made by the Brothers Vasilyev from factual material supplied by Furmanov, commissar of Chapayev's Red Division. It is the simple story of a peasant who becomes a great military leader under the stress of the Civil War. It was made by Lenfilm at Leningrad and has created a tremendous furore in the Soviet Union.

So much for the material facts. Artistically, it returns the Soviet Union to its position at the head of the movie world. If I speak in superlatives it is because I have waited twelve hours for the effects of *Chapayev* to wear off, and I am still physically stirred by it. There are no tricks, no striving for effect, no high points of fake drama. It is so funny in spots and is played throughout in so humorously natural a manner that an audience which has only the English titles finds itself roaring. This is life as it really is – a compound of fun, tragedy, and courage. Boris Bobochkin as Chapayev is miraculously cast and turns in a performance that belongs among the best ever seen on any screen.

As the picture opens, Chapayev is bouncing over the countryside in a droschka, picking up his men anew and gathering his wandering forces about him. He is a roistering, warm-hearted fellow who sings with his men and rules them with an iron hand. He can barely read and write, but he is a born leader and tactician. Moscow sends Furmanov to be commissar with the division, and Chapayev is not pleased with that. Furmanov halts the looting by Chapayev's men and throws Zhikharev, second in command, in gaol. There is a showdown which is halted by the appearance of the peasants coming to thank Chapayev for the return of their animals. The Reds are, after all, not like the Whites, who rob and kill. The rich humour of the scene only points the more important fact that the Bolsheviks were able to defeat their enemies because they won the confidence of the countryside by these very means. Chapayev can do nothing but accept the thanks of the peasants, but he sees the point. He calls a meeting of his men to admonish them on how they shall act in the future. The old peasant (Boris Chirkov) who has headed the thanks-delegation is there again. He is after information this time.

'Are you a Bolshevik or a Communist?' he asks Chapayev, and Chapayev is stumped. He looks around for Furmanov's help, but Furmanov lets him fight it out alone. The answer he finally gives will roll you in the aisle. I won't spoil it for you.

The scenes with Pyetka (Leonid Kmit, and a great job he does) are equally hilarious and human. Pyetka is his orderly and also his pal. He thinks Chapayev is the greatest general in the world. Chapayev admits it. Later he proves it. The White Army prepares to attack. Chapayev outlines his defence and stations his men. As the battle starts, he is informed that his cavalry leader has been shot and there is mutiny among the men. He goes to curb the mutiny and lead the charge. The battle scenes are the most thrilling I have ever seen. The sight of the White Army marching in steady, deliberate file across the plain, moving with the inevitable force of a wall of water and accompanied only by the deadly reiteration of the beat of a drum, is so menacing and nerve-racking that the spectator not only clings to his seat in terror, but understands the effect the spectacle must be having on Chapayev's untutored men. They break and flee, but are brought back by Furmanov. Anna, the only girl with the division and the chief machine gunner, holds the enemy in check until Chapayev can arrive with the cavalry.

It is in the story of Anna that you begin to understand how great the film is. Hollywood would have made her a combination of Joan of Arc and Carrie Nation. The Russians are really a stupid people. There she is, a pretty girl among a company of soldiers, an ideal place for the love of two men to clash over her. Joan Crawford, dressed in a military creation by Adrian, could have made something of the role. The Soviet directors throw it all away. Anna (who is really Maria Popova and is now famous in Russia) does her job as a soldier, in love with Pyetka as he is in love with her, but never once steps out of character to make a screen holiday for those who can never believe that 'human nature' is anything but a matter of a kiss being more important than a continent.

Furmanov is recalled to Moscow and another commissar is sent to replace him, and Chapayev is resting on his laurels when disaster overtakes him. His sentries fall asleep during the night and are overpowered. The Whites pour through to headquarters. Anna rides for help while Chapayev and Pyetka man the machine guns and hold off the enemy forces. A field gun finally brings their retreat in ruins about them and Pyetka manages to get Chapayev away, grievously wounded. Pyetka stays on the river bank to halt the Whites while Chapayev starts to swim the river to safety. Pyetka's ammunition gives out and he is killed from the high bank. Chapayev sinks to his death from machine gun bullets with the farther bank almost within reach. The Red cavalry arrives almost at the same moment and drives out the Whites.

It is the secret of the greatness of the film that we never conceive of the death of Chapayev as defeat. A brave man is dead, but from what has gone before, from the very fineness of his men, there is never any doubt that victory belongs to his cause. There is not a word of 'propaganda', not a gesture or accent which seeks to divert the spectator from the plain intent of the action. Chapayev is dead, but Chapayev lives as a symbol. The Soviet world has its Chapayev, its Dimitrov; Nazi Germany has its poor pitiful Horst Wessel. Who can

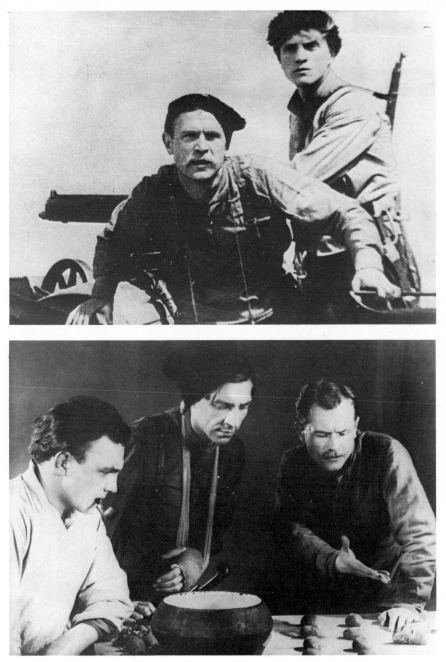

Chapayev

doubt, who can ever doubt about the future! What can all the Hearsts, all the Soviet-haters, all the oppressors of the earth do against one Chapayev!

Never have I been so envious of those who understand Russian. The lines were brilliant even in English translation (and I want to say a word of praise for those English titles) but the people around me at the Cameo were chuckling continuously at phrases which the translator obviously couldn't include for lack of space. There are dozens of episodes I could mention – the scene with the veterinarians; the scene where Pyetka is trying to mix machine gun instruction with love; the scene where Chapayev reproaches his assistant for allowing a bullet to hit him; the beautiful scenes in the farmhouse where Chapayev and the soldiers sing and talk of life and death; the scene in White head-quarters with Colonel Borozdin (I. N. Pevtzov, another masterly characterization) playing Beethoven sonatas at the piano while his body servant pleads mutely for the life of his deserter-brother. It is all there and it is marvellous.

If I have the faintest criticism (and I have racked my head to think of something which might allow me to retain my standing as a critic of severity), it would be that the character of Furmanov (Boris Blinov) is slightly overdone. He seemed a trifle too pleased with the success of his education of Chapayev, but I am quite prepared to hear that nobody but myself has been aware of it. I am not well enough acquainted with Russian music to know if the songs are folk-songs or were written for the picture by G. Popov, but in any case they are hauntingly beautiful and placed with such rightness that they seem an inevitable part of the story.

I can't close without another word about Bobochkin who plays Chapayev. If you can recall Wallace Beery playing Villa, you will get some notion of the horrible quality which would have been brought to such a part by an American producer. Bobochkin is gruff and hearty without being grotesque. He jumps on people in the severest manner and they are not at all afraid of him. He sings, he jokes, he dominates his men and leads them, but he is always exactly himself, without a false note – a shrewd, uneducated peasant who happens at the same time to be a great man. They will be talking about this characterization when all the American character men have gone to join Alice in Wonderland; because Bobochkin is playing not a character out of a book, but a man out of life, with the variations all of us realize we only rarely see depicted.

A Midsummer Night's Dream

After a series of triumphs having to do with Hooray for the Army, Hooray for the Navy, Hooray for the Irish and Marion Davies, the Warner Brothers have got round to Art. Not only have they discovered it; they have practically surrounded it and captured it. The furore which has accompanied the producing, promoting and exhibiting of *A Midsummer Night's Dream* could, if properly harnessed, have prevented the Ethiopian War. It revealed that not only were the Warner Brothers conscious that they had done something admirable but that they were scared to death by their bravery. After $1,500,000 had been spent, the full force of the idea descended upon them that they were not only tackling Shakespeare but also fantasy, the two Deadly Sins of the Cinema. The result has been a frantic campaign joined in by the entire film industry, including the office of Mr Will Hays and the assembled battalions of press agents of all persuasions and degrees of competence. Briefly, if *A Midsummer Night's Dream* doesn't go, Art is through in the movies.

To the credit of the Brothers Warner, it may be said that they have done their part. They have engaged Max Reinhardt to direct the picture and Herr Korngold to adapt the music of Mendelssohn. They have lavishly thrown in every actor on the Warner lot. The fact that many of them are not actors doesn't alter the generosity of the gesture. The Warner Brothers have given the picture every opportunity but they have run into a difficulty which has often thwarted them: author trouble. The truth is that judging from its showing in this one film William Shakespeare will not do in Hollywood. I say nothing about how *A Midsummer Night's Dream* read in the original script or how it played in the stage version. I know only that as a film it is a nonsense fable and the great bore of the century.

The greatest limitation of the screen is that it is compelled to show too much. It is also its greatest strength, but not when doing fantasy. Because the stage is unable to do much more than hint at the forest and the fairies, the imagination of the spectator has a chance to create his own pixie world. In the movie it is not possible to hint at the forest and the whirling vapours and the downy tufts of turf; they must be there for all the world to see. But when you can see them, they become ridiculous. The whirling vapours become nothing but a cloud of steam pumped up by a crowd of stage hands, the flittering nymphs become nothing but a ballet trained by Albertina Rasch, the prancing in the moonlight becomes as embarrassing as the little groups of dancers who leap aloft on the lawn at summer college sessions.

A Midsummer Night's Dream

What saddened me most was the collapse of the comedy. I had always thought that the strolling players were pretty funny and when it was announced that James Cagney was playing Bottom, and such excellent gentlemen as Frank McHugh and Joe E. Brown were to accompany him, I sat back in expectation. Since I will die rather than admit that Mr Cagney is not a great actor, I must blame it on Shakespeare or Reinhardt. Something is wrong and it isn't me and it isn't Cagney. It isn't even Joe E. Brown. I will laugh at Joe E. Brown in an ordinary comedy, which is about as far as anyone should be expected to go in proving a sense of humour. Just to be on the safe side, I'm going to blame it on Reinhardt. The scene in the cellar when they are rehearsing is always on the verge of being funny, and the scene in the castle during the performance before the nabobs is funny because of the contrast of the players in that elegant setting, but it is so horsed about in direction that it loses the fine goofy effect it needs.

If anything can save the film it will be Mickey Rooney who plays Puck. Reinhardt does his best but he can't quite ruin Mickey. The kid is a typical little Harp with a mocking laugh which would drive a giraffe mad and he is practically perfect for the part. Reinhardt, by the way, is going to do well in Hollywood. If one laugh by Puck is good, he must have not fifteen extra laughs of the same general tenor but five hundred. If a few clouds of steam are effective, he must have clouds of steam repeated at intervals of seconds over a period of what seems days. Reinhardt is colossal, he is gigantic and his direction in this picture is pedestrian and unimaginative and dull.

Who else is in the picture I don't remember. There are a host of lads and ladies dressed in court costumes and of course the two young couples who get all balled up when the magic curse is put upon them, but it all matters very little. They wander about in the woods and Mr Cagney wears his head of an ass with the aplomb of one who can play in anything, and there is the fairy queen and the tough Oberon and miles of fantasy and gauzy ladies and I wished to heaven it would end so I could get out into the God-given exhaust smoke, clatter and literal hellishness of Broadway.

But this is not to say that it will not be a success. It is going to be a success or everybody at Warner Brothers is going to get fired. The publicity push behind the film is tremendous. It makes one realize what will happen when the movies really get into their Fascist swing. The film is being used as a study course in thousands of schools. If you look closely you will see long lines of students, with their quarters clutched hotly in the palms of their hands, marching down to the movie house to do their part for culture.

This feature of the business interests me very little, however. I'm more concerned with the future of the movies. If *A Midsummer Night's Dream* fails as Doug and Mary failed in *The Taming of the Shrew*, it will be final proof to the intellects of the industry that the people will not support good pictures. Because a play which Shakespeare himself could surely never have taken as anything but a pot-boiler fails to succeed with a modern audience, it will prove to Hollywood that the age of the public is short of nine and that anything more intellectual than *Top Hat* cannot hope to make money. Secretly, I hope they prove it. If there is anything I don't want Hollywood to do it is to begin dealing with ideas. There was a time when I cried for a more serious Hollywood approach to art but I'm aware now of my error. Any radical who urges them to deal with current problems or current ideas is crazy. By the very nature of the industry – its tie-up with the big bankers, its dependence on exhibitors of every blend of intelligence and every prejudice, with its fear of the moron and the churches – they are forced to keep on the side of general opinion, forced to deal with events of importance in a way which cannot help being obviously or insidiously reactionary and Fascist.

Peasants

In all possible ways I am the right person to be reviewing *Peasants* because with the exceptions of two pictures seen on my vacation I have stayed religiously away from the cinema for months. One picture seen in a little Vermont town was *Love Me Forever* with Grace Moore, which if not the worst picture ever filmed is a certain indication that judgment has left me entirely. The point I am making is one I have made often before: to wit, that familiarity with motion pictures breeds tolerance. Coming upon them after a long absence, one is likely to blink the eye and be amazed that such nonsense can be accepted peaceably by human beings. After a period of regular attendance, the spectator begins to make the comparisons which are fatal to his intellectual integrity. He begins to convince himself that while the particular movie before him is awful, it is not worse than something seen last week.

In brief, I should be prepared to feel that *Peasants* was nothing but an ordinary Soviet programme picture, fit for proletarians and maniacs who have been misled by the Comintern. The plight of my friends, the New York newspaper reviewers, was even more complicated than my own by reason of the appearance on the same day

Peasants

with *Peasants* of Marion Davies's *Page Miss Glory*, which naturally
required first attention. It will be difficult for them to live down the
memory and I refrain from adding to their miseries by predicting that
their grandchildren will not rest happy under such a pall. The truth is
that *Peasants* is a masterpiece. Not the best picture of the year; not
the finest production of the Soviet new season; not the most successful
example of the new Soviet screen technique. I mean none of these
mealy things. I mean that *Peasants* belongs among the great motion
pictures of all time. It is an achievement of stupendous proportions
because it succeeds in dramatizing ideas rather than adventures. To
those who complain that it is slow moving, I can only answer that
John Erskine might have written a more sprightly *Growth of the Soil*,
but thank God Hamsun did it.

In its more rounded form, *Peasants* is the supreme drama of
collectivization. More concretely it is the story of a pig farm.
Ordinarily, I am not attracted to pig farms. Until I had seen *Peasants*
I would have resented the idea that I could have the slightest interest
in a pig farm. Friedrich Ermler, the director, won the Order of Lenin

and gets the Grand Badge of Forsythe for what he has done in this picture.

The beginning is confusing. After an opening in the barn when the news comes that the pigs are to be killed or taken away because the farm can't feed them, it shifts to a meeting of the kolhoz, where all is in an uproar. The spectator is likely to resent his inability to pick out the heroes and villains immediately. It is only later that he realizes his bewilderment is matched by the befuddlement of the farm workers at the seemingly contradictory forces. Thinking that they are doing the only thing possible in the circumstances, the peasants distribute the pigs, while a few of the more loyal and clear-headed members try to keep the drove together. Good intentions are no guide; there are bitter fights between peasants who have only the best interests of the farm at heart. It is only with the appearance of the political representative from the tractor station, that order is restored. Ermler is superb in showing that the machinations of the kulaks are not the slinking treacheries of the usual stage villains but the subtle guiding of willing workers with wrong advice.

But there is no justice in spoiling the story for those who are yet to see it. The loyal girl (E. Yunger) is married to a man whose hatred of collectivization is a profound and pathological thing. His father has been exiled to Siberia, his brother has been shot for killing a peasant on a collective farm, his mother yearns only for the day when she can have her old individual farm back. Ermler is fair. The cards are not stacked. Not only does he show the man as an intelligent and sincere believer in his ideas but he allows the spectator to sympathize with him. It is a problem. Is it to be the old Russia with its cruelties and black superstitions and hopelessness (the kulaks having, indeed, a better life than they will temporarily have under collectivization) or is new Russia to go forward, even if the road onward is rocky with difficulties? It is a fair problem and it is handled honestly. The result is a human and dramatic document so powerfully and fundamentally moving that there are only a few motion pictures within memory which remotely compare with it. I will not mention the Hollywood product, even the finest Hollywood product. There is no fair comparison.

There is no salty, colourful central character such as Chapayev, but it is not needed and indeed would be incongruous in a picture based on collectivization. Always the farm is there and the people who belong to it. We have the girl and her tortured husband, her brother, the tractor agent and dozens of peasant characters looking as if they stepped fresh from a photograph by David Octavus Hill, the old Scottish master. The scenes in the clubhouse are so human, so warming, so jolly and real that I will never again think of a farm without centring all my thoughts on Ermler's peasants. These are the people who, according to reports of hostile Soviet visitors, never smile, never laugh – who will never again enjoy themselves as human beings. If that is true, the very least we can agree upon is that they are surpassingly fine actors. Not only do they laugh but I have heard no heartier laughter in years than that which came from the audience on the second night at the Cameo Theatre, at the episode where the men eat dumplings until it seems they must pop.

What is it about these people which makes them so human and palpitantly real? If they are merely actors, why is it that they convince me so completely that they were never off a farm in their lives? Nothing is idealized, nothing is glossed over by Ermler. When the girl is accidentally killed by the husband who becomes literally terrified at her dreams of a child who will carry on the common work of the farm, there follows a scene of horror which might have been taken out of an old Russian novel but which, in the circumstances of the man's state, seemed so inevitable and brutally logical that, in retrospect, it would have been difficult to conceive of anything else he might have done. What I am saying is that *Peasants* is flawlessly right in feeling and mood and temper. It is a great work of art and a triumph for the Soviet screen.

The New Gulliver
When they started telling me about a new motion picture based on Swift's *Gulliver's Travels* and done with puppets, I said to myself: 'I love the Soviet Union, I love every single solitary citizen of that great land, I love the Old Bolsheviks, the ex-Trotskyists, the Young Pioneers and the Dam on the Dnieper, but puppets, marionettes. . . . No, by God!'

This is because I have never liked puppets even when they were good. I haven't liked them whether done by Tony Sarg, the Yale Puppeteers or the Italian . . . what's the name . . . Piccoli? I was once dragged to the Italian puppets in Chinatown and found them the most boring thing in the world next to a book review by Herschel Brickell. Any child of mine who preferred Tony Sarg to Mickey Mouse or James Cagney would be left out of the will and indeed given very little food until he repented.

I can hear the sceptics saying: 'This is the usual Forsythe trick of building up the opposition to such a point that when he turns about he practically floors the reader with the revelation.' I can hear them saying it and they're right. I hate puppets and I think *The New Gulliver* (Cameo), which is done mostly with puppets, is not only great but bordering on the miraculous. The point must be that they're not puppets at all but a new race of human beings. A gentleman named Ptushko has taken several years out of his life and fashioned a set of individuals of such astuteness and discernment that I can think of whole races who would do the world a good turn by retiring and allowing the Ptushko people to take over in their place.

What these incredible Russians have done is take the old story by Swift and return it to its original form as a satire rather than a fable for children. It starts out with a group of Komsomols being rewarded for good behaviour or good deeds or something. (I saw it before Julian Leigh did the English titles and my knowledge of Russian is so slight that when I once thought I was ordering food in a Third Avenue Russian restaurant I received a very hard look from a waitress and the manager came up and stood menacingly by the table.) Among the prizes given the boys is a copy of *Gulliver's Travels*. They go off in a boat for a picnic on a nearby island and when one of the boys starts reading the book aloud, another boy (V. Konstantinov) falls asleep and dreams the Gulliver legend.

He is first engaged in a battle on board ship with the lusty crew, the ship is wrecked, he is washed ashore and when he awakes he finds himself pinned down by the tiny cables of the Lilliputians and half of the nation sitting on his chest. This is where the real picture begins. Gentlemen, I tell you; you've never seen anything like it! I'm not good on technical matters and I pass on only what I've been told. The puppets aren't on strings; perhaps that's where they've always gone wrong with me before. As I understand it, each motion of all those hundreds of Lilliputians was photographed individually just as is done with the Mickey Mouse cartoons. In any event, there are motor cars with gun turrets, soldiers, pompous officials, innocent passers-by.

The scene shifts to the King's palace where His Majesty, looking as charmingly half-witted as Alfonso, is being prompted by his Prime Minister, who is keen enough to allow the royal moron to mouth the phrases while a phonograph (concealed) grinds out the words. But somebody leans on the record and cracks it, with the result that the needle sticks and keeps repeating the same phrase. The audience of loyal court followers see nothing out of the way in this but the Prime Minister finally gets the thing halted. These scenes and the succeeding ones in Parliament are satire in the grand manner.

What follows is a public entertainment in honour of Gulliver, with an opera singer looking exactly like Bee Lillie burlesquing an English concert-hall queen, with dancers and a culminating conceit by which the Lilliputians, to do their very best for this visitor, trot out *their* company of midgets! It's the biggest laugh I've had in years. I don't want to spoil the picture for you by giving it in detail. The lady who writes for *The New Yorker* from Paris under the name of Genet was annoyed at the thought of the Russians making a class problem out of the Swiftian fable, but she surrendered to the point of saying that 'for technical sorcery, for the magic of Ptushko's animated mechanical actors, the film is astounding, fantastic, an engineer's and technician's delight.' This is going rather far for *The New Yorker*, but she rounds to in great form by adding, 'as a work of art, or even propaganda, it is vexing'.

It is perhaps rationalization on my part but I feel that the battle between the workers and the royal nitwits makes the film. There is a great to-do with guns, explosions and advances and retreats in the latter sequences of *The New Gulliver* and it keeps the picture alive. I'm afraid Genet hasn't read her Swift in late years. As a matter of plain truth, the Lilliputian episodes wear very thin. After you have the first shock of delight in the transposition of everything from a large scale to the midget scale, nothing much happens until Gulliver walks out and takes the ships in hand. Ptushko, as an artist, must have realized that. If he had been an artist working for the New York Theatre Guild he might have taken such liberties as are taken, and successfully, by Alfred Lunt and Lynn Fontanne with Shakespeare's *The Taming of the Shrew*. Being a Bolshevik and interested in other problems, he took such liberties as struck him as being important for the audience he was addressing.

But what of it and why the discussion? *The New Gulliver* is a knockout for sheer entertainment and the greatest technical achievement the screen has seen since the early days of David Wark Griffith and the fade-out. It has been taken over for American distribution by Oscar Serlin and Joseph Burstyn, and the chances are that audiences which have never seen a Russian film will have a chance at this one. If they don't enjoy it, it will be a clear sign that there is nothing left for the United States but one last earthquake and zoop! the country disappears between the Atlantic and Pacific Oceans.

Graham Greene

Born 1904. Balliol College, Oxford. Three months on the *Nottingham Journal,* four years on *The Times*, which he left in 1930. Film critic of *The Spectator*, 1935–7; literary editor and film critic of *Night and Day* from 1937 until a remark about Shirley Temple led to a libel suit and the magazine's closure. Many of his novels have been filmed, including *Brighton Rock, The Heart of the Matter, A Gun for Sale* (as *This Gun for Hire*), *The End of the Affair, The Power and the Glory* (twice), *Our Man in Havana, Stamboul Train* (as *Orient Express*), *The Quiet American, The Comedians. The Fallen Idol* was his own adaptation of one of his stories, and *The Third Man* was an original screenplay.

The Garden of Allah: Charles Boyer, Marlene Dietrich

7. Graham Greene

Abyssinia

The best film in London is *Abyssinia* at the Rialto, the finest travel film I have seen, made by a Swiss expedition and explained in an admirably plain commentary. Here is the last medieval state in all its squalor (the flies swarming round the eyes and nostrils as though they were so much exposed meat in a butcher's shop), its dignity (the white-robed noblemen flowing into the capital followed by their armed retainers, the caged symbolic lions, and the Lion of Judah himself, his dark cramped dignity, his air of a thousand years of breeding), its democratic justice (the little courts by the roadside, on the railway track; the debtor and creditor chained together; the murderers led off to execution by the relatives of the murdered). This film, alas, may prove the last record of an independent Abyssinia. It leaves you with a vivid sense of something very old, very dusty, very cruel, but something dignified in its dirt and popular in its tyranny and perhaps more worth preserving than the bright slick streamlined civilization which threatens it. I don't refer particularly to Italy, but to the whole tone of a time whose popular art is on the level of *The Bride of Frankenstein*.

St Petersburg

A new Russian film. How exciting it seemed in the days when questions were asked in Parliament, when *The Times* refused to review the Film Society, when pictures banned by the censors were passed by labour councils, and bright knowing people went to Whitechapel to see the best films. But the old tricks are beginning to pall: the romantic use of scenery, the long whiskers of depraved aristocrats shot from one angle, the short whiskers of simple peasants shot from another. Here again are the satirical photographs of heavy statues, though the Communist cameraman is finding it increasingly difficult to get a new slant on the horses and the emperors. The moral of *St Petersburg*, of course, is just as impeccable as the moral of *Mother*: the poor musician who can't get a hearing in the capital is Good, and the rich insensitive patrons of music are Bad. You can tell how bad they are by their jewels, their busts, the cherubs and the chandeliers and the pictures of naked women. For a Communist is nothing if he is not a Puritan. At the end of the film the poor musician hears his song sung by convicts on their way to Siberia, and knows that he has done something for Russia.

It is a naïve, jerky, sentimental film, sometimes genuinely moving, sometimes absurdly inept. Like most Russian films it is best when it is most savagely satirical, and the scenes in which the rich old patron listens with a scared covetous appreciation to the new revolutionary tune, and in which the Duke of Baden's violinist catches the dowagers in the boxes and stalls with his mannerisms and little tricky melodies, are admirable. It is the serious Socialist idealism that is embarrassing, the sentimental simplification of human nature, the Dickensian plot. Oh, we feel inclined to protest, we know that you are on the right side, that your ideals are above reproach, but because you are virtuous, must there be no more cakes and ale?

Song of Ceylon

Song of Ceylon, made by the G.P.O. Film Unit and directed by Mr Basil Wright, is introduced as a second feature into the Curzon programme with little notice from the ecstatic connoisseurs of classic tragedy, although it is an example to all directors of perfect construction and the perfect application of *montage*. Perfection is not a word one cares to use, but from the opening sequence of the Ceylon forest, the great revolving fans of palm which fill the screen, this film moves with the air of absolute certainty in its object and assurance in its method.

Abyssinia; St Petersburg

Song of Ceylon; Warren William in *The Case of the Lucky Legs*

It is divided into four parts. In the first, *The Buddha*, we watch a long file of pilgrims climb the mountain side to the huge stone effigies of the god. Here, as a priest strikes a bell, Mr Wright uses one of the loveliest visual metaphors I have ever seen on any screen. The sounding of the bell startles a small bird from its branch, and the camera follows the bird's flight and the notes of the bell across the island, down from the mountain side, over forest and plain and sea, the vibration of the tiny wings, the fading sound.

The second part, *The Virgin Island*, is transitional, leading us away from the religious theme by way of the ordinary routine of living to industry. In *The Voices of Commerce* the commentary, which has been ingeniously drawn from a seventeenth-century traveller's account of the island, gives place to scraps of business talk. As the natives follow the old ways of farming, climbing the palm trees with a fibre loop, guiding their elephants' foreheads against the trees they have to fell, voices dictate bills of lading, close deals over the telephone, announce through loud speakers the latest market prices. The last reel, *The Apparel of a God*, returns by way of the gaudy gilded dancers in their devil masks to the huge images on the mountain, to a solitary peasant laying his offering at Buddha's feet, and closes again with the huge revolving leaves, so that all we have seen of devotion and dance and the bird's flight and the gentle communal life of harvest seems something sealed away from us between the fans of foliage. We are left outside with the bills of lading and the loud speakers.

The Case of the Lucky Legs
It is curious how little the cinema has done for the detective public; perhaps that public is not large enough to tempt the film magnates, consisting, as it chiefly does, of crossword puzzlers and tired intellectuals. There have been a few unsuccessful attempts to transfer Sherlock Holmes to the screen, there was even a rather deplorable effort by an English company to film an adventure of Lord Peter Wimsey, but the only sustained detective characters on the screen are Mr Warren William's Perry Mason, Mr Warner Oland's Charlie Chan, and Mr William Powell's suave suède impersonations in such agile and amusing films as *The Thin Man*, and *Star of Midnight*. Of course the cinema cannot go in for the really dry donnish game; the type of detection which depends on a Bradshaw's time-table has to be excluded, for a cinema audience cannot be expected to carry a series of mathematical clues in mind. Detection is almost necessarily the weakest part of a detective film; what we do get in the Perry Mason

films is a more vivid sense of life than in most detective stories, the quality we get in some of Mr David Frome's novels, in all Mr Dashiell Hammett's, and in a few of the early works of Miss Sayers.

Perry Mason is my favourite film detective; he is curiously little known, perhaps because his films, as 'second features', are usually not shown to the Press. *The Case of the Lucky Legs* is an admirable film, but it is thrown in as a makeweight at the Regal to the appalling film, *I Give My Heart*. Perry Mason is a hard-drinking and not very scrupulous lawyer. He owes something to the character established by Mr William Powell: there is the same rather facetious badinage with a woman assistant, but he is, I think, a more genuine creation. Mr Powell is a little too immaculate, his wit is too well-turned just as his clothes are too well-made, he drinks hard but only at the best bars; he is rather like an advertisement of a man-about-town in *Esquire*, he shares some of the irritating day-dream quality of Lord Peter Wimsey. I find the cadaverous, not very well-dressed Perry Mason more real in his seedy straw hat with his straggly moustache; one does not find him only in the best bars; he is by no means irresistible to women; his background is the hiss of soda rather than the clink of ice. He is far more likely on the face of it to be a successful detective than Mr Powell's character because he belongs to the same class as his criminals. Often indeed, as in his latest case, they are his clients. For I can never really believe that a good detective will be found in the Social Register or that Lord Peter would be capable of detecting anything more criminal than a theft by a kleptomaniac duchess. To those who do not yet know Perry Mason I recommend *The Case of the Lucky Legs* as good Mason if not good detection, better, I think, than *The Case of the Curious Bride*.

Rose of the Rancho
Miss Gladys Swarthout is the latest singer from the Metropolitan Opera House to 'go movie' and to my mind, which cares little for music, the most agreeable. *Rose of the Rancho* is a very long way indeed from being a good film, but at least it is without the bogus seriousness, the artiness, the pomposity of Miss Grace Moore's and Miss Pons's pictures. There is nothing operatic about it: no love-life of a prima donna, no blithe Dôme or wistful Rotonde, no first appearance in New York threatened by unhappy Romance. It is just a commonplace Western (the scene is actually New Mexico) with galloping horses and last-minute rescues and masked riders, and a secret federal agent who falls in love with the bandit. One could do

very happily without the music altogether, for Miss Swarthout is quite as attractive as any other star dummy, whether she is wearing a mantilla as Queen of Santa Something *festa*, or, as the mysterious leader of the patriotic brigands, black riding breeches. And one could do very happily, too, without Mr John Boles. I find Mr Boles, his air of confident carnality, the lick of black shiny hair across the plump white waste of face, peculiarly unsympathetic; and never more so than in this film as he directs his lick, his large assured amorous eyes, towards Miss Swarthout and croons:

'I call you a gift from the angels,
For I feel in my heart you're divine'.

That is about the standard of the lush last-century melodies which interrupt rather oddly the gun-shots, the beating hoofs, the traditional American dialogue that one begins after a while to welcome rather wearily like very old friends whose conversation one has exhausted – 'Siddown won't you – Thenks.' 'Wise guy, huh?'

If You Could Only Cook

I do not think anyone need await the release of *If You Could Only Cook* with any impatience. It is produced by Mr Frank Capra, who made *It Happened One Night*, and it bears a few agreeable Capra touches, a few situations which might have had wit if the main performance had been less earnest, less conceited, less humourless than that of Mr Marshall, who plays the part of a millionaire on holiday posing as a butler. Not a bright situation, though Mr Capra, with the help of such players as Mr Leo Carrillo, Miss Jean Arthur and Mr Lionel Stander, might have made something of it. But fantasy droops before Mr Marshall, so intractably British in the American scene. He does, I suppose, represent some genuine national characteristics, if not those one wishes to see exported: characteristics which it is necessary to describe in terms of inanimate objects: a kind of tobacco, a kind of tweed, a kind of pipe: or in terms of dog, something large, sentimental and moulting, something which confirms one's preference for cats.

Kliou the Tiger

'Into her unfinished basket Dhi – the daughter of the Quan – was weaving dreams of her beloved one.' That is the kind of film the Marquis de la Falaise has brought back with him from Indo-China. Oh, the appalling conceit, one longs to exclaim, as the horrid Technicolor browns and greens stain the screen, of these travellers with movie cameras who, not content to photograph what they see, presume on a few months' acquaintance to write a tale of native life, to say *what* dreams. . . .

This to my mind is the worst type of travel film. Better the travelogue, the 'views of old Japan', the cherry tree blossoming to point the wisecrack. Far better, of course, the plain statement of fact, such a film as Mr Smythe's *Kamet*. Best of all – there has been only one of this kind – *Song of Ceylon*, where the plain statement has the intensity of poetic experience. Mr Basil Wright was content to accept the limitations of ignorance, of a European mind, to be 'on the outside, looking in'; the film is a visual record of the effect on a sensitive Western brain of old communal religious appearances, not of a life which Mr Wright pretends to *know*.

'Thrice five suns had risen over Klien-hara, since last the forest had swallowed them up.' The Marquis de la Falaise is speaking again, and of course the caption is followed promptly by the sixteenth sun, an improbable ochre dawn. . . .

But perhaps what annoys one most in this cheap vulgar film is the waste of good material – not such good material as Mr Zoltan Korda brought back from Nigeria to waste in *Sanders of the River*, for the Marquis has no eye whatever for the significant (an elephant or a tiger is always more important to his melodramatic mind than the men and women of the Moi tribe, though equally good shots of tigers could have been made in Hollywood; indeed . . . but to that doubt later), still fairly good material: the houses on stilts, the poor patches of cultivation at the hill foot, gentle lovely youth, ugly diseased age and a little of the ordinary life that goes between. The Marquis has preferred to dramatize, to use what – for want of a more accurate word – we must call imagination. 'Into her unfinished basket . . .' and the strange faces can hardly restrain their smiles at the curious awkward emotional Western thoughts they are made to express. But first the prologue: the lonely French outpost on what we are told is the edge of 'tiger-infested' jungle, 'fever-ridden' swamps where live 'the mysterious' Moi, 'a very savage and dangerous tribe': the Marquis emerging in shorts and topee from a shrubbery and recounting to the lonely officer over a sundowner his traveller's yarn, which consists of the love story of Dhi, the daughter of the Quan, and Bhat, the hunter. The Quan is mauled by Kliou the tiger, and a medicine man tells the tribe that, unless the tiger is killed, the Quan will die. So Bhat goes out with his spear to hunt the man-eater and win his bride.

And now we come to the Problem of the Tiger so admirably

photographed (the other wild animals, even the elephants, the pythons, the water buffalo, 'most treacherous of horned beasts', present no such difficult dilemma). We are told that for filming in Technicolor 'long-focus lenses cannot be used, so the pictures showing close-ups of tigers were genuine close-ups – not pictures taken hundreds of yards away. The Marquis vouches for the authenticity of every shot, the entire picture having been filmed in the jungle without any studio or specially staged scenes being added. The tigers are real tigers [certainly one had not thought of them as stuffed], photographed in their natural surroundings.' So definite a statement leaves us with a painful dilemma: we see the tiger leap upon the Quan, we seem to see the man mauled. None of the scenes, we have been told, were staged; the Marquis with eighteenth-century imperturbability must have continued to shoot his film within a few feet of the struggle. How are we to help doubting either his accuracy or his humanity? And the little well-shaven gentleman in shorts and topee emerging from that fever-ridden swamp has all the appearance of a kindly man.

The Petrified Forest

'Dramatize, dramatize.' Those were the words which used to ring in James's ear whenever some anecdote at a dinner table touched his creative brain, but how seldom are they heard by even the most distinguished contemporary dramatists. Mr Sherwood, for instance. . . . I seldom go to the theatre, but even I have heard of Mr Sherwood as a playwright of uncommon ability, and it was with great hope that I visited *The Petrified Forest*. The opening movement of his drama is very promising: the lonely filling-station on the edge of the Arizona desert; the old garrulous owner who had once been shot at for fun by Billy the Kid and had kept a soft place in his heart for killers ever since: his grand-daughter with her taste for poetry who feels her life drying up in the dust storms: her father, an officer in the vigilantes, trying to get excitement from his fake uniform and bogus drills: the huge dumb hired hand with his eyes on the girl: and then the arrival of the educated down-and-out, the girl's outbreak of sudden starved love, his departure with his food unpaid for and a dollar the girl had given him from the till, and finally disaster breaking in with a killer and his gang on the run from Oklahoma, and the down-and-out's deliberate return.

There is good dramatic material here, but Mr Sherwood doesn't see his play as certain things happening but as ideas being expressed, 'significant' cosmic ideas. As for the plot, the drama, these are rather low-class necessities, like the adulteries in Mr Charles Morgan's novels. The down-and-out, so that he may express the ideas, must be an unsuccessful author, the filling-station girl – to interest him – a painter of untrained talent, for whose Art he sacrifices his life (Mr Sherwood is nothing if not literary). The hero leaves the girl his life-assurance money and then forces the killer to shoot him, though why, if he hadn't a cent in his pocket, was the life-assurance for five thousand dollars fully paid up, or if that be explainable, why had this homeless and friendless tramp not cashed it for its face value? But first all through a long evening, with the sad simian killer (the best character in the play) sitting above with his beer and his pistol, the self-pitying post-War ideas have to be bandied about. 'Dramatize, dramatize', one longs to remind Mr Sherwood, as more and more the concrete fact – the gun, the desert, the killer – gives place to Life, Love, Nature, all the great stale abstractions. It is as if Othello had met the armed men outside his door not with 'Put up your bright swords or the dew will rust them', but with some such sentence as: 'Nature, my men, is having her revenge. You can't defeat Nature with your latest type of swords and daggers. She comes back every time in the shape of neuroses, jealousies . . .' and had let Desdemona and the affairs of Venice, Iago and the one particular handkerchief vanish before Woman, Life, Sex. . . .

So this drama slackens under the weight of Mr Sherwood's rather half-baked philosophy. The moral is stated frequently, with the tomb-stone clarity of a leading article, when it ought to be implicit in every action, every natural spoken word, in the camera angles even (but this is not a film but a canned play). There remain in this picture a few things to enjoy: the killer himself, with his conventional morality, his brooding hopelessness, his curious kindness, is memorable, but not so memorable nor so significant (the word which I am sure means most to Mr Sherwood) as the murderer in *Four Hours to Kill*. That killer was a profound and legendary figure, this one the ingenious invention of a clever writer. Miss Bette Davis gives a sound performance, Mr Leslie Howard faithfully underlines the self-pity and the bogus culture of a character embarrassing to us but obviously admired by his creator, and everyone works hard to try to give the illusion that the Whole of Life is symbolized in the Arizona filling-station. But life itself, which crept in during the opening scene, embarrassed perhaps at hearing itself so explicitly discussed, crept out again, leaving us only with the symbols, the too pasteboard desert, the stunted cardboard studio trees.

Herbert Marshall and Jean Arthur in *If You Could Only Cook*; Leslie Howard and Bette Davis in *The Petrified Forest*

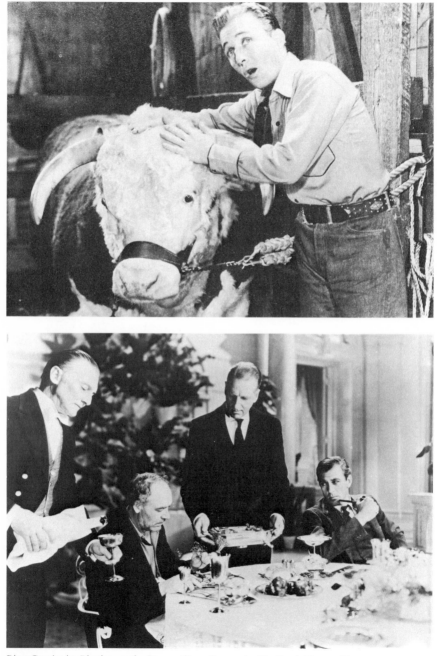

Bing Crosby in *Rhythm on the Range;* Gary Cooper in *Mr Deeds Goes to Town*

Rhythm on the Range
Bing Crosby as a cowboy: Bing Crosby crooning a prize bull to sleep
on a freight car: Bing Crosby more than ever like Walt Disney's Cock
Robin: it needs some stamina to be a film reviewer. Only the conviction that a public art should be as popular and unsubtle as a dance
tune enables one to sit with patient hope through pictures certainly
unsubtle but not, in any real sense, popular. What a chance for the
creative artist, one persists in believing, to produce for an audience
incomparably greater than that of all the 'popular' novelists combined,
from Mr Walpole to Mr Brett Young, a genuinely vulgar art. Any
other is impossible. The novelist may write for a few thousand readers,
but the film artist *must* work for millions. It should be his distinction
and pride that he has a public whose needs have never been met since
the closing of the theatres by Cromwell. But where is the vulgarity of
this art? Alas! the refinement of the 'popular' novel has touched the
films; it is the twopenny libraries they reflect rather than the Blackfriars
Ring, the Wembley final, the pin saloons, the coursing.

> 'I'm not the type that I seem to be,
> Happy-go-lucky and gay,'

Bing Crosby mournfully croons. That is the common idea of popular
entertainment, a mild self-pity, something soothing, something gently
amusing. The film executive still thinks in terms of the 'popular' play
and the 'popular' novel, of a limited middle-class audience, of the
tired business man and the feminine reader. The public which rattles
down from the North to Wembley with curious hats and favours, tipsy
in charabancs, doesn't, apparently, ask to be soothed: it asks to be
excited. It was for these that the Elizabethan stage provided action
which could arouse as communal a response as bear-baiting. For a
popular response is not the sum of private excitements, but mass
feeling, mass excitement, the Wembley roar, and it is the weakness of
the Goldwyn Girls that they are as private an enjoyment as the Art
Photos a business man may turn over in the secrecy of his study; the
weakness of Bing Crosby's sentiment, the romantic nostalgia of
'Empty saddles in the old corral', that it is by its nature a private
emotion.

There are very few examples of what I mean by the proper popular
use of the film, and most of those are farces: *Duck Soup*, the early
Chaplins, a few 'shorts' by Laurel and Hardy. These do convey the
sense that the picture has been made by its spectators and not merely
shown to them, that it has sprung, as much as their sports, from *their*

level. Serious films of the kind are even rarer: perhaps *Fury, Le Million, Men and Jobs*, they could be numbered on the fingers of one hand. Because they are so rare one is ready to accept, with exaggerated gratitude, such refined, elegant, dead pieces as *Louis Pasteur*: the Galsworthy entertainments of the screen: or intelligently adapted plays like *These Three*.

'People want to be taken out of themselves', the film executive retorts under the mistaken impression that the critic is demanding a kind of Zola-esque realism – as if Webster's plays were realistic. Of course he is right. People are taken out of themselves at Wembley. But I very much doubt if Bing Crosby does so much. 'They don't want to be depressed', but an excited audience is never depressed: if you excite your audience first, you can put over what you will of horror, suffering, truth. But there is one question to which there is no answer. How dare we excite an audience, a producer may well ask, when Lord Tyrrell, the President of the Board of Censors, forbids us to show any controversial subject on the screen?

Perhaps I ought to add that *Rhythm on the Range* is quite a tolerable picture with a few scenes which do deserve to be called popular cinema and an excellent new comedian, Mr Bob Burns. I think one might even find a place, in one's ideal popular cinema, for Mr Crosby: he represents permanent, if disagreeable, human characteristics of nostalgia and self-pity: I would have him bobbing about at the back of the scrimmage like a worried referee – or like an Elizabethan clown crooning his lugubrious reminders.

Mr Deeds Goes to Town

Mr Deeds is Capra's finest film (it is on quite a different intellectual level from the spirited and delightful *It Happened One Night*), and that means it is a comedy quite unmatched on the screen. For Capra has what Lubitsch, the witty playboy, has not, a sense of responsibility; and what Clair, whimsical, poetic, a little precious and *à la mode*, has not, a kinship with his audience, a sense of common life, a morality; he has what even Chaplin has not, complete mastery of his medium, and what Clair, whimsical, poetic, a little precious and *à la mode*, has it. Like Lang, he hears all the time just as clearly as he sees and just as selectively. I do not think anyone can watch *Mr Deeds* for long without being aware of a technician as great as Lang employed on a theme which profoundly moves him: the theme of goodness and simplicity manhandled in a deeply selfish and brutal world. That was the theme of *Fury*, too, but Capra is more fortunate than Lang. Lang expresses the theme in terms of terror, and terror on the screen has always, alas! to be tempered to the shorn lamb; Capra expresses it in terms of pity and ironic tenderness, and no magnate feels the need to cramp his style or alter his conclusion.

Mr Deeds is a young provincial who inherits twenty million dollars from an uncle he has never seen. An ardent tuba-player in the local band, he makes his living by writing verses which are printed on post-cards on such occasions as Mothers' Day. The uncle's solicitors, who have absorbed, with the help of a Power of Attorney, half a million dollars of his money, hope to continue the process with his un-sophisticated nephew who is quite unexcited by his fortune and only wants to do good with it. They bring Deeds up to town. Wealth educates Deeds, he learns the shabby side not only of business but of art, with the help of the opera directors and the fashionable poets; he learns, too, the deceit which may exist in ordinary human affection (the girl he loves, and who loves him, is all the time writing newspaper articles which make front-page fun of the activities of the Cinderella Man). A revolver and a would-be assassin's nerveless hand educate him socially, and he is arranging to use the whole of his fortune in providing ruined farmers with free land and free seed when society – controlled by racketeers – strikes its last blow at the elements it cannot absorb, goodness, simplicity, disinterestedness. Claimants are found to dispute his sanity and to try to remove the management of the estate from his hands.

It sounds as grim a theme as *Fury*; innocence lynched as effectively at a judicial inquiry as in a burning courthouse, but there is this difference between Lang and Capra: Lang's happy ending was im-posed on him, we did not believe in it; Capra's is natural and unforced. He *believes* in the possibility of happiness; he believes, in spite of the controlling racketeers, in human nature. Goodness, simplicity, disinterestedness: these in his hands become fighting qualities. Deeds sees through opera-directors, fashionable intellectuals, solicitors, psychologists who prove that he is insane merely because he likes playing the tuba and isn't greedy for money. Only for a few minutes in the courtroom does he lose heart and refuse to defend himself: he is never a helpless victim, like the garage man behind the bars watching the woman lift her baby up to see the fun, and he comes back into the ring with folk humour and folk shrewdness to rout his enemies for the sake of the men they have ruined. The picture glows with that humour and shrewdness, just as Lang's curdles with his horror and disgust; it is as funny, most of the time, as *Fury* was terrifying. It is not a question

Housing Problems

of truth or falsehood: two directors of genius have made pictures with curiously similar themes which present a conviction, a settled attitude towards life as it is lived. The pessimist makes a tragedy, the optimist (but how far from sweetness and complacency is Capra's optimism) makes a comedy. And Capra, as well as Lang, is supported by a perfect cast. Every minor part, however few the lines, is completely rendered, and Mr Gary Cooper's subtle and pliable performance must be something of which other directors have only dreamed.

Nutrition

We are apt to forget, among the gangsters and the grand passions, that the cinema has other uses than fiction, and yet it is the Gas Light and Coke Company which is responsible for the most interesting film I have seen for a long time. The Company deserves the highest praise. For the second time it has undertaken a work which should have been the responsibility of the Ministry of Health. There is no gas propaganda in *Nutrition*, any more than there was in *Housing Problems*. Both pictures are the work of Mr Edgar Anstey, who is contributing some-

thing new to the documentary film. The documentary film has sometimes hovered too uneasily on the edge of art and story-telling. The
G.P.O. Unit in *Song of Ceylon* produced the most aesthetically
satisfying film ever made in this country, but there have been times – in
Night Mail, for example – when the demands of instruction and the
instinct to create a work of art have conflicted. The final sequences in
Night Mail were aesthetically satisfying, but earlier in the film one was
aware of hesitation: we were shown too many technicalities for atmospheric purposes, we were shown too few for understanding.

In *Housing Problems* Mr Anstey was superbly untroubled by the
aesthetic craving: he used the camera as a first-class reporter, and a
reporter too truthful, too vivid, to find a place on any modern newspaper. He produced a poignant and convincing document simply by
taking his camera and his microphone into the slums, the terrible
tiny peeling rooms, up the broken stairways, into the airless courts,
and letting the women talk in their own way about the dirt and rats and
bugs. The method was simple, certainly, but it cannot have been easy;
it must have needed human qualities more common among Russian
than English directors. (Compare the characters in *Housing Problems*
with the frightened ironed-out personalities with censored scripts
whom the B.B.C. present as 'documentary'.)

Nutrition has everything which *Housing Problems* had (the same
human interest handled with the finest, self-effacing sympathy), and a
great deal more beside. It goes deeper and speaks with more authority.
It takes the statistics, the categories of food (energy, body building,
protective), and presents the problem at different dramatic levels: the
chemist in his laboratory examining his rats (the small undersized
piebald creature, who scrambles in a scared way beneath his plump
capitalist companion, has been fed on a typical working-class diet),
Sir John Orr on his experimental farm, the medical officers of Bethnal
Green and Stockton-on-Tees in conference, the street markets, the
Bluecoat boys on their playing fields, the working-class boys in their
back streets. Professor Julian Huxley speaks the admirable, quite
unpolitical commentary, which is interrupted occasionally for Mr
Herbert Morrison to describe what the London County Council is
doing for elementary schoolchildren, for medical officers to discuss the
proper balancing of diets, for working women themselves to speak
with a sad courage of their housekeeping, of cabbages at sixpence a
pound, of the inevitable hungry Thursdays. It is the foods which build
and the foods which protect that are most expensive: the energy foods,
which the children need least, are cheapest, and who can blame the

parents if they choose to give their children the foods which will at least prevent them *feeling* their starvation? And a long parade goes past the camera of cheerful child faces above under-developed bodies.

Mr Anstey has had no aesthetic end in view: he has wanted to explain the problem clearly and to make the fight for better diets personal by means of showing the actual sufferers, the actual investigators, but there is always an aesthetic delight in complete competence. Conrad once wrote an essay in praise of the literary merits of the official Notices to Mariners, and as the film reaches its end, the summing-up of the commentator coinciding with a quick repetition of images, one is aware of having attended not only a vivid and authoritative lecture but a contribution to Cinema.

Romeo and Juliet

'Boy Meets Girl, 1436' – so the programme heads the story of *Romeo and Juliet*, which it tells with some inaccuracy; but this fourth attempt to screen Shakespeare is not as bad as that. Unimaginative certainly, coarse-grained, a little banal, it is frequently saved – by Shakespeare – from being a bad film. The late Irving Thalberg, the producer, has had a funeral success second only to Rudolph Valentino's, but there is nothing in this film to show that he was a producer of uncommon talent. He has made a big film, as Hollywood recognizes that adjective; all is on the characteristic Metro-Goldwyn scale: a Friar Laurence's cell with the appearance, as another critic has put it, of a modern luxury flat, with a laboratory of retorts and test-tubes worthy of a Wells superman (no 'osier cage' of a few flowers and weeds); a balcony so high that Juliet should really have conversed with Romeo in shouts like a sailor from the crow's-nest sighting land; a spectacular beginning with the Montagues and Capulets parading through pasteboard streets to the same church, rather late, it appears from the vague popish singing off, for Benediction; Verona seen from the air, too palpably a childish model; an audible lark proclaiming in sparrow accents that it is not the nightingale; night skies sparkling with improbable tinsel stars; and lighting so oddly timed that when Juliet remarks that the mask of night is on her face, 'else would a maiden blush bepaint my cheek', not Verona's high noon could have lit her more plainly.

But on the credit side are more of Shakespeare's words than we have grown to expect, a few more indeed than he ever wrote, if little of the subtlety of his dramatic sense, which let the storm begin slowly with the muttering of a few servants rather than with this full-dress

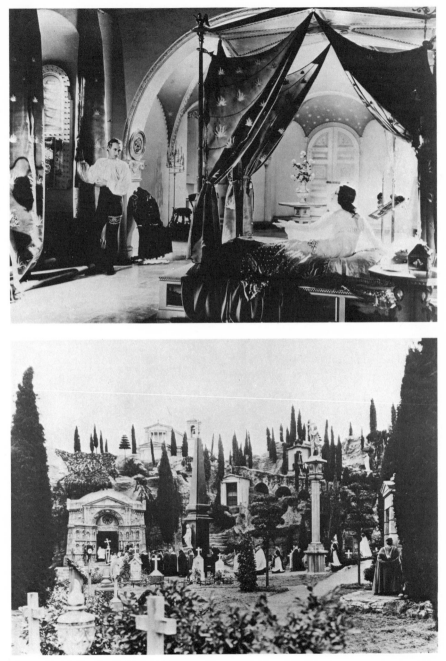

Romeo and Juliet: Leslie Howard, Norma Shearer

riot. The picture has been given a Universal Certificate, and one was pleasantly surprised to find how safely our film censors had slumbered through many a doubtful passage: even 'the bawdy hand of the dial' had not disturbed the merry gentlemen's rest. The nurse's part has suffered, but more from Miss Edna May Oliver's clowning than from a censor. This part and Mercutio's suffer most from overacting. Mr John Barrymore's middle-aged Mercutio is haggard with the grease-paint of a thousand Broadway nights. Mr Basil Rathbone is a fine vicious Tybalt, and Mr Leslie Howard and Miss Norma Shearer speak verse as verse should be spoken and are very satisfying in the conventional and romantic and dreamy mode (one still waits to see lovers hot with lust and youth and Verona fevers, as reckless as their duelling families, 'like fire and powder which as they kiss consume').

It is the duels and violence which come off well, Mercutio's death and Tybalt's, and, more convincing than on the stage, the final fight with Paris in the tomb, but I am less than ever convinced that there is an aesthetic justification for filming Shakespeare at all. The effect of even the best scenes is to distract, much in the same way as the old Tree productions distracted: we cannot look and listen simultaneously with equal vigilance. But that there may be a social justification I do not dispute: by all means let Shakespeare, even robbed of half his drama and three-quarters of his poetry, be mass-produced. One found oneself surrounded in the theatre by prosperous middle-aged ladies anxiously learning the story in the programme for the first time; urgent whispers came from the knowing ones, as Romeo went down into the Capulet tomb, preparing their timorous companions for an unexpected and unhappy ending. It may very well be a social duty to teach the great middle-class a little about Shakespeare's plays. But the poetry – shall we ever get the poetry upon the screen except in fits and starts (the small scene between Romeo and the ruined apothecary he bribes to sell him poison was exquisitely played and finely directed), unless we abjure all the liberties the huge sets and the extras condemn us to? Something like Dreyer's *Passion of Joan of Arc*, the white-washed wall and the slow stream of faces, might preserve a little more of the poetry than this commercial splendour.

The New Gulliver
The new, the Soviet Gulliver is a long way after Swift. The inventor of the Yahoos would have been bitterly amused by the blithe Bolshevik optimism of Mr Roshal and Mr Ptushko, the inevitable victory of the Lilliputian proletariat, the Victorian sense of Progress. But even if the

theme seems to us a little dusty, like the sermons of Charles Kingsley, the execution and invention awake our admiration.

The New Gulliver begins like *Alice in Wonderland*, as an idyll of a summer day. The best workers in a corps of Soviet children have the honour of being the first to sail the little yacht they have built. They land on a small island off the shore and the boy leader reads *Gulliver* aloud, a bowdlerized *Gulliver*, I feel sure, in this brave new world where virtue is always victorious. With the sound of the waves in his ears the boy falls asleep and dreams. . . . Only in dreams (but I doubt if the authors intended to point this moral) can he escape – unhappy Gulliver – from triumphant virtue to a world where evil can still put up a sporting fight. After a battle and a shipwreck ('Save my box. It has all my schoolwork in it'), he is cast ashore on Lilliput. Lilliput is oppressed by a King, a Parliament and at least one priest, and there are numerous police spies and armament manufacturers. An exciting old world, but one already on the point of learning dialectical materialism. The workers plan the Revolution in a cave on the sea shore, and there they find Gulliver's exercise book washed up by the sea and on the first page a Soviet slogan. The rest of the film shows the triumph of the workers assisted by Gulliver. There are moments of delightful satire: the Chancellor putting a small gramophone under the robe of the king who cannot make a speech ('my people are muddled, are muddled, are muddled . . .' creaks the record as the needle sticks in a crack); the tiny queen hastily packing her hats at the news of the workers' seizure of the arsenal.

The invention is often delightful (one wonders how such humour in detail can exist with so humourless a philosophy), and the marvellous ingenuity of the puppets is beyond praise. One soon begins to regard them as real people and to give critical applause to the performers who amuse Gulliver at dinner: the ballad singer (an exquisite parody), the elderly mezzo-soprano, and the troupe of ballet girls with their black gloves and transparent fans. The doll world is pure pleasure, a child's dream with its inconsequence: the tiny tanks manœuvring on the shore with frigates attacking from the sea, the periwigged ladies listening to the radio, the cameraman in check plus-fours filming the royal procession; sometimes a child's nightmare: the gross idiot faces, the evil king with his loopy laugh, the arsenal with its white-hot furnaces and pounding machines in the caves underground. But Gulliver wakes, that is the profound difference, wakes into the bright, happy, virtuous Soviet day; he has not to live on, like his poor ancestor, among his native Yahoos.

The Garden of Allah: Charles Boyer, Marlene Dietrich

The Garden of Allah

Mr Charles Boyer, a renegade monk from a Trappist monastery in North Africa, Miss Marlene Dietrich, a lovely orphan heiress suffering from world weariness ('Go to the desert', she is told at the convent school to which she returns for advice and prayer. 'In the face of the infinite your grief will lessen') meet in a Moroccan dance hall. A desert soothsayer does his best to warn the woman against her doom ('I see a camel by a church door, and then a tent in the far desert', as he describes it with surrealist fervour), and so does the local Catholic priest, who distrusts this man who is apt to stagger uneasily back at the sight of a crucifix. 'This is the land of fire', he says, 'and you are a woman of fire.' Nobody talks less apocalyptically than that: the great abstractions come whistling hoarsely out in Miss Dietrich's stylized, weary, and monotonous whisper, among the hideous Technicolor flowers, the yellow cratered desert like Gruyère cheese, the beige faces. Startling sunsets bloom behind silhouetted camels very much as in the gaudy little pictures which used to be for sale on the pavements of Trafalgar Square. Needless to say – but many thousand feet of film are expended in saying it – the pair are married by the Catholic priest (according to the Church of England service), and there, waiting for them outside the church door, is The Camel, the foredoomed camel, ready to carry them, with an escort of twenty-five armed Arabs, on their honeymoon – to that Tent in the Far Desert. There Fate has a coincidence in store for them in the person of a French officer lost in the Sahara with his men. 'We are a lost patrol', he succinctly explains to the lady in a low-backed evening dress who is waving a lighted torch from the top of a ruined tower (the surrealism of this film is really magnificent). He recognizes the former monk (he had been a guest in the monastery), and sitting together on the Gruyère cheese, silhouetted like camels, the lovers make the great decision to renounce all. The Catholic priest (Mr Aubrey Smith, who has kept a straight county bat to the bodyline bowling) shakes hands all round at the railway station, the monk slowly wends his way up an avenue of cypresses, a grey glove flaps from the window of a four-wheeler. Alas! my poor Church, so picturesque, so noble, so superhumanly pious, so intensely dramatic. I really prefer the *New Statesman* view, shabby priests counting pesetas on their fingers in dingy cafés before blessing tanks. Even the liqueur made at this Trappist monastery is Mysterious. Only one monk at a time knows the secret of its making, and when Mr Charles Boyer disappears from the Monastery the secret is irrecoverably lost. The thought that this sweet and potent drink will

The Plainsman: Gary Cooper

be once again obtainable during licensed hours mitigates for us the agony of the parting.

The Plainsman
Mr Cecil B. de Mille: there has always been a touch of genius as well as absurdity in this warm-hearted sentimental salvationist. *The Crusades, The Ten Commandments* were comic and naïve, but no director since Griffith has handled crowds so convincingly. Now – startlingly – Mr de Mille seems to have grown up. *The Plainsman* is certainly the finest Western since *The Virginian:* perhaps it is the finest Western in the history of the film.

The story is of the Indian rising after the Civil War when General Custer's forces were annihilated, with Mr Gary Cooper as a famous Scout, Wild Bill Hickok, the lover of Calamity Jane. Mr de Mille has never before handled stars of Mr Cooper's and Miss Jean Arthur's quality, and another unexpected trace of sophistication, the music is by George Antheil. Indeed one might wonder whether Mr de Mille's name had been taken in vain if it were not for the magnificent handling of the extras in the big sets: the brilliant detail, depth and solidity of the dockside scenes at St Louis, the charge of the Indian cavalry. A few great spectacular moments in the history of the film remain as a permanent encouragement to those who believe that an art may yet emerge from a popular industry: the long shots of the Battle of Bull Run in *The Birth of a Nation*, the French attack in *All Quiet*. Some of the scenes in *The Plainsman* belong to that order.

That might have been expected, and the excellent dialogue may be a fortunate accident; what takes one by surprise in a de Mille film is the firm handling of the individual drama: the silent moments in the cleared street of the shabby frontier town when Hickok crosses the road to meet his would-be murderers: the final poker game he plays in the barred saloon with the white prisoners he is keeping for the military to hang, the air of doom while we wait for the inevitable shot in the back from the little treacherous bowler-hatted comic behind the bar: and most surprising of all the brilliant satirical sequence when the armament directors, whose new repeating rifle has been put on the market too late for the Civil War, discuss how to dispose of their unwanted stocks and the cynical old Pickwickian chairman persuades them to sell to the Indians 'for hunting purposes'. This actor's performance, when the news of Lincoln's murder comes roaring down the street, is superb: the conventional shocked regrets, the roaming, faintly speculative eye. It is a pleasure too to see Mr Charles Bickford back in one of his rough scoundrelly parts as the trader who smuggles the rifles to the Indians. Only in the character and treatment of Buffalo Bill Cody does the dreaded softness of the traditional de Mille intrude.

Otis Ferguson

Born Worcester, Massachusetts, 1907. After four years in the Navy finished high school, took an A.B. at Clark University, subsequently obtained an M.A. from Columbia. From 1934 on the staff of *The New Republic,* for which he became film editor. Member of the National Board of Review of Motion Pictures.

Three Songs of Lenin

8. Otis Ferguson

Three Songs of Lenin

In Vertov's *Three Songs of Lenin* the Soviets come forward to bury the great leader in Westminster Abbey, with something of the atmosphere of Patriots' Day. Objectively, it is an attempt to idolize, not so much a man as his concepts; it is thus rather limited in appeal. Washington in boats with his ragged army, Lincoln freeing the slaves – these things could be dramatized in some fashion. But when Lenin tots up a column of figures to give some of the Eastern peoples economic freedom, what are you going to do about it in terms of pictures? Near the end of the film there is a moving section of Lenin's Russia today, with men working, tractors, forges, the dams, etc.; but on the whole it seems poorly melted newsreel material with a poetic cast. I would not have brought it up except that it has gone the way of many foreign films in its reception here, and got its most honourable citation on the grounds of its being pure cinema.

And this suggests the subject of film criticism in general, which is really the subject of this piece. The appreciation of pictures is much like all other forms; but there is the sad fact of its having thus far got so little intelligent consideration that intelligence, when it appears, tends to become the high priest guarding marvels. Everyone goes to the movies, to laugh or to delight his heart; they are a part of common experience – and very common at that, usually. Now and then one is good, but in thinking of it we do not think of art. It's just a movie; we only went for the fun. So when someone comes along and says down his nose, Art in the cinema is largely in the hands of artists in cinematographic experimentation, we think, Mm, fancy such a thing, I wonder what *that* is like. When someone, almost holding his breath, says, Well, there is surely no better *montage* (or *régisseur*) than this *montage* (or *régisseur*), we are apt to be discouraged: Oh damn, I missed it again, all I saw was a story with people and action. And when someone says of *Three Songs of Lenin*, This is pure cinema, implying that you couldn't say more for it, we think, Well, well, can't miss that surely.

The pay-off is that *régisseurs* are in ordinary life directors, that *montage* is simply the day-in-day-out (in Hollywood) business of cutting: all you need, except for the higher technical reaches, is a pair of shears and a good sense of timing. As for pure cinema, we would not praise a novel (in which field by this time you must, to be intelligent, be intelligible, or perish) by saying merely that it was pure *roman*. I do not wish to pull rabbits out of the hat, but here is a fact: you too can make pure cinema.

Given the proper facilities and scientific advice, anyone can, me for instance. Out of my window I can see a rather mean-looking tenement. Doors, windows, a sidewalk. Just above it, rising over it, is a tall very recent building, elevator apts. electrolux, 1 2 3 4 5 rooms, etc., but wait, we'll not open there. We will catch the meanness of the mean street by opening on pages 18–19 of *The New York Times* for last week, dirty and blowing along the mean sidewalk in the morning wind. Dust, desolation. The paper blowing and on the sound-track a high piccolo note – wheeeeeee – and the street empty, deserted, it is morning. Now (take the shots separately; cut and paste them together afterwards): the sky (grey), the house (sleeping), the paper, the sky, the house, the paper (whee). Follow the paper down to, suddenly, the wheel of a milk truck (Ha! truck – life, the city stirs; throw in tympani under the piccolo for the city stirring) which goes down to the mean house, stops, the driver gets out: follow him with one bottle of Grade B up three flights of mean stairs to a mean door where – stop.

Down in the street the driver comes out, yawns. Up the house front slowly to a top-floor window where a man, tousled, yawns. As the truck drives off its wheels turn, gain speed, and suddenly there are other wheels (the city awakes): trucks pounding down the Concourse, the subway, the 'El', street cars and the trucks pounding, the 'Els', the subways and now (on the sound-track, the piccolo goes a fifth higher) you cut in the big dynamo wheels, all the wheels, all the power houses, wheels and wheels. Rah, *montage*. Then from the dynamo out (space, motion, speed) to – what do you think? An electric grill in the big stinking apartment house, with a coloured servant in white, frying bacon and looking at the dumb-waiter. Title: WHERE ALL IS THAT MILKMAN NOHOW? Now down to the milkman, taking in a bottle of heavy cream (flash: SERVANT'S ENTRANCE) to the dumb-waiter; now back to the poor house, and out over the city and up over the high proud bulge of the apartment house to the high grey clouds, over the city, over the rich and poor getting up, getting their separate service from the milkman. And on into a great dither of wheels, clouds, gaping windows, yawns, men walking – into plush elevators, on the hard mean sidewalk, faster, faster, everybody getting into motion, the same city, the same sky, the two remote worlds rich and poor. For special effect, let us say, a kid coming out of the door of the mean house, with pennies for a loaf of whole-wheat, and running past the feet and in front of the wheels, and tripping up on the broken cement, falling, smack. Close-up of the head showing a splash of blood spreading on the mean stones, and flash to the apartment house, up, up, to a window, in through the window to the cream being poured into the coffee, being drunk in bed, in silk pyjamas, spilling, a splash of coffee spreading on the silk pyjamas.

Any good? I'm afraid not. But it is pure cinema. Pure cinema can be anything: the important thing always is whether it is done well, whether you can pile one thing on another in a clear beautiful moving line. The wonderful and humbling thing about the movies in general is the skill and sure judgment behind this mechanical transfer of images to strips of celluloid, of a certain number of feet of celluloid into a moving series of images that will have a certain effect on those who watch. It doesn't matter whether the result is a story or a Significant Experiment: what we have got to single out is the difference between a picture that catches you up in its own movement, and a picture that stammers, stands doubtfully, hammers at a few obvious meanings, and leaves you with a feeling of all the mechanism used to capture emotion, without the emotion. *Three Songs of Lenin* may have been attacked with a new attack, may be an awesome experiment. My point is that it is not a good picture, and my quarrel with movie criticism is simply that if it was, those who thought so have not done one thing to show why.

Love Me Some Other Time

Serious music has had quite a career in the movies already, apart from its frequent use for purposes of accompaniment. There have been such awful things as the short subjects depicting the sad love life of Tchaikowsky, Liszt, *et al.*; an occasional recording of fragmentary symphonic performances; the more effective full-length works such as the recent *Unfinished Symphony* and the still supreme *Constant Nymph*. And now in this same highbrow field comes Miss Grace Moore, bringing art to those who faint by the wayside for the lack thereof, and furnishing the text for today.

Grace Moore films – first *One Night of Love*, now *Love Me Forever*, and practically endless future possibilities: *Two Loves in One Night*; *How Lovely, Lovey*; *Love Me Tomorrow*; *Love Me on Friday*, etc. – these films threaten to become a tradition, and therefore cannot be turned aside lightly, but may be studied with profit. They have, so far at least, these significant elements in common: (1) a great deal of care for the mechanics of music, that the sound shall be recorded clear as a bell; (2) one original theme song and the balance Puccini; (3) a story that has seen better if not more romantic days; (4) a comic relief in the person of Luis Alberni; (5) a smash ending in the Metropolitan itself (the old house ringing with merry sound and the old art-lovers in boiled shirts loving it to the point of epilepsy); and (6) the continued presence and histrionic splendour of Miss Grace Moore, one-time auxiliary of the New York Opera (I mean *the* opera).

The show, in fact, is built entirely around Miss Moore, who shapes up as follows: A trained voice, cool, thin, mechanically perfect but without much colour, beautifully recorded. A youthful figure; a face not lovely but with enough regularity of planes to be called pretty, if you like – somewhat reminiscent of that other national darling, Miss Mary Pickford, and best expressive of a certain arch emptiness. In carriage rather moosey, by which I mean no offence but simply that she has neither graceful motion nor a natural disposition of members in repose, always giving the impression (without quite doing it) of standing pigeon-toed or crossing space at a gallop. She is not an actress, but acts the part of an actress, a sad cross between the best schools of elocution (not to forget gesture) and the worst Wagner. Failing as an actress, she might well fall back on a natural dignity of her own – but no, she must be vivacious, irrepressible, girlish; she will only be herself in so far as a well marked tendency for flouncing and stiff mummery is herself. She must give it this, she must give it that; she must talk on the tonsil.

One Night of Love: Grace Moore

Analysis of anything so complex as a personality is always difficult
and usually unfair, because when everything is said you either like a
person's type or you don't like it at all; but I imagine even the best
friends of this gorgeous creature would admit that when it comes to
stage genius and stage presence there are scores of little girls in
Hollywood who can run wide circles round her. Miss Moore is here
solely for her music. And her music in *Love Me Forever* adds up to
one chorus of the theme song, two arias from *La Bohème*, a few rounds
of 'Funiculi, Funicula'; 'Il Bacio', and a participation in the *Rigoletto*
quartet (computations based on *Variety*, which is wise in many
matters).

In actual running time, that is, her use to the picture is very small.
Yet the whole story has to be tailored to her; she is its star, she must
have dramatic moments, playful moments, cosy, homelike moments,
close-ups, medium shots, long shots, follow shots – the works, in short.
And every time she begins to vibrate in the vocal cords, the effect is
supposed to slay whole roomfuls of people and you sit there and
watch them slain, and no mistake. Leo Carrillo (low gambler and high

flier and good in a stock interpretation) is also slain and gives up all for her; and that makes the story, which in turn makes up the picture, which thus gets to be makeshift, unoriginal and (particularly in the part of Miss Moore) quite ham.

Everything in *Love Me Forever* is jettisoned in favour of the elaborate production and recording of the big punch numbers. But here at last in these numbers, descending in the vestments of art on the American movie, we have something, have we not? There must surely be something here, at long last? Briefly, what we have in these big numbers is a first-rate and literal copy of an eighth-rate (and outdated) treatment of distinctly third-rate music. And that is about all.

Such purely popular musicals as Warner's new *In Caliente* are built along the same lines – except that their popular music does not, like that of Puccini, represent some of the best and most enduring of their time and place. Their story is equally foolish and sketchy (in the latest, it revolves about the troubles of a dancer in falling in love with a critic who once panned her); their emphasis is also placed on lavish production numbers – of which, for a welcome change, there is only one really big one here. But *In Caliente* has a lot of good spots in the relations between Pat O'Brien, Edward Everett Horton and (aptly enough) Leo Carrillo, and in Dolores Del Rio it has the presence of a woman ripe with charms and a constant pleasure to the eye. And in all the musicals, however bad, there is an absence of this stuffy insistence on Art, an absence of this self-conscious strain that is invariably in evidence when the movies – so astonishingly at home in newspaper offices or stokeholds, in hospitals, on the ranch, at police headquarters, in the Foreign Legion, anywhere – get completely out of their water into the rare and awful air of artistic creation, as pronounced upper case.

Average musicals are pretty dull, but so are these Moore pieces pretty dull, and what is worse they have a holy smell of uplift about them. And all this (at last) through a medium in which, to mention only the native achievement, Walt Disney, not three months ago and with very little acclaim, blended music with his pictured story in such a bit of sheer genius as *The Band Concert*; in which, about the same time, there was performed offhandedly a little stretch of cartoon called *The Kids in the Shoe*; in which Duke Ellington has fixed up an arrangement of *The St Louis Blues*; and before the cameras of which Louis Armstrong has performed upon his brash and lovely horn. What the hell, I say, love us some other time can't you, Grace; we can hardly be bothered.

The Marxian Epileptic

In terms of rhyme, reason, good taste and formal plot structure, *A Night at the Opera* is a sieve, a leaky ship, and caulked to the guards with hokum. It has three of the Marx Brothers and absolutely no pride. It seems thrown together, made up just as they went along out of everybody else's own head – it steals sequences from René Clair, it drives off with whole wagonloads of the Keystone lot without so much as putting the fence back up; it has more familiar faces in the way of gags and situations than a college reunion – it has even got a harp-and-piano specialty, which it goes through with dead solemnity for about fifteen minutes. In short, *A Night at the Opera* is a night with the Marx Brothers, who have a zest for clowning and a need to be cockeyed that are either genius or just about enough to fit them all out with numbers and a strait jacket, and who troop through this impossible hour and a half of picture with such speed and clatter as to pin up a record for one of the most hilarious collections of bad jokes I've laughed myself nearly sick over.

The film could have been grand satire on Lawrence Tibbett in *Metropolitan* or Grace Moore in the love-me-love-my-tonsil cycle; but satire, like the cherry-stone clam in the colonel's slipper, was too much. It has a pretty idea and starts off with a fine edge – the Italians are a singing race, so open on Italy singing. And then the Marx Brothers, in the onward march of their stealing everything in sight (you couldn't have kept a camera or a chorus girl on that set ten minutes running), steal the idea and the edge. The romance is handled straight, the love and singing scenes being cut out like slabs of mince pie. And the picture has no line or continuous pitch of its own at all.

Yet many of the individual scenes show much sure generalship in the way of galloping through it, one, two, three and putting over the big punch before you can get your breath, and keeping the boys in focus, all the boys all the way (try this some time – that terrific walk of Groucho's would get out of focus like a clay pigeon). In the good spots the action is kept swift and disentangled, evenly spaced and in clear relief. Groucho has just squeezed into a third-class stateroom with a trunk big enough to hold two brothers and a tenor, who pop out of it as soon as the door is wedged shut, and then people begin to pile in – manicurists, cleaning maids, retired majors, stewards with trays, the engineer's assistant, the engineer looking for him. They begin to get about seven deep and the laws of physics are insulted right and left, Groucho still the host, sarcastic and regal with a cigar, the other two still swarming up the chambermaids, everything still piling up and

A Night at the Opera: the Marx Brothers, Margaret Dumont

bulging the walls until just the second when the rich matron, never so outraged but blackmailed into it, sweeps along to her assignation with Groucho and arrives square in front of the door, which breaks out like a shot and they all spill out clear across the ship, like a tubful of blueberries.

Or take the opening night at the Metropolitan. The issues at stake here are too many to recount, but the impresario is lashed in his closet upstairs, Groucho is wearing his tails and addressing the throng from the rich matron's box, and the others have slipped sheets of popular music under the second page of the overture score. Everything is in place, the horseshoe, the music lovers, the maestro's wee baton (ha!); the orchestra is just rising into one of those ripe overture chords, the second-chair men snaking the page over desperately, and down comes a full brass choir on 'Take Me Out to the Ball Game', and Harpo has got hold of a baseball and is passing it clear across the pit to Chico, and the hubbub keeps warming up and the ball passing until one of them snatches what must have been a violin but looks like a cello and lines it clear out of sight into the wings, and Groucho is dropping his top hat excitedly off the box into the orchestra, whistling with his fingers to get it back up – Hey Shorty, he says to the music-lover in a stiff shirt, Hey! Hey Shorty.

This is wonderful while it lasts but it gets anti-climactic as it extends through all the scenes of the opera; and that is the way the picture as a whole goes. There will be stretches of dull clowning, of the boy getting next to the girl; and then there will be something like that perfectly irrelevant four feet of film where the set has three cots and two Marx Brothers asleep, and the third cot has right in the middle of it an alarm clock. One, two, three – you just get time to count the cots and the alarm clock explodes and Harpo automatically raises a twenty-pound mallet and comes down, whango, right through the works of the clock with his eyes still closed, and that is all. That is the way it goes with the picture as a whole, a breakneck crazy business, made violent and living by the presence in it of some impenitently ham and delightful bad boys.

The Marx Brothers' type of humour is frequently not their own; but what is never anyone else's is their ability, when they have got a laugh, to put it over the plate and halfway through the catcher's glove. Having no controlling idea, they cannot make their comedy stick – i.e., you realize even while wiping your eyes well into the second handkerchief that it is nothing so much as a hodge-podge of skylarking, and soon over. Their picture is done the minute it fades on the screen. But the boys themselves are still with us, and I estimate an average period of ten days to three weeks, as the picture gets around, before the American public will be able to open its garbage can in the morning and not duck involuntarily, anticipating that a Marx Brother will pop up and clout it over the head with a sackful of tomatoes.

This fact and the exuberant antic that carries it along will remain for a while as a vague monument, in something more than wax, to a colossal burning energy spent on anything and nothing. With the definite exception of Groucho, who would be funny in still photographs, the Marx Brothers are an uninventive, stupid bunch. They are very much like somebody exploding a blown-up paper bag – all bang and no taste; but they are also irrepressible clowns with a great sense of the ridiculous. They tear into it by guess and by god, they rush through it as though it were meat and they starving; their assurance, appetite and vitality are supreme; they are both great and awful.

Hollywood's Half a Loaf

The boys in Hollywood must get bewildered if they turn to the right sort of left criticism occasionally. In the day-to-day course of their business they've developed an art of screen fiction that is equalled no-where; but the comment on this is the prevalent formula: Hollywood slickness. They learned first and learned for keeps that camera spectacularism is more of a hindrance to a picture's motion than the mantle of art itself; but the comment here is the dark question: Ah, where is the camera of the exiled Pflugg, of Pirojok or Pissé, or of the superb Pckzy, who has eliminated motion and whose amazing study of decomposition may be seen tonight through individual stereopticons at the New Museum of Social Modernes? And so on.

The boys get their worst drubbing on the score of content – and even more so when they attempt to include some they have long been reviled for not including. When they made *Black Fury* they made it as good a strike picture as they knew how, but localized the issue and otherwise pulled teeth to the end of selling it here and abroad. So when the social-hopers got hold of this picture, which made the idea and need of strikes more understandable and real to more people than any picture ever released, they went angrily on, reducing their own principles to the final absurdity of the proposition that anything not a whole loaf is necessarily an anti-loaf, or rat-biscuits.

The two sides don't get together. Movie people tend to understand things in surface terms rather than basic principles. But their command of surfaces is supreme, so that when in their best stride they show a thing, there is no need for thumbing back through Marx to find if it is safe to believe, let alone laudable: the thing exists by itself for its moment on the screen, unquestionable. Whereas the professional content-sifters have all the correct principles in their little black bag, but small comprehension of how a story is set in motion or of its possible effect on audiences.

M.G.M.'s picture *Fury* is a powerful and documented piece of fiction about a lynching for half its length, and for the remaining half a desperate attempt to make love, lynching and the Hays office come out even. But I doubt if those who see it will carry the whitewash part of it so long in their minds as the straight action of the introduction and middle. The boy (in the person of Spencer Tracy a homely human boy, a little old and clumsy and hulking) sees his girl off on the train and goes back to his two kid brothers, whom he is trying to keep out of dangerous mischief in their unemployment, and to the routine of his job where he is scraping pennies toward his marriage. The three chaps get a gas station and make it go; the boy buys a cheap car; and finally he starts out to get his girl, after months and years with his dull pain of wanting her.

206

Fury: Spencer Tracy

But a small-town force picks him up for a kidnapper: a mistaken identity that will clear up in a minute – but doesn't clear up. And then the mob begins to work and we get about the finest exposition of ferment in motion that has ever been done. The gossips, the trouble-makers, the stout citizens. Gatherings in bars, easy talk, the dynamite of outraged womanhood and other standard American (i.e., easy and dithering) ideals, and the spark to set it off. And then the crowds gathering – only a few active ones, the rest coming to gawp and joining in – the mounting hysteria and march on the jail, and suddenly the jailhouse, the object, giving pause. The sheriff with his lean figure and white hair standing out on the steps, trying weak reason and invective, invoking state troops and rallying his scared deputies. And in the middle of this stupid growing fury, with such fine submental types as Bruce Cabot in the foreground, this picture has the true creative genius of including little things not germane to the concept but, once you see them, the spit and image of life itself – as witness the kid hanging on to one of the vantage points attainable by kids, and during a lull in the crowd's roar giving out a fair imitation of Dave

Fleischer's theme line: 'I'm Popeye the sailor man (*wheat wheat*).' It goes beyond the thick noise and action of mob fury as a concept, to the macabre sidelights – the kids, the hurled tomato, the women's taunts – that make it not only more likely but more terrible.

Anyway, failing to get him, they fire the jail, and his cell window is framed, small and high and desperate, when his girl finally arrives to witness what they are doing to him with fire and smoke and mob frenzy – only they had to dynamite the burning jail to cover up their guilt before the troops arrived, blasting the place open and allowing him to make a secret getaway, burning his side off. Then we go on to the trial, which is tense, especially in the introduction of newsreel action and stop-action shots of riot, but marred by a nance of a district attorney and by confusing plot trends. By now they are trying to change a lynching picture into a love and personal-vengeance story.

Even in its powerful moments this is not the story of a typical lynching – there is no race angle, there is a dimly implied class angle, there is no mutilation and the man escapes. And then minor discrepancies: the sheriff has a strange sense of justice and, insulted and stoned by his townspeople, stands like Jesus Christ with a rifle, I mean he won't shoot; but after being slugged and thrown out of his own jail he perjures himself to conceal the identity of even those rabble-leaders already shown to be public enemies and thorns in his side. The Governor is justice incarnate (the evil genius is some unnamed political boss); and that strike-riot squad sometimes referred to as the National Guard is shown here as a national guard. But even if these facts cannot be considered cancelled by such incidental edges as the comment on the newsreel, on the radio announcer, the editorial bit about how we are always hanging our own community troubles on foreigners, etc., they have bearing only on how typical and agitationally useful the story is, not how true it is to the strange facts and contradictions which may be called either the exceptions to historical rule, or the actual stuff it is made from.

For those who already have all the dope on lynchings, *Fury* will have nothing to say, and will not say all of that; for those whose business it is, it will prove matter for angry discussion. But who is to be educated around here anyway? That handful of liberals and last-gaspers who have known all the answers these many years? The people to get to are those who don't even know the questions yet, and on these little will be lost by a movie company's trying to eat its cake and sell it to the chains too, so long as on the one subject they treat, however obliquely, terror is made true and the truth terrible.

Wings over Nothing

Secret Agent is a Gaumont-British film on the old formula of love and spies and war-time. But it is the work of Alfred Hitchcock – which makes all the difference. The rapid development of this genius in the form – his eternal inventive sense, wit and good taste and flair for swift, open movement – is already making some big names look rather lower-case. Mainly against him so far is his material (easier to concentrate on good effects if you don't have to make your story come out even). In *The Man Who Knew Too Much* the story about the people shown was so unlikely and maudlin as to spoil the picture for me – even if there hadn't been an amateurishness about much of the direction that can only be explained now by crediting Hitchcock with the rare quality of developing his strong points to the exclusion of all else. *The 39 Steps* went far beyond this: it was a delightful film, really a miracle of speed and light. But its story was hokum, you had to accept that at the start and keep on accepting.

And now in *Secret Agent* there are still a lot of holes – the hero's squeamishness, unlikely in war-time; the general reluctance of deadly enemies to kill anybody who would interfere with plot development; the British War Office's cueing in feminine interest by sending some silly society girl out to ball up deadly missions and practically lose the War. But in general there is a lot of sounder stuff – still on the surface, but present at least and with motivations. Madeleine Carroll makes fine capital of her first breakdown and subsequent near-hysteria. And John Gielgud is right for the character of one of those backbones of empire, brave and decent enough to get into a horrible spot of conflicting loyalties (Dash it, man, and all that).

Best of all is Peter Lorre's study of the assassin as artist. As satyr, humorist and lethal snake, he shows, here as always, a complete feeling for the real juice of situations and the best way of distilling this through voice, carriage, motion. He is one of the true characters of the theatre, having mastered loose oddities and disfigurements until the total is a style, childlike, beautiful, unfathomably wicked, always hinting at things it would not be good to know.

His style is most happily luminous in the intense focus and supple motion of movie cameras, for the keynote of any scene can be made visual through him. In close-ups, it is through the subtle shifts of eyes, scalp, mouth lines, the intricate relations of head to shoulders and shoulders to body. In medium-shots of groups, it is through his entire motion as a sort of supreme punctuation mark and underlineation. A harmless statement is thrown off in a low voice, and it is felt like the

Secret Agent: John Gielgud, Peter Lorre, Madeleine Carroll

cut of a razor in Lorre, immediately in motion – the eyes in his head and the head on his shoulders and that breathless caged walk raising a period to double exclamation points. Or the wrong question is asked, and the whole figure freezes, dead stop, and then the eventual flowering of false warmth, the ice within it.

And Alfred Hitchcock is the kind of director who can make the finest use of such character effects, neither exploiting nor restricting. The vital imagination behind almost every detail shows in the fleet economy of the opening sequence: the false funeral, the Chief, the mission. It seems hardly three minutes before everything is known, and the scene gathers itself into premonition merely through the wide, dark flight of stairs being seen from that angle, with the men at the top. Then the scream, the horrified servant girl running up, then back to the door and Secret Agent Peter Lorre in hot and sly pursuit – a perfect entrance.

All the usual expository sediment of a play, that is, runs off in solution like brook water here; and presently we are in Switzerland, spy meets girl-spy with some fetching and varnished by-play, and here is Lorre again, barking like a spaniel, breathless with the devastation brought about in him by sight of anything wearing pants that don't show, and already established as a major and mysterious force. And then the absolutely stunning sequence in the church. The organist being their agent, they come in, light the candle signal, wait and wait, and there is no answer but the sustained organ chord of minor thirds, which swells and becomes tremendous as they creep up on the organist, to find him strangled across his keys. There follows the flight to the belfry and that beautiful shot looking down from there – the space and dwarfed perspective, the twisted form sprawled on the stones and the pulling of the bell rope.

After this comes one of the finest suspense foundations I know of: their singling out the wrong man and hoaxing him up the mountain to his certain death. The hard intention is set off against the humour on the surface, the act against the result. The mountain, Gielgud's revulsion and quitting of the expedition to watch through a telescope, the house back home with the wife complacent in her German conversation class but anxious over the husband's dog, who worries the door and whines – and the visual bridge between these in Madeleine Carroll. And finally the three scenes merge in one as the act is framed in the telescope, a terrible moment of space and falling and cloud-shadows over the snow, the dog's howl rising over the picture above and bringing the camera back to the quiet, terrified home scene below.

Garbo and the Night Watchmen

There is no space for going into the manner in which superimposed images, throwbacks in character, blended contrasts and camera positions and well-paced cutting, constantly heighten effects. Or for any analysis of just how Hitchcock and his camera can load the simple entry of a building with suspense and terror. But something should be said of the use of sound, which is not equalled anywhere else: the music in the church, the howl of the dog, the disembodied voice in the rhythm of the train wheels (he mustn't, he mustn't, he mustn't, he mustn't), the deafening factory and steeple-bell noises, etc. Then there is the growing discord of the peasant-dance scene, after the murder, where the voices go from sweet to wild and the accompaniment becomes the metallic scream of coins whirling in bowls.

In all matters of treatment, the director of this film hardly has a rival. And whatever may be said for the boys who start out with a conviction and philosophical good-will large enough to cancel out all the unimaginative heaviness of their execution, I still think Hitchcock should be rated among the best if only for what he can teach them. In a latter-day fashion, he is a pioneer of the movie, increasing the range of its plasticity and power: he can take something that is practically nothing and make it seem like music and give it wings.

All the World Loves a Winnah

There is nothing on the screen this week, there is nothing anywhere this week, that for implications and sheer electric excitement can come up to the pictures of the Joe Louis–Max Schmeling fight, run off at the Yankee Stadium in New York, the night of 19 June, as a foregone conclusion and box-office flop. People had stayed away in droves – from what turned out to be one of the fights of the century. But in any event it is here now in pictures. They had cameras well placed, both on a special elevated stand and just below the ring looking up; they had sound equipment to catch the crowd's roar outside in the dark and the abrupt, pregnant explosion of the major blows inside this unnatural square of light; they got all of it and have edited the several prints so that both the flow of action and its crucial points are developed on the screen, until tension is heavy in the audience and the illusion of attending the actual thing is complete.

The picture tells a more accurate story than could be got from even the first row of ringside seats: the camera eye is not subject to human excitement and fluctuations (if a handler leaps up in imprecation or horror it does not stray off), and what is more it is a collection of eyes seeing several sides, from right or left, close or far, capable through editing of registering the most significant.

In the picture you can see the biding restraint and driving power of arms and shoulders, the bodies weaving, surging, braced. You can see in perfect focus the deadly precision of Joe Louis, weighing 198 pounds and moving like 140, also his one-two-three routine – a left to the body followed through, by some powerful flex of shoulder, into a left hook to the head, and the right coming in through the opening, bam. You can see in slow motion every step and blow following the first blow to stagger this fighting turret, the long-range salvo against the bones forward of his left ear which sent the Brown Bomber scuttling off backwards in queer little half-circles on his heels; and Schmeling moving up on him in a fury of attack and Louis melting under those blows like butter, seeking cover where there was none, blown wide open with a left and seeming in the slow motion to hang there for seconds as the right came in like a train of cars, bouncing him on the canvas.

In the camera record you can see the several low blows struck by Louis subsequently, and along with the worst of them the somehow touching picture of his remorse and mute reassurance to Max (one doesn't talk through a clenched mouthpiece) by throwing arms over his shoulders with futile pats of the glove. And you can see the kill as clear as crystal – Louis coming out wavering but still to be reckoned with as usual, his being driven back around the ring, knocked silly with the final direct hit, toddling like a baby under the pelting gloves, and then the last completely safe powerhouse sending him halfway around and down like a brick chimney.

These pictures of the fight must be among the best ever made; they are a night with the gladiators, a round trip to Mars, they are practically everything. And yet there is missing from their flat black-and-white motion across the screen something vital – whatever it took to make the fight a fight and the air charged with uncertainty, everybody there with his nerves strung like a harp. Without the crowds and smoke and sharp cries growing through the preliminaries, the atmosphere becoming heavy as the fighters climb through the ropes in their bath-robes, the colour and rough tangibility and spirit of the place, the recorded action becomes more like a waxworks, however true to life – a little ghoulish, like the acting out of a murder.

For one thing, the picture has been cut down so subtly that you would not know it if there were not the fact of its running time (33 minutes as against almost 40 of actual fighting, let alone introductions, throwbacks in slow motion, credit titles and shots taken between gongs); and in cutting they have somehow deleted the suspense we felt in the stadium, those interminable seconds of the first few minutes, where lightning might strike with the next move and few moves were made, the fighters feeling out and testing and blocking, many people yelling and the question silent in the air, When will it come?

For another thing, we know the outcome now; we are here only to see the bloody flux of its execution. The Brown Bomber having, as a matter of record, been practically grounded in the fourth round, we have no terror of him now. Joe Louis, as seen after the event, appears merely as a stubborn, doomed hulk, going through the motions and postponing the end, pitiful or ludicrous as the case may be.

Well it wasn't that way with us in the stadium, where the idea of Joe Louis as the invincible torpedo died hard. We had been told. This Negro heavyweight is a sensation – young, purposeful, on the up-grade, backing weight with speed, and speed with dynamite in both shoulders (speed and weight without that special slugger's leverage in the muscles of the shoulder and back are no good), and rounding it all off with an unflustered command of all the blows and their combinations and the angles from which they may be swung. And what is more, Louis is a killer, always has been a killer, sullen and cruelly efficient and heavy of eye. He doesn't grin, slap backs; doesn't have to.

Whereas Max Schmeling is thirty now, pretty old for a fighter. He has been The Champ but is champ no longer, and was never very glorious. What has he got? A right, a clumsy technique, and lead in his pants. So the sports-writers have a lot of fun with him. Well, well, one more day before they lay Maxie in his pine box. Der Big Max will come in like a lion and go out like a light they say, and laugh. Spare a laugh for poor old Max, with one doubtful right arm and one foot in the grave.

And so it took quite a long time for the idea to sink in that the newspaper boys must have been talking about somebody else. And still the tension held, for even after the seventh round the fight was no certainty, there were no wise guys at the time who jumped up and announced that the fight was in the bag. That man was still worth watching, and when he flicked a shoulder you could see Schmeling's head go back, hard. Louis was instinctively game and a living danger so long as the feet held up under him, and even in the last round managed to throw in a long right that would have mowed the whole working-press section down like a row of wooden soldiers. But not Max, he couldn't get Max down, and so as the people gradually caught on that Louis might be the Brown Bomber but old Max was out-fighting and outlasting and gradually knocking the heart out of him, they began to shift, until Joe Louis as the peepul's favourite was lost sight of, during the last two or three rounds, by all except the Negroes in the audience, who were silent and seemed dazed.

The people weren't very decent about this fight. You wonder what they go for. You go yourself and are nervous as a chicken, more scared of Joe Louis than anybody who faced him in the ring. You watch the fight and don't know if it's Friday evening or San Francisco. And if you have a taste for imagination you imagine how the world of these two has shrunk to a right glove and a left glove and a tough weaving head above them, the yelling night air of the place falling away to a stillness of inhuman exertion and inner counsel (watch his right, watch his right, back a little and shift, watch watch . . . just over the cheek-bone, just below the ribs), to an almost visual chart of moves to make or block, and then the false move and the rain of blows, the giddy lights and whirling universe and gloves as big as box cars (get clear, get clear now, stay up, clinch for cover and stay up). And then the gradual shift to blackness, a nightmare of circling and blocking and striking out automatically, the body no longer under control as such, the remote movements of arms and legs coming as a dim surprise but as of no moment, the iron gloves in front and a painful brief rest in the seconds' corner with acid restoratives and rubs and slaps and out again. And then a heavy jar (get back, get away out, stay off) and then the big guns and a fall through space, thousands of faces through the ropes, a convulsion (*three, four, five* – the count, get up, knees up – *seven, eight* – knees up, try, move, get up) and the knees giving like jelly and the floor coming up and the body gone into it, nothing but distant noises, lights and rest with a bad throbbing.

But do people feel it this way, is there some such feeling for the tragedy of a man's being pounded groggy and the senses practically blown out of his body, some kind of awe or pity or something? It must be there is some, but it is certainly not vocal. Max Schmeling hasn't a chance, so they come in yelling for Joe Louis (here and there a rebel voice going counter to the crowd); then in the theatre they know Louis was beaten raw, and so come in yelling for Max (slug him, Maxie, oh, it's murder, oh, slug him). And for that pitiful figure of a man wobbling around out of his senses with the head being blasted off his shoulders, for that proud two hundred pounds of fighting power and skill, tottering and fumbling and shooting its weak lefts at the moon, there is no more compassion evident than shows itself in the laughter to see him bounce grotesquely on the floorboards, the hoots for his rubber knees, the final anxious clapping and rooting for the kill.

Of course the boys are fighters in a prize ring, it's their job, they are paid for it: no use getting soft on the subject. But all this turning of coats to be on the winning side, all this mirth and high spirits in the face of a man's ambition and body being broken under spotlights – this is callous, knavish, the presence of it in this theatre disheartening, somehow obscene. It would seem that the main part of our boasted interest in boxing as an art and sport is simply a desire to see blood let and tissue bruised. And as to another one of our pet national qualities, may we not put it that we are always cheering for the underdog just so long as we can find an underdog who is a ten-to-one shot to come home ahead and on top – the winnah.

Hail but Dead End

Having gone up to see *The Thin Man* once again before Metro called it in to clear the way for the sequel, I can report that in spite of a tattered print this is still an ace picture, beautifully timed and executed, shrewdly invested in character, and with its conflict, meanings and sentiments seeming to have been photographed in a bowl of light, so easy and lucid is all its motion. But the reason for looking it up now is that in the two and a half years since its release this picture has been playing around almost steadily, has somehow been more in the public eye than other films just as good, and has become a myth.

So I am afraid that when Metro comes along with its new *After the Thin Man*, figuring that you can take a list of the same key names, dial them out like a telephone number and have immortality on the wire, people are going to be disappointed. Not only because there is no formula by which a true natural can be duplicated, but because *The Thin Man* itself has already passed out of flawed reality into the awe and perfection of legend.

But before they put it in mothballs for good, a few remarks on this picture might be read into the record. In the first place, it is the best of its type but the type has limitations. I have just read the book for the first time and find that Albert Hackett and Frances Goodrich did a wonderful job of reshaping the story, softening it up considerably but humanizing it even more, giving a local habitation, etc. – in fact, their treatment, with its inserts of gaiety and underlineation of dramatic points, definitely overshadows the original source. Nevertheless, they had to deal with the problem of all detective novels: the need at the end to unravel for the audience all the strands of plot they have been

William Powell and Myrna Loy in *The Thin Man;* William Powell, Spencer Tracy and Jean Harlow in *Libelled Lady*

Libelled Lady: Jean Harlow

weaving together with such care for the audience's mystification all along. And so there is a banquet scene in which all the motives and the culprit have to be revealed, and in a hurry, to the inevitable detriment of plausible human values and straight logic. It should go without saying that if so many emotional lives are to arrive at a simultaneous crisis believably, the whole story must lead up to such a climax, not around and away from it.

But while it is also true that stories depending for success on a surprise twist at the end must forfeit, when the end is already known, the long-term values of a second reading (thus daisies and reviewers of murder-mysteries won't tell), *The Thin Man* is still good, seen for the second or third time. It is not only a handsome piece of craftsmanship, it has appeal and a cocky good humour. Recall Miss Loy's grand entrance, Christmas morning on the air-rifle range, the life and doings of Asta the terrier, and that expansive party, packed with types and droll situations and lines – e.g., the conference in the bathroom ('That's all right, we're only chatting'), William Powell saying why nonsense he used to bounce her on his knee and the lush following him around with happy hope, 'Which one, can I touch it?' And the predominant sentiment, being the tanned leather of an equable married life rather than the friskier calf of boy-chases-girl, was a fine and refreshing change.

Yet from being tender and being gay the film was never permitted to go soft or forget that it was a pretty tough case, with murders and stool pigeons, the law working its victims over and Edward Brophy giving off that classic address: 'That'd be very smart. . . . Me that a police captain's been in a hospital three weeks on account we had an argument. The boys would *like* me to come in and ask 'em questions. Yuh. They's like it right down to the end of their blackjacks.' Add the fearful visit to Wynant's shop, Wynant with his hawk face rising in the elevator, and his shadow, as the Thin Man, projecting all across the picture. So there was the drama and the fun too, one being the flesh, the other the hard necessary bone, neither conflicting. All in all it was a miracle of co-ordinated talents – writing, casting, acting, W. S. Van Dyke's direction and the staff men under him, on cameras and in the recording and cutting rooms, who assisted in catching the spirit of every scene, from cocktails and jazz pianos to gunfire.

It was a miracle but also a dead end: it can hardly be bettered and there is no constructive use in imitating it. In the way of light pictures, the best body of work so far (outside of Chaplin and Capra and such unclassifiables as *Sing and Like It*, *The Milky Way*) is the Paramount comedy cycle. I mean the MacMurray–Colbert–Lombard type of pictures, which hit the top two years ago in Wesley Ruggles's *Gilded Lily*. The line has since gone to seed – *Hands Across the Table* (next best), *The Bride Comes Home*, *The Princess Comes Across*, etc. – but is potentially good stock and surely worth more deliberate care than something which has reached its limit.

Libelled Lady is Metro's best and latest entry in this field, a frothy thing like all the rest, with touches of feeling, little stagnation and considerable laughter. The plot is one of the chestnuts of romance: William Powell and Myrna Loy are really meant for each other but are slower in finding it out than the audience, because he is the fixer for a metropolitan paper, trying to frame her into dropping a libel suit that runs to millions. Spencer Tracy is the managing editor, Walter Connolly is the millionaire father, Jean Harlow is the bride who never quite gets married, a little stormier than her part but none the less doing valiantly on the barricades, or should it be breastworks?

The situations step right along, first with fireworks between Powell and Tracy, next between Powell and Loy, and finally among all five principals. There is a tendency to work out one incident at a time for its own sake, but everything hangs together nicely and we all leave the theatre in a fine humour, feeling that newspaper men and rich daughters may be pretty tough nuts, but love is the thing that will crack them – and if the same is not demonstrable by facts, who cares? Also everybody is telling everybody else, Did you get the part where he was saying, Why, don't you worry about *him*, he's just like my brother, and Jean Harlow came back at him, Maybe so, but he's not *my* brother; and what was this she said to the taxi driver when he told her I can go faster lady but the cab can't, and a dozen others – the snapper-answer method here prevailing over sustained flights of dialogue. It is too long for its story, holding off with needless complications and then resolving too glibly; and it is a bit mean to some of its characters. But it moves and sparkles, has some good-natured swipes at things and may be remembered with some affection. Given the genius spent on *The Thin Man* it might still be no more stunning; but given more it should be better and – because it runs in a straighter channel to start with – true comedy.

Swing High, Swing Low

Looking at pictures and studying what is said about them, one occasionally gets the feeling of men working along out there in Hollywood, shaping the mechanisms of a complex art delicately and

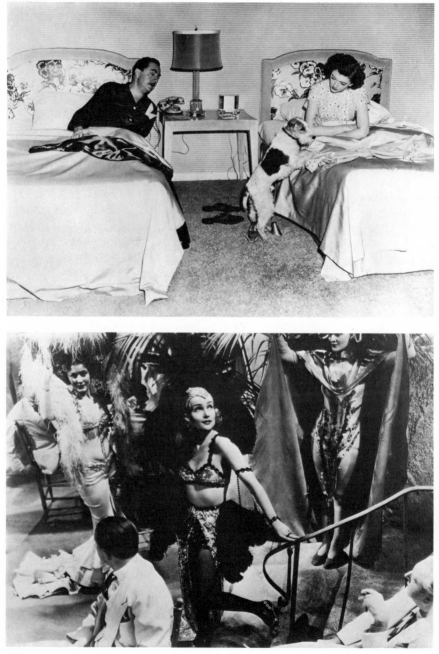

William Powell and Myrna Loy in *Song of the Thin Man*; Carole Lombard in *Swing High, Swing Low*

getting no more reward (outside the trade, that is) for their labour and vigilance and aspirations than a blundering imprecise praise or the customary blanket dismissal of all their works. The men make their way in the industry of course, earning titles and fat bonuses and a chicken in every garage; but while that ought to be enough for anybody, I am wondering about the good film-makers who must know very well that the same rewards would flow, and often twice as fast, if they made pictures atrociously. It must make them rather cynical to see that about the only way a director can become recognized as a good artist, among the very people who give out the loudest yells on the need for improvement in Hollywood, is to get out of Hollywood altogether: either go abroad and grow an accent or stay at home and join a Group.

Mitchell Leisen makes good comedies; indeed there is enough concentrated filmcraft in his current *Swing High, Swing Low* to fit out half a dozen of these gentlemen who are always dashing around in an independent capacity making just the greatest piece of cinema ever. The picture will play the big time and there will be press raves and an audience of millions; but one doesn't begin to speak of art until a picture becomes unavailable because of an unfamiliar language or a lumbering scowlike motion that tickets it for the 600-seater houses. Take the new imported version of *The Golem*, which is an example of art as nobody could deny. It has the great Harry Baur and it manages a fine atmosphere of the Ghetto and sixteenth-century Prague and it tells a good yarn. But outside of a surface approach to sociology it isn't a patch on the creative effects of *The Bride of Frankenstein*. James Whale's *Frankenstein* played into the New York Roxy, though, and the Roxy seats around 6,000; it was more thrilling in practically the same way, but since it didn't have to be played up in a shoe-box theatre as art, it was played down in the normal circuit as a thriller. And that was all.

Swing High, Swing Low is romantic comedy shading into tragic effects, the story of a happy-go-lucky Canal Zone soldier who plays the trumpet without knowing how good he is, and falls in love with the lady without knowing how deep a responsibility *that* sort of thing is. It is all fine until an agent books him into New York and he begins to live high and forget about everything, or put everything off. Misunderstandings, too many bars, and presently he is a down-and-outer, and presently (for the happy end) he isn't. The reasons for the failure of this story as truth are various and as follows: (1) the shift from comedy to near-tragedy is thin and difficult ice here as anywhere,

(2) coincidence is made to explain turns of the story that should really have proceeded from the weakness of character just as it stood, (3) the trumpet music is so thin and colourless that it is a drag on the story rather than the buoyant influence it should have been.

The faults are easy to catalogue; the virtues are those of good film comedy and about as easy to describe as running water, having the same continuous flow and play of light and change without effort and joy to the senses. Not just dialogue; not just the people who put it over; not just the situations they are put in; not just the clear development and right focus of everything in the cameras. It is a little of each of these and a lot of something else, some sunny genius for the total effect.

You can pick out a spot like the complex visual play of the sequence where Carole Lombard is busy building a fire in the oven and Messrs Butterworth and MacMurray are busy rousting a six-foot bed through a three-foot door, and it goes on and on (not the bed, however) and everybody talking and saying What? and dropping the bed – I thought I'd die. Or take the little duel where the rival chippie starts out to freeze Carole by announcing her contract with the El Greco in New York, 'Which naturally everybody has heard of the El Greco,' she says. 'Yes, dearie, but has the El Greco heard of you?' Carole says from off-stage where she is changing a dress or something. 'Oh of course, sugar,' the chippie says, 'they must just know me by reputation' – and Carole comes out fastening a strap as demure as sin itself: 'Yes, dearie, I'm afraid everybody must know that' and goes into some feminine business or other before the girl can get her breath, 'My *angel*, isn't that a stunning hat – is that a *feather*?' and gets away. Or take the way they mount the scene where MacMurray is trying to put on an airy good-bye and the camera frames both her against the door and him going down and starting back up the steps, the contrast of plane and position of each helping to bring out the unspoken juxtaposition of their private worlds. Or you could mention the auxiliaries to comedy: Charles Butterworth, Jean Dixon, the game-cock, the flair for the unexpected but completely human that shows in the lines. You could go on and mention each thing in turn, but that wouldn't be the half of it because one thing merely leads to another, just as in life, and this leading-on motion (or continuity) becomes a sort of fourth dimension to the whole, in all its intangible, persuasive charm.

Cecelia Ager

Born in Grass Valley, California. University of California at Berkeley.
Contributor to *Harper's Bazaar* and *Vogue*.

A Day at the Races: Chico Marx

9. Cecelia Ager

Whistling in the Dark

Always Una Merkel's been clown to some other girl's romance, always that funny gangling kid standing by to make the heroine exquisite by contrast. Well, comedy relief has a heart, too, a curly blonde head that longs to rest on a strong masculine chest, lips that yearn to be bruised with kisses, arms that ache to embrace, and so on. At last comes *Whistling in the Dark* to reward Miss Merkel's valiant service in the cause of laughter. Now she can be the heroine herself.

'Tis said that love makes lovers beautiful; Miss Merkel proves that's true. Certainly it teaches them new flattering ways of doing their hair. Miss Merkel, for instance, combs her marcel waves straight back off her forehead, lets them ripple into soft curls across the sides and back. Bangs soften her coiffure and give it witchery; love and improved make-up are responsible for the new load of piquancy in her pert face.

There's another saying knocking around that fits Miss Merkel too, something about taking the bitter with the sweet, and so, though she's the feminine lead in the picture, they've forgotten to give her clothes lead-importance. She wears one dress through most of the picture, and it happens to be very dull, even oldish. Dark crepe with dolman sleeves and silver ball buttons down the shoulders, an uninteresting bateau neckline, and a belt that droops a little dowdily in front. Miss Merkel is the sort of girl, however, to appreciate that one can't have everything, so she doesn't let her frock depress her, but seizes her opportunity and soars.

Parachute Jumper

Bette Davis in *Parachute Jumper* seems convinced she's become quite a charmer. Slowly she raises her eyelids to sear the hero with her devastating glances, then satisfied, she smiles a crooked little Mona Lisa smile. Unfortunately, this procedure takes place while Miss Davis is wearing a curious pill-box hat that perches on her head at an angle slightly comic. The hat, and her own self-satisfaction, interfere with the effect.

To make matters still more troublesome for her, Miss Davis must keep to the neat but not helpful black-and-white frocks of a job-hunting stenog. Finally she gets work, and an evening dress, too, from a dope-smuggling employer. The dress is black satin swathings about the hips, little more than a drop shouldered ruffle for the completely backless bodice. A bit too-too for Miss Davis's slender figure.

Claire Dodd, the story says, engages her chauffeurs on their biceps appeal, then gets to the point the day they start work. Miss Dodd is too young and pretty to need to be so aggressive, but the story says she is.

Hallelujah I'm a Bum

Madge Evans is a fortunate girl, and that's because she's such a very nice one. She's fortunate in *Hallelujah I'm a Bum* – for not only Frank Morgan, but Al Jolson is mad about her. Because she's such a nice girl, the story arranges for her to have amnesia, so she can return their adoration each in turn. When she's got a memory, she loves Mr Morgan, when she's lost it, she loves Mr Jolson. It would never do for a nice girl to be a two-timer, and a nice girl couldn't fail to find both Mr Morgan and Mr Jolson charming. If it seems a little mixed up, that's because the rewards of virtue have been absent from the screen for such a long time that hardly anyone recognizes them any more.

Being true blue, regular and wholesome takes up so much of a nice girl's time that she has very little energy left for the less worthy pursuits – of style, for instance. Miss Evans pauses long enough in her devotions to right to fix herself up with a flatteringly expert make-up

Una Merkel in *Whistling in the Dark* ; Bette Davis in *Parachute Jumper*

Madge Evans in *Hallelujah I'm a Bum;* Loretta Young in *Grand Slam*

that realizes what fine, frank eyes she has, but that's all the attention she can spare for vanity.

Her clothes are neat, of course, and ladylike, but flair is the shallow province of hussies. Miss Evans has a couple of decent suits that will do very nicely, and a light satin one-piece dress for times when she's expected to be a little seductive. That satin dress just proves that nice girls really ought to stay in their own backyard. It clings so desperately in several places that it becomes a little embarrassing. Oftentimes nice girls are that way because their figures don't give them any choice.

Grand Slam

When *Grand Slam* is all said and done, of course it is safe for husbands to play bridge with their wives – if the wife is as pretty as Loretta Young. Too, they must love one another madly, and be temporarily separated because their love is so overwhelming it drives them to deranged jealousy. By fulfilling these few requirements, husbands and wives may play bridge together in security. They don't even have to play a system; their love will show them the way.

This is all made clear to the audience and to Miss Young – after she runs the gamut from hat-check girl to wife of a bridge expert, with its corresponding change from neat and becoming black frocks with flattering white collars to fancy draped and beaded costumes over-anxious in their frantic designing to indicate elegance. Bridge brings Miss Young a lot of clothes, but her concentration on the game permits her no time to choose them either wisely or well. Only once, and then only after she has not been playing bridge for some time, does she appear in a costume which does something kind for her. It is wide-striped crêpe, simply cut and moulded in diagonal lines, with a wide decolletage softly hung with swags of the same material broadening Miss Young's slim shoulders so that they achieve the current smart silhouette. Her evening wraps are long and fitted at the waist, but their distracted, indecisive use of fur defeats their groping towards chic.

Glenda Farrell doesn't play bridge. She's not quite bright enough for it, therefore her costumes are simple, pictorially stylized, as all good picture clothes should be. Helen Vinson, again, is devoted to bridge and bridge players, so her clothes, too, are riotous with detail. She's not quite as good a player as Miss Young, however, so her clothes aren't quite as fancy, just fancy enough to be dull.

Ladies They Talk About

Once in every Barbara Stanwyck picture it has become the custom for

Barbara Stanwyck in *Ladies They Talk About;* Bunny Beatty, Mae Beatty, Constance Bennett in *Our Betters*

Miss Stanwyck to blow up in a shattering emotional scene. *Ladies They Talk About* respects tradition.

Miss Stanwyck therefore suffers a continuous series of treacheries from practically everybody in the cast, so that when the time comes for her to do her stuff, she'll have gathered a goodly store of ammunition. Meanwhile, of course, she lets off little sparks along the way, but she takes proper care to save the full punch for the finish. She permits the audience to suspect she has a temper right from the beginning, and then stuns them with what she can do when she's really mad.

Miss Stanwyck is a bad, bad girl in *Ladies They Talk About.* She's sent to San Quentin for it and meets a lot of other naughty girls there, Lillian Roth, Dorothy Burgess, Maude Eburne, Cecil Cunningham. They're bad all right, but they've got mighty strong personalities.

And San Quentin's not such punishment at that, more like a finishing school for young ladies. Each girl has her own room which she may decorate to suit her individual flair. Portable phonographs are allowed the pretties, Pekinese dogs if they like, plenty of cigarettes and cigars, and though they must all wear cotton dresses, in the privacy of their own rooms they may put on black lace chemises and sheer mesh stockings, the more pleasantly to muse about their sweethearts. Ruth Donnelly, the matron, is just like a house mother, only she has more sense. Helen Ware is no more strict than a Dean. The girls have their little feuds, but no worse than those at boarding school. Sometimes the girls have to work in the prison laundry, which is really a post office with the letters concealed in the clothes they wash instead of in post boxes. Yet girls are just girls. Miss Stanwyck doesn't like it there somehow. She looks very well during the time she spends at San Quentin. Her hair is always neatly waved and coiffed, her make-up never neglected, but she doesn't appreciate it. She just sulks and pouts and wants to get even all the time.

Our Betters

Constance Bennett flings herself into the hoity-toity snobsy-wobsy elegance of *Our Betters* like the prodigal hot-footing it home. Here's a role that says of her though once she was trusting and dewy with good intentions, life had made her relentless, clever, unscrupulous, triumphant. It's an unsympathetic part, but Miss Bennett is always a little unnatural in sympathetic roles. Somebody's got to show the younger generation how to get on in the world, and Miss Bennett's peerless at that. She plays the foresighted, arrogant Pearl with uncanny understanding. She's so sure in her characterization, she makes it practically an autobiography.

Our Betters is terribly smart, violently upper class. Insistently it shrieks toniness, graduation from Hollywood aristocracy. Its houses have not only drawing-rooms and boudoirs, they have libraries, with books in them, too. Some of its rooms are Empire, some Georgian, it even has a Directoire foyer. Positively nothing is modernistic, that's how swell it is. Constance Bennett, Anita Louise, Phoebe Foster, are presented at court and top anybody Their Majesties have seen, that's how utterly ornamental they are. Miss Bennett wears a white Schiaparelli suit with a three-quarter casual coat and a dark high-necked blouse that smart New York shops plan to stun their customers with this spring, that's how fashion-wise it is. Miss Bennett wears ropes of black pearls with a dark crêpe dress, that's how up in really blatant luxury she is. Every detail is so painstakingly indisputable it sets up a positive nostalgia for the other side of the railroad tracks.

Violet Kemble-Cooper is completely authoritative, continuously effective in her richly exaggerated characterization. Phoebe Foster and Anita Louise screen nicely, but in a cast with Miss Bennett and Miss Kemble-Cooper their lack of flair is too apparent, sets them aside as well meaning, but none the less bores.

King Kong

Despite all her experiences with picture beasties, Fay Wray can't seem to condition herself against the horrid old things. She's just as terrified at King Kong, she screams quite as shrilly as if she couldn't remember from her past encounters that she will surely be saved at the end. She won't learn, Miss Wray, she won't learn. All that's come of her former run-ins with monsters is the overnight change of her hair from black to blonde, but it doesn't help. The curious attraction she has for man-beast combos is not to be denied by superficial hair-colour transformation. It's made matters even worse for her. Blonde, she looks even more the part of Beauty in the fable, *Beauty and the Beast*, so what can the beast do but act good and beasty.

In *King Kong* Miss Wray actually puts on the legendary costume of Beauty, a medieval robe of sheer cloth of gold that falls gracefully off her shoulders and clings devotedly about her hips, girdled snugly with gold braid. She wears it presumably the better to rehearse her part in the film she's engaged to make on the mysterious island; but really and truly that costume is a plant, a hint to the audience in case they've forgotten the fable.

Miss Wray's reaction to Kong makes mincemeat of the fearless modern girl theory. She's not only scared to death, but she completely loses her head. She won't learn that Kong is really her friend. No, she screams and writhes and wriggles and kicks every time she's cradled in his love-lorn paw. Even when he scales the Empire State building holding her firmly in one hand, she carries on so vehemently it seems she wants to be let go so she can be dashed to the ground eighty storeys below. She just has no foresight. Strange girl, Miss Wray.

Night Flight

If *Night Flight* were to give you more than a hint, a teenchy-weenchy suggestion as to the kind of gals Helen Hayes and Myrna Loy are (*Night Flight*'s little women who wait at home while their husbands soar the skies), what would become of its restraint, its well-bred artistic economy, it would like to know. *Night Flight* means to be art, Hemingway kind of art. So away with embroidery. Let the facts be bare and brief.

If the audience can't tell that Helen Hayes loves her husband from watching the good housekeeping details of her preparation for his return, if they can't tell that she's a little bird at heart from noting her love for radio music, if they don't get her spirituality from observing the lack of allure of her routine chiffon and lace négligé, if they don't realize that she's a little soldier from heeding her gallant apprehension when she learns her husband's plane is late, if by this time they haven't learned to love her themselves – it's their hard luck. *Night Flight*'s not going to lead an audience by the hand.

And if they can't see that a flyer's mighty fortunate to have Myrna Loy for a wife, the way she asks no questions, the way she accepts his arrivals and departures, the way she looks at him, but, above all, the way she looks, warm, gentle, yielding – but the chances are the audience sees. For one thing, Miss Loy's photographed more tenderly than Miss Hayes. For another, she doesn't have to play any painfully playful little scenes pretending her husband's dining with her when everybody knows he's up in the skies bucking storms.

Man of Two Worlds

In all her screen career, Elissa Landi has never been tossed the flattery that heaps at her feet in *Man of Two Worlds*. To Francis Lederer, a poor Eskimo, her photograph is more anaesthetic than ether, more soporific than morphine. He looks at it while his fractured leg is set and feels no pain. And Miss Landi's voice, wafted on radio waves

King Kong: Fay Wray

Elissa Landi in *Man of Two Worlds*; Irene Dunne in *This Man is Mine*

from London to an ice-bound Arctic exploration ship, makes brave men swoon. Mr Lederer faints dead away when first he hears it.

It develops that Mr Lederer believes, in his simple, straightforward manner, that Miss Landi is white magic, sort of a goddess. She looks divine, anyway, in her white tea-gown with classic draperies and Grecian girdle outlining her Diana-esque figure. Besides, she's doing her hair in the same short curled coiffure swept up and off her forehead that was so very becoming to her as a legendary Amazon in *The Warrior's Husband*. Were it not for the fact that her mouth twists human-like when she talks, and that she has to speak a kind of pidgin English most of the time – everybody in the picture talks pidgin English sooner or later because of the Eskimo – were it not for carelessness anybody might consider Miss Landi a goddess. A stylish goddess who fastens her tweed suits with large wooden initial clips.

Steffi Duna plays a young lady Eskimo without powder, mascara or lipstick, who chews large hunks of blubber with genuine relish. But though it is Miss Duna's lot to suffer all the realism in the film, it doesn't get her down. She is sweet and appealing and even charming.

This Man is Mine

She's still noble, Irene Dunne in *This Man is Mine*, but she is loosening up. She says 'jake' once, and saying it, makes it sound like a swear word; she smashes a glass in temper, but smashes it against the fireplace, where its destruction will cause the least untidiness; and, most revolutionary of all, she confesses an ardent dislike for – what is this world coming to? – her mother!

This Man is Mine would have you sorry for Miss Dunne because her husband walks out on her. Oh, only temporarily. Catch any man getting away from capable Miss Dunne forever – but just the same it would have you sorry for her. Sorry for her, when she always goes about telling him how much she loves him and makes him tell it back to her, when she takes away the books he's reading, coyly rumples his hair, and sits down on the sofa beside him for a nice long homey chat. She likes to talk things out, Miss Dunne, and anything she likes to do, though she's only a little woman, gets done.

She's bold, even daring, in this picture because she's pretending to belong to that country-club set – but beneath it all it is to be feared that she is the clear-eyed, level-headed, silent sufferer of yore, expensively suburban in a series of ladylike costumes shot through with timid allure, the sort of clothes that shops advertise 'for young matrons' and which are bought by just matrons.

Constance Cummings, before she makes her entrance, has it said of her that she's a 'man-eater, glamorous, and fascinating'. And then she has to come on. And in a beige cloth coat with full puffed sleeves of summer ermine and a large white straw hat. But despite her billing and her own helplessness with clothes – she's of the opinion that chic is attained from startling, unrelated detail – Miss Cummings creates a characterization that registers, even if it does lack subtlety. She reveals a new sense of humour and progress toward being an actress.

It's nice having Kay Johnson back to see how well she's looking in her new banged coiffure that gives her face a becoming roundness, and to hope that by next time she remembers that she must not use too much lip-rouge, for too much makes her mouth look unhappy and old.

I Found Stella Parish

Kay Francis is handsomely prepared in *I Found Stella Parish* to do some right dressy self-sacrificing for her child. For each self-sacrifice she has a pretty dress. For one of them she even has a pretty suit. It's grey, and the lapels are worked all over in grey soutache braid to match the soutache-braided crown of her grey felt casual hat.

Miss Francis is an actress on the stage in the beginning of the picture, and someone mighty smart thought it would be nice for her to be acting in a play that happened in ancient Greece, so the ladies could see the very source of the current classical mode. Whereupon Miss Francis wears some costumes that look quite authentic in the play's Grecian setting – save that one of them's got a Greek key-design in rhinestones – and at the same time look like she's going to a party when she's photographed standing in the wings. One of the play's costumes is virtuous folds of white velvet, caught by jewelled buckles across her arms into sort of peek-a-boo sleeves, which gives it the right to have a V neckline extending smack down to her waist in front, but the topography of Miss Francis's figure doesn't make such carry-ings-on dangerous anyway. Along with this creation that knows how far it dares go, and goes it, Miss Francis wears a sleek white wig with stylized ringlets fashioned into bangs and imperious and eminently suitable diadem.

Miss Francis is so taken up with sacrifices for the sake of her child and the sadness they plunge her into, that she has very little oppor-tunity to smile as frequently as her fans have grown to expect. But smiling less, she acquires poise, and besides she has a lot of crying to do, glamorously.

Kay Francis in *I Found Stella Parish;* Rosita Moreno in *The House of a Thousand Candles*

241

The House of a Thousand Candles

Until *The House of a Thousand Candles* came along and showed them, American young women probably didn't realize the fun to be had out of saving the fate of Europe. Probably never realized how easy it is, just whisking nimbly behind curtains in the master spy's apartment, listening to the dastardly plot, then whisking out again to the rescue.

All it takes is a figure slim as Mae Clarke's, dressed in white satin because taffeta rustles; a yen for a British attaché that's strong enough to send a girl chasing him straight into the master spy's clutches; and the awareness that any dame who wears an all-over sequin costume with tulle flounces massed on her shoulders like Rosita Moreno's has got to be a secret agent no matter how much she slinks, yelping she's Raquel, the dancer, the Toast of All Nations. No dancer would be caught dead in that costume; Miss Moreno is; so she's no dancer. Not even though she can dance, and has an accent besides.

It does help, Miss Clarke points out in addition, to have friends spotted all over Europe who wear the same size clothes you do. That's for when you jump on trains in evening clothes and without baggage, you should have something different to wear the next night. Not so different, however, that it doesn't display your hip-line with equal conscientiousness.

Camille

Greta Garbo dies beautifully in *Camille*. You can actually see her do it, sense the precise moment when her lovely spirit leaves her fascinating clay. Though it's Robert Taylor himself who's talking awful dramatic at the moment, you pass him up. You don't pay any attention to Taylor. It's Garbo's face that absorbs you. It grabs at you all through *Camille*, but it's got you complete; you're all tied up when she dies. Complete, even though it looks like she's going to take quite a time dying, loping and staggering from bed to chair and back again. It's a magnificent face; death, and canny lighting and photography, revealing its epic bone structure, showing you that its baffling allure has solid foundation – it's structural, architectural and not, as you may have feared, disbelieving, something you just made up.

Garbo in *Camille* shows up Dietrich in anything as a smooth mask with interesting hollows in her cheeks and a low voice that reads 'yes' with a rising inflection. Garbo in *Camille* has character and shading and, surprisingly, warmth. You don't just admire her in *Camille* – you like her. You find her human at last. You are actually, actively, sorry for her – nor does she sacrifice any of her natural dignity to win your

Camille: Garbo

sympathy. It's that, in *Camille*, she realizes her potentialities as a great actress. She no longer need depend upon a provocative personality; now every nuance has meaning, is felt, is true.

There is fine showmanship in the externals of her portrait. Just as her cough grows progressively more frequent, chilling you the first time you hear it with its portent of doom and reiterating its ominous message each succeeding time, so does the colour of her costumes change from white in the carefree beginning, to grey when the forces of tragedy gather momentum, until at last sable black with all its dark meaning appears. First, in an all-black velvet dress and large black hat that she wears for her journey to the country. Then, when it seems that she is to be happy, white again in cannily picturesque lawn dresses with only a black cloak to remind you her fate is sealed; black again after her renunciation – shimmering black net with sequins, but black. For her death, so that you are not too miserable and may find solace in something, a white gown, ecclesiastical in feeling with its monk's cowl, sending you to religion, there to take courage to bear it. Adrian has never been more touching, nor, fortuitously, more decorative.

Garbo's coiffure also acts: the frivolous curled bangs that cover her forehead in the beginning are gradually lifted until at the end the whole serenity of her brow is revealed; there is something spiritual about this process too.

Lenore Ulric, new to pictures, shows Laura Hope Crews, who's been in pictures a lot, that an actress can register raucous vitality without becoming a noisy bore. Even Jessie Ralph is toned down in *Camille*, which makes Miss Crews's violently discordant carryings-on the more singular and distressing.

Three Smart Girls

Pure youth rarely gets on the screen. The chances of its coming to the studio at all are few – since pure youth is not itself concerned with making a profession of its youthfulness – but still it is possible for it to arrive at the studio in its natural state, whereupon the usual treatment it meets is a good lousing up. In the processes of making a picture, it's doomed to adulteration.

Too much make-up, elaborate coiffures, fancy clothes, unsuitable scripts, insensitive direction – even glamour. Either Hollywood doesn't understand children, or just doesn't like them for themselves alone. Extraordinarily precocious things are thought up for Shirley Temple to do, and her mass of curls is relentlessly cultivated. Bobby Breen is terribly emotional for a boy of his age, and his deep marcel waves are burnished to a blinding shine. Therefore the sympathetic and simple handling awarded Deanna Durbin in *Three Smart Girls* is all the more remarkable, and the picture's good taste virtually sensational.

No attempt is made to make Miss Durbin look or act like Joan Crawford, nor read her lines like Myrna Loy. She is asked only to behave like what she is – a nice girl of fourteen. Realizing that she can't sing all the time, and seeking something with which to fill in the gaps, her picture's producers have hit upon the daring scheme of letting her natural bloom of youth suffice.

And so Miss Durbin's eyelashes are of a normal length and her liprouge unobtrusive. She is given opportunity to be sweet and spirited; she is guarded from being cute. Her clothes are simple and suitable for her age; they have none of the strident salesmanship of a wardrobe selected by a stage mother.

Of course, *Three Smart Girls* has its glamour get-ups all right, but such is the iconoclasm of the piece that they are all assigned to the villainesses. The nice girls dress like nice girls – it is the dames who dress like picture actresses, who wear leopard-skin tunics with turbans to

244

Deanna Durbin in *Three Smart Girls;* Joan Crawford in *The Last of Mrs Cheyney*

match. Binnie Barnes has, too, a pale tawny short fox jacket, which she wears over a dark cloth dress with a dark Oriental toque mystic with a beige veil; also an exotic coiffure built on Tudor headdress lines. Alice Brady as well looks very expensive in a deliberate way, but all it avails them is hisses and frustration. *Three Smart Girls* goes for naïvety and sincerity, but it can tell the real thing from the phoney.

The Last of Mrs Cheyney

It is comforting to see, in *The Last of Mrs Cheyney*, that Joan Crawford has at last attained the manner she's been striving for. She put up a good fight, against what to anyone less determined might seem utterly insurmountable odds, and her final victory is an inspiration to us all. Now everybody, Miss Crawford and her audience, can relax. She emerges from the struggle freed of nearly all her feeling of inferiority (though why she should have felt that way the least bit is baffling, since after all she is a picture star, and picture stars are absolutely top aristocracy today); purged of nearly all the little giveaways that used to worry her so and drive her to an enormous and stridently active elegance in her fierce longing to wipe them out.

Now she quietly looks any actor, no matter how English, straight in the eye, confident of the mastered casualness of her own pronunciation. Nobody's coiffure is more cleanly swept-off-the-brow, more intent upon character and therefore disdainful of artificial coquetry, than hers; nobody's wardrobe more starkly simple – but only on the surface, mind. That calm and repose she's now achieved, that feeling of firm ground beneath her feet, must not be mistaken for just pure simplicity. Far from it. It wells from knowledge – from knowledge, at last, gained the hard way. No more do 'beans' – for 'beens' – jut out from her speech naked and terrified; no more do unresolved trimmings distract from the compact and self-contained silhouette of her clothes. Still self-conscious, but with a new self-assurance that shows her self-consciousness is only an expression of her awareness of her duty of high-class-example-setter to her public – instead of the mark of self-doubt it used to be – now Miss Crawford goes about doing right things, wearing right things, with deafening poise. Now her quality asserts itself from the inside out, instead of insisting on itself with externals; and the whole show is much more convincing, besides being a lot easier on everybody and cosier to watch.

True, she still keeps her eyes open to their widest range, but surely she has been severe enough with herself to warrant indulgence in this small holdover from her old ways. There is enough blackboard correctness in *The Last of Mrs Cheyney*, enough horror of vulgarity as it is. After all, only one of Miss Crawford's costumes, the hostess dress with the short Persian jacket, fits rather too tightly across the hips; there are no furs; her jewels, if large, are chastely set. There is enough restraint.

John Meade's Woman

The sulks are not a pretty thing, but they are arresting. People who make faces get more attention, doing it, than people who look pleasant, and so, fortunately for *John Meade's Woman* and for her own debut in pictures, Francine Larrimore turns out to be an excellent glowerer.

In *John Meade's Woman* Miss Larrimore is supposed to be burned up all the time. Miss Larrimore burns splendidly, giving it a nice direct attack, zinging right into it and without any co-operation from the script either. Single-handed she gets everybody to keep looking at her and wondering – since the script never explains, and she's too choked up to – what's eating her. All through the picture she keeps them wondering, a remarkable feat indeed.

From what goes on in *John Meade's Woman*, it seems Miss Larrimore is cut out for a career of intensity. She hates hard and she loves hard and if they both look like the same thing, it's because she's so very intense she gets all tangled up. She's so intense, in fact, it's a little difficult to tell in the picture when she's stopped being drunk and has gotten sober, and vice versa. However, the heroic degree of Miss Larrimore's intensity is piquant and fetching in so petite a figure and delicate a face. She photographs nicely and in the future, no doubt, her knack for outbursts will not be so extravagantly exploited.

When You're in Love

Grace Moore sings 'Minnie the Moocher' in *When You're in Love*, but the swingers will remain quite calm. When prima donnas get what they trust is hot, they also get cute. They hit the notes on the head, but they also 'interpret' the lyrics as if they were doing 'Mammy's Little Coal Black Rose' as a gracious encore on a concert programme. They read it with expression, which is nice, but it does interfere with the relentless beat of the rhythm. They pause to draw a well-trained breath before they've 'sent' in a scat chorus, which throws the whole thing off, and they are also apt to want to sway with the frenzy of the music, to prove their common touch, but their tossing muscles are prim and maintain their inhibitions no matter how desperately the prima donnas yearn for abandon. Miss Moore's 'Minnie' is an adorable drawing-room stunt; however, 52nd Street can take it or leave it.

Head Over Heels in Love

Before *Head Over Heels in Love*, one could think that Jessie Matthews dressed so badly because nobody around the studio dressed well. One can't think that any more. Whitney Bourne dresses well in *Head Over Heels in Love*, but Miss Matthews dresses worse than ever. Now some new explanations of the Matthews-bad-dressing phenomenon will have to be thought up, like only villainesses dress good in English films (Miss Bourne plays an American picture star), or Miss Matthews is sweet but badly advised, or Miss Matthews is very headstrong and dresses that way because she likes it. Perhaps the last explanation is the right one, for Miss Matthews has been so very consistent about wearing nothing that does anything for her. All of which is a grave situation, since Miss Matthews happens to have a natural frame for style.

It would almost seem in *Head Over Heels in Love* that she louses up her possibilities on purpose. She has a bony chest, so she wears deep wide-V neckline to give every knob a break. She has a well-shaped head, so she coiffs her bobbed hair to stick out and away from the smooth contour of her crown and thus conceal it, even wearing a poke-bonnet with a shirred brim and no crown so that her hair can stick out good and thoroughly. It's been years since a chorus girl in a third-rate floor-show would even dream of tying floppy bows on her tap-dancing slippers, so now Miss Matthews is just taking it up. She has a lovely waistline, gracefully and accurately placed, so she wears white satin blouses and black velvet shorts that stop somewhere around her hips in an effort to move her waistline down. Her dancing is delightful and her legs superb, so she sings all the time so that everybody will be sure to note that her teeth are large and irregular and her lower jaw unequal to the arch of her upper. Fundamentally it's so agreeable to watch Miss Matthews, it really ought to be made a bland delight.

Personal Property

It used to be the girls who took the baths in pictures.

It used to be the girls who lolled, tantalizing, in cloaks of delicate soap bubbles. It used to be the girls who, spending the night away from home, stumbled about adorable in borrowed pyjamas, oh so much too big for them. It used to be the girls who fetched the pretty photography, who got the seductive make-up, who drew the glamour lighting, who wore the clothes.

It used to be the girls who laid in bed and drove everybody mad with just the thought of it. It used to be the girls who had the irresistible

Jessie Matthews in *Head Over Heels in Love*; Ann Harding and Binnie Hale in *Love from a Stranger*

bedroom doors, who waited deliciously apprehensive and wide-eyed behind them. It used to be the girls who stuck the flower between their teeth.

However, this was before Robert Taylor, before the advent of a manly beauty so overwhelming, all the old traditions tottered before its might. Now in *Personal Property* it's Robert Taylor who takes the bath.

In *Personal Property* one may have Mr Taylor in a lather or rinsed, one may quiver to the way he wraps his robe close to his splendid chest and beautifully modelled loins, one may sigh as he ties the belt snug to his waist with such dashing disregard of the buckle. One may learn how he achieves his magnificent coiffure, how he coaxes with his own two hands his lustrous black hair into that proud, clean-swept line, one may even watch him clean his nails.

Although it does leave out the method by which Mr Taylor nurtures the lovely shape of his eyebrows, it is a stirring performance that Mr Taylor gives in this sequence – natural, confident, and yet deeply hygienic – and it provides the flaps with a high standard for comparison. Nor, while educating the flaps in the details of what to keep on longing for, do Mr Taylor and *Personal Property* forget the matrons. They can always be a mother to him, *Personal Property* shows them, consoling them with several scenes of Taylor and Henrietta Crossman kissing one another full on the lips with an ardour far more burning, as a matter of fact, than the feeling Taylor puts into the lone fade-out clinch he accords Jean Harlow.

But then, *Personal Property* executes so conscientiously its mission of pandering for Taylor, it can hardly be expected to take full care of Miss Harlow, too. Miss Harlow's already been made. Besides, *Personal Property* knows it can always be sure, for her part, of her own natural gift for conjuring up the illusion of strip-tease without any of the bother of going through the motions.

Love From a Stranger

Ann Harding, scared to death, is all right; it's Ann Harding, natural, that's so harrowing. This conclusion is available in *Love From a Stranger*, in which Miss Harding is charming for the first two-thirds of the picture, while one tears one's handkerchief to tatters – and frightened for her life for the rest of it, when at last one may relax.

Miss Harding's natural charm makes many people subjected to it uneasy, because she herself takes it so big. Her slightest 'thank you' is never an expression of courtesy, it's undying gratitude; her 'come in' to a knock on the door heralds the Coronation Procession; her 'I'm going to take off my bonnet' sings of a duty about to be done, to be done valiantly, with head held high though the whole world may be against her. Whatever she does or says, it's to make somebody else a little happier. If she just can't meet people on equal ground, it's because she's so much better, wiser, kinder, than they – her superiority fairly pushes her into a position of condescension. With so much inherent nobility to carry around, it would be tough for anybody to be casual. However, understanding it doesn't seem to make it any easier.

But Miss Harding is a competent actress, and so when she gets scared to death, fear takes possession of her to the exclusion of her charm, and when she shrieks, she no longer rings out. The crescendo of her fright leaves no time for love-of-humanity looks and only terror shines from her eyes, and she becomes, by contrast, quite soothing. One's tension consequently disappears, and with Miss Harding screeching and shuddering, the experience turns out to have a happy ending after all.

Another Dawn

Everybody in *Another Dawn* suffers from a stiff upper lip, which may be why everybody in *Another Dawn* is crazy to die. Because, just before they fold up, they see the angels and then their lips relax into a happy smile, which must be terrific relief.

So everybody's so eager to get popped off by Arab snipers, they double-cross each other only for a chance to get in range. Common soldier and officer alike are obsessed with the urge to be targets, though as befits their superior station, the officers' urge has some high-class complications provided by Miss Kay Francis.

Officers Errol Flynn and Ian Hunter are very sensitive, and their natural British yen to stop bullets with their persons may very well be increased by an unconscious desire to be dead before the prophetic fashions Miss Francis wears become universal.

Ardently searching the horizon – because she's supposed to be a deep one – Miss Francis pretends she doesn't know what she's got on, but there aren't many people who have Miss Francis's ability to be unaware of what she chooses not to be aware of. So, while she's having a soul, she's also got a mess of draperies, the very latest thing for desert sand-storms. So late, in fact, that nobody ever thought of them before, figuring, with stodgy practicality, that a sand-storm is enough trouble without a lot of silken stuffs swirling around. But Miss Francis's floating scarves, dervish skirts and feather capes do have a certain merit, ballooning in the sirocco; watching them sort of hypnotizes people, and keeps their minds off the spiritual things she says.

A Day at the Races

There ought to be a statue erected, or a Congressional Medal awarded, or a national holiday proclaimed, to honour that great woman, Margaret Dumont, the dame who takes the raps from the Marx Bros. For she is of the stuff of which our pioneer women were made, combining in her highly indignant person Duse, stalwart oak, and Chief Fall Guy – a lady of epic ability to take it, a lady whose mighty love for Groucho is a saga of devotion, a lady who asks but little and gets it.

Disappointment can't down her, nor perfidy shake her faith. Always she comes back for more though slapsticks have crippled her, custard pies spattered her trusting face. Surrounded by brothers who are surely a little odd, she does not think so. To her, her world of Marx Bros. pictures is rational, comprehensible, secure. Calmly she surveys it, with infinite resource she fights to keep on her feet in it. Equally ready for amorous dalliance or hair-pulling, for Groucho's sudden tender moods, or base betrayal, all her magnificent qualities are on display in *A Day at the Races*, where once again her fortitude is nothing human. It's godlike.

Modern Times

This section rounds up the nine star-gazers and sets them to work on a single comet. Several reasons made *Modern Times* seem ideal for this choice. It was the ranking box-office film of its year and has probably been seen by more readers than any other film here mentioned.

But chiefly, the character is the most famous in screen history, and whatever doubts a critic has to resolve, Charlie Chaplin is not one of them. Most people made up their minds about him long ago, and about this character at least all critics expect to write nothing less than the truth.

A.C.

Modern Times: Chaplin

10. Modern Times

Robert Herring

To laugh presupposes a belief in evil. Therefore, a wish to avoid, prevent or change it (the means used to do this are, of course, the fundamental jokes). To prevent is also to fight, to laugh is not to allay fears but to master them, and why we don't laugh (much) at crooners, Warner musicals, Tom Walls, Lionel Barrymore, Beryl Mercer, George Arliss – and Grace Moore – is because they represent not fears, but the suppression of fears. Arliss turns his hat round, from Nelson to Napoleon. That, in the long run, isn't funny. But we laugh at Laurel, Hardy, Chaplin at intervals, Keaton long ago, Disney when we can and Jeanette MacDonald for the sheer fun of the thing, because these are our terrified selves. With this difference – which separated Hamlet from Yorick in every place but the graveyard – that they show it only in action. When a Chaplin goes berserk, says 'Grr, you big sissy' and walks off in a way that shows he is only a small one, we laugh for three things; he has said 'Boo' – so we can; he is smaller than us – so we needn't say 'Boo'; he walks off – which is a comfort to remember as possible. But when he reads his more high-falutin' fan-mail and goes philosophical, as in *City Lights* or *The Circus*, we did not laugh, because his chief concern is pity for the little fellow. We cannot pity little fellows. First, because we're afraid of them and next, because we despise them. We're afraid they will make us small, too, just because we aren't (sez we). So we won't allow them anything that makes them admirable. We know that we admire in order to be frightened after. We laugh, because we were frightened first. Only after, when by laughing at the tramp we've lost our fear of ourselves being rebuked and refused, will we elevate him at the end. And that final iris of Chaplin *is* elevation. Apart from all technical and dramatic convenience, it is the halo which it is essential for him to be given. His strength lies, not in his gag-making and tear-jerking, but in his ability to create the essentialness.

He abuses that ability. But when he makes a film in which he comes out as a worker among workers, it doesn't mean it's because he thinks the wind is blowing that way, first turning on the Left. Nor does it mean that he's as out of date as his critics, who count the proletarian appeals and say 'We aren't moved any more'. It does mean that he's late, because we've had *Hey Rup* and Clair's had fiercer fun in a factory. But the reason he's late is that he has, it seems to me, been fighting out an equivalent for Man-Loses-Hat. It may not be insignificant that, in these modern times, man loses head.

There is plenty of loose thinking in his film. But Chaplin, like most of those who write most about him, is not a thinker. In his better moments he doesn't set out to be, and I submit that *Modern Times* has a good many better moments. It's romantic, all right all right, because things have happened and he's felt them and he's taken a long time. But the film is the result of those happenings and of the happening of himself faced with those things. That is the first point about it; he is one of the few who goes on happening himself.

He dare now be one among his fellows, instead of an aspirant among those who aren't. He's less frustrated, more happy – and one shouldn't, say those who think he made the film for them, be happy about social problems. With a fixed idea of what those demand, they don't see what a comedian deducts. These, however, are just the people who swallowed his last two pictures, hook, line and what-not. Sinker? You've said it. They swallowed those, not for what they were, which was not a mouthful but a regurgitation, but because they had been misled by what had been belatedly said about the films before that. *Modern Times* is judged by what was said of *City Lights* and *The Circus*, which is being about as tired as Chaplin was then.

I hold no special brief for Chaplin. I'd laugh as much with Cantor if his box-office would let me, and I still think Grace Moore is often as funny as Jeanette MacDonald, let Norma Shearer act what she will. But if I can laugh with Chaplin, I know I can laugh. That, it seems to me, is a greater victory for him than the Marxes should claim when I laugh at them. They, being surrealist, are so life-like. Chaplin isn't.

Chaplin's is not the world as I know it at all. I find his chief attraction is the stylization of movement, which has on me the same effect as does the first performance of the annually returning Ballets Russes after winters of wavering danseuses whose andantes are not so good as their intentions. Chaplin, when he moves, moves from something to something. It is not a fluttering in space (as with prima donnas, when they 'act'), but a bridge between times. The times get mixed (as when we have close up of *le Charles* in toupee alternated with mediums of Chaplin today). The joints between also creak somewhat. That is what comes of making your films when you like, as you like, over a period of years which your renters don't like. But that very same cause, the interference of personal life (Lord, these artists) has let him abandon being sorry for himself in this film. The reason he's not, is that he's dealing with something that has for long frightened him. Russia's done that, too – but it took her five years to plan something else. Chaplin is serious enough to be silly. 'Work (*Modern Times* says), till you feel you'll go mad.' We know that. 'Then go mad.' We don't know that. It makes us more powerful to feel that we can. The boss doesn't know that he has under him a flock of potential lunatics. Chaplin, at last growing up, rags not the routine of modern life, but the answer we give it. No wonder his film is labelled 'dis-Kordant' by those to whom Clair's inspired mischief with social breakdown in *Le Dernier Milliardaire* got under the skin.

At the same time, no one can condone the repetition, the fake machinery, the naïve suggestion that music instead of speech is using sound, and why does he use mime to illustrate his song, anyway? No one can say that the Chaplin of today is Chaplin. *That's* Fred Astaire. He does the same things, gives us, from a different approach, the same joke that Chaplin did. Indeed, just as man-losing-hat isn't in a sense as funny now as man-with-hat, he carries mime one step, two steps, quick-step further. He jokes mime by dancing. Underneath that, he gives us that side of us that is afraid that people won't like what we've got – in his case, gaiety, confident perkiness and a belief that it'll work out all right if you're not hit in the same spot twice. He gives also our other permanent fear that we'll lose or won't get what we most

Modern Times

want. Ginger Rogers isn't a girl, simply. If she were, the Astaire films might be just another off-white-drawing-room off-drama. But Rogers, incidentally what passes as romantic element, is primarily *partner* – first, dancing (that being his language, as *gaminerie*, save the mark, is Chaplin's) and then as one who most understands what he most likes and can do (dancing, again). Being therefore what is loved, Rogers is also what can most misunderstand and most hurt. Fear and non-fear, and what one loves in order not to fear. This, mixed up with Astaire's other asset of loosening our fright, not of being fools on the floor, but of getting out of time, losing step, losing balance. He, an ordinary little man, can dance as he can. Therefore we, who are ordinary, can hope. His dancing does not remove him from us. It makes him ordinary plus. Genius in any form does not make the exponent cease to be ordinary. It merely makes them something else as well.

We, because of that, can laugh at the ordinariness and all the mishaps it involves. We identify ourselves with ordinariness; being identified, feel we have the genius. Feeling that, can forget ordinariness. Its fears and our fears of it. We laugh. At the end, forgetting what was originally the side most like ourselves, we feel that *we* wouldn't get into such scrapes, aren't ordinary at all and leave – consoled, because our fright has been funny.

Don Herold
Charlie Chaplin still walks funny.

His *Modern Times* is merely an elaboration of the old joke about the man in the Ford production line who laid down his wrench to scratch his ear and threw the whole factory out of gear, but Chaplin still walks funny. *Modern Times* is a funny picture, a terribly funny picture, but its ingenuities are simply the ingenuities at which many in Hollywood are adept, many including Laurel and Hardy and Harold Lloyd and the Marxes and a hundred gag men. It is not a great picture. It is not a profound, significant picture.

The one great thing about it is Charlie Chaplin.

And, at that, there is a great deal of bunk about Chaplin – not in Chaplin, but around and about Chaplin. He is not (that is, not in his *pictures*) a deep-searching, penetrating philosopher or a subtle sociological observer and satirist. His calling his picture *Modern Times* and his inclusion of a lot of complicated Joe Cook machinery and Goldbergian gadgets, and alternate shots of people in a subway and sheep in a run-way, do not make him one of our great sociological cynics. The observation that people are sheep is not new or deep.

But the fact remains that though Charlie Chaplin is often just a clown, he is oftener a great artist and a master pantomimist. The smartest comment ever made on Charlie Chaplin was uttered by M. M. Warburg, director of the American ballet: 'After all, the greatest ballet dancer this country has produced – one of the world's greatest – is Charlie Chaplin.'

Many critics have raved some pretty banal stuff about Chaplin's profundity. Well, he may be as profound as the devil over a bottle of Scotch, but I maintain that *Modern Times* is simply a succession of swell gags with overtones of ballet – not overtones of technocracy or undertones of any other *ocracy*. Chaplin is not only a genius, but he is practical showman and business man enough to keep his pictures on a pure clowning basis.

One time in Los Angeles, between chukkers of a tennis tournament, my attention was caught by a man on the fringe of the crowd under the stands, a man looking into time and space with the lonesomest, saddest, deepest eyes I've ever seen – an isolated thinker in a crowd of silly, buzzing picture people. I finally realized that this was Chaplin, and I knew that I'd love the guy, that I'd like to sit and cry gloriously far into the night with him about the ugh and phooey of man.

But that Chaplin and the Chaplin of *Modern Times* are two people, and I am a little impatient with many motion-picture writers who try to make them the same.

The authorship and conception of *Modern Times* are superficial and commercial. The picture itself is little more than a succession of robust belly laughs, and some of them pretty old. Chaplin steps on a loose board with a brick on one end, and unconsciously socks a cop with the brick – that's a fair sample.

But Charlie Chaplin still walks funny – as funny as all get out – he dances – he capers – he frolics – he rises in elation and falls in abject despair – and it all adds up into humorous beauty, into ballet art at its highest and best.

John Marks

The new Charlie Chaplin film, *Modern Times* is misnamed. Primary humour the world over consists in suddenly supposing things to be what they aren't, calling a spade a tuning-fork and playing up to the mistake. We learn so laboriously to recognize objects and emotions that we laugh to see them travestied, looking different. Chaplin was always a master of pathos. But the pathos seems to have overtaken him at last. The title of his new satirical farce is pathetic. . . . It was slow in the making, late to appear, and now, dear me, it's ten years behind the times.

It is the new 'Charlie Chaplin', though, with a vengeance. Charles Chaplin wrote, directed, and produced it, the Charles Chaplin Film Corporation issues it, and it stars Charlie Chaplin. Only the jokes are René Clair's (the best ones, that is) and the music ('composed by Charles Chaplin') contains echoes, generous excerpts, from tunes that have gone before. In *City Lights* it was *La Violetera*; here it's *Titine*. This shows that Chaplin has a fitting sense of period – and a natural fondness for old favourites, which, to judge by the reception accorded to this film, we all evidently share.

Although most individual scenes in *Modern Times* have the giddy speed of the custard-pie comedy, it is a slow film, because it is silent – except for the already famous gibberish song sequence (which is funny, but, when we have waited so long for Chaplin to speak – and to speak incoherently – not funny enough). Chaplin persists in forcing silence on all the other members of the cast as well. Silence means sub-titles, and sub-titles are slow: they hang up the action and alter

Modern Times: Chaplin and Paulette Goddard

the jokes; it takes a little more than twice as long to see a man gesticulate, and then to read the gist of what he said while he gesticulated, than it does to see and hear and at the same time find out what we need to know. When an accident occurs in this film a caption is tacked on to a comprehensive and comprehensible shot to tell us, in answer to Chaplin's question to a bystander, that a night watchman has broken his leg. We needed to know who was hurt; then why not *say* so, and save time? Chaplin may be above speech; but the talkies aren't. To ignore the sound-track, to use it only for a vaguely musical accompaniment no better than a piano, drum, violin and trombone in the orchestra-pit, is to strike the cinema dumb, or at least to muffle it.

The result of this gagging is that the comic 'gags' come out: pantomime is all that's left – and wit of idea, if you can find it. Here the wit is largely borrowed from *Le Million* and *A Nous la Liberté*, and there is a fine flash of fantasy which should have belonged to the Marx Brothers. The rest of the jokes are antics, often exquisite, because Chaplin has few equals as a mime, and sometimes genuinely comic, because he has none as a mummer. His movements have a graceful precision in clumsiness; and this most certainly produces comedy of a sort. To dive into a pool of water a foot deep isn't funny, though Charlie's diving makes it so; to lean against something that gives way is merely unexpected – it is humorous only when the foolishness of your fall is disproportionate to the pride (the dignity, the confidence, or the bombast) which went before it. Chaplin contrives this reversal jest again and again; and it makes us laugh. But occasionally his ballet movements have a subtler psychological significance, and achieve wit as well. It is witty to express panic by having to *hobble* away, on roller-skates, from the suddenly discovered danger of a yawning abyss, which one has gracefully glided past, blindfolded, two seconds previously. But such subtlety in pantomime is necessarily rare, even with Chaplin. *Modern Times* gets us no further on Chaplin's obstinate and sentimental journey back into silence than we were with *City Lights*; indeed, not so far. It's much less funny.

Meyer Levin

As Mr Chaplin wanted critics to get an audience reaction, and there was no preview of *Modern Times*, I was unable to present an early review. I notice that the 'critics' in all but the liberal and revolutionary press chose completely to ignore the nature of the film. 'Here is Charlie back again, the same old Charlie, still king of pantomime', they said, suggesting that it was just another Chaplin picture, to be enjoyed because it brought back memories of old.

Modern Times is the sum of Chaplin's work, finally given social orientation. It suggests a collected complete edition, revised by the author in the light of mature judgment, a farewell work, but I fervently hope that instead it is merely a work marking a milestone in his career. A 'from now on'.

Chaplin's inclusion of his classic roller-skating act and his waiter-juggling-a-tray act suggests the idea of the definitive edition. His adherence to sub-titles and silence further suggests a connection with his previous work that would have been unnecessary if he meant to break into something entirely new, with this film, rather than conclude something old.

I think the reception of the film will have proved to him that he could have kept all of his stylistic simplicities without adhering to the crudities, such as the often unnecessary sub-titles. His voice, as revealed in the nonsense song, seems to me to be quite compatible with the character of Charlot, and I don't think he would be risking destruction of the classic cinema image which he has created if he now added dialogue to his films. It would have to be a Charlot type of dialogue, fragmentary, perhaps rhythmic.

In casting himself as a factory workman who is driven insane by the speed-up on the assembly line, who finds authority in the shape of a big cop hovering over him at every turn, who finds gaol the only possible home, Chaplin has of course finally identified the wistful Charlot who went through so many slapstick adventures unidentifiably. He always reminded everybody of somebody. Nobody could quite place him. Innumerable tracts were written about the ways in which he symbolized the soul of hopeful inferiority. Now it seems that we should have known all along that Chaplin was meant to be the average man, the average worker.

To my mind, *Modern Times* divides into two parts. The opening sequences, from the sheep-into-the-factory scene until his attack of insanity, form a complete photoplay, developed step by step without a scrap of extra footage to the logical climax. This includes the inspired eating-machine sequence, which is in itself the greatest satiric commentary on mechanized civilization I have ever encountered. The screen-projected face of the factory manager, following him around even when he goes to the washroom for a smoke, is another supremely ironic and original piece of business. The ballet-movement of the workmen in the speed-up sequence contributes to the ironic interpretation.

But once he leaves the factory, the film becomes episodic. Some of the incidents, as noted above, seem to be included more because of their relation to Chaplin's previous work than because of their relation to the idea of the film. The skating episode, in which a blindfolded man teeters on the edge of a sheer fall, exploits the philosophized fundamental fear in man, the idea that we go through life tight-rope-walking over an unknown abyss. The act in which he is a waiter trying to deliver an order across a crowded dancing floor again exploits a philosophized truism, the idea that we are continuously frustrated in our goals by the uncontrollable whim of the crowd that pushes us around, carries us away from our destination. This, too, is unrelated to the theme of the picture.

It occurred to me that Chaplin might have made even greater use of the device of the factory manager on a screen, representing the worker's consciousness of being watched. The apparition could have followed him outside the factory, into the gamin's shack, everywhere.

Paulette Goddard as the gamin illustrated the idea-form of Chaplin's pictures. For Chaplin's appearance happens to fit perfectly the

Charlot-idea he has created. Miss Goddard was excellent, but not 'right' as the gamin. She did everything correctly, and with spirited understanding; but to me at least her features happened to be too intellectual. However, this is an extremely minor distraction and certainly no fault of hers.

Alistair Cooke
'Streamlining a water closet cuts neither wind resistance nor ice and has nothing to do with the science of aerodynamics' – Fortune, November 1935, on the Modern Interior.

On Tuesday morning of last week one of those squat rumbling Channel steamers was chugging across the sea with strange passengers aboard. No stranger, perhaps, as human beings, than the daily crew of cigar merchants, wine tasters, ailing people going off to find the sun. But however queer they looked they had more things in common than a blustering wind. And though they spoke many languages, their profession was the same . . . that is, if film criticism rates as a profession. They came from Berlin and Paris, Stockholm and Rome, from Holland, Belgium and Czechoslovakia – and it is possible that if there had been an outbreak of fire, there is not one practical sentence of English that they could all be sure of repeating. But as this boat pulled in to our tight little isle, a German – a twinkling, inconsequential little man – cocked his head up at the moon – it was a good moon – and began to sing to himself. In a minute or two another man came up and hummed alongside him. Soon a small group of them, French and Austrian and German, had forgotten all about security by poison gas and encircling each other's country, and they were all leaning overboard singing hard and high and slightly out of tune. It was an old song, a song about the moon shining bright on a man with a bowler hat. And this curious crew of critics, who should have been fast asleep in Amsterdam and Prague before getting up to see their daily film, were coming to London for ninety minutes' entertainment. They had come to see how the moon was feeling, after twenty years, about the man with the still unmended trousers. They had come to say whether Charlie Chaplin stood where he did in 1915, as the world's funniest and most famous man.

Five years have done a lot to the movies, but not so much as they have done to us. Our hearts may go on beating on the left sides of our chests, telling us all sorts of touching and heartening things. But our eyes take advice from none of the other senses. And one of the discouraging things about the movies considered as an art, one of the countless cues for the psychologist, is this optical sophistication that delights in, then wearies of new conventions almost before the other senses have taken any account of them. And what chiefly makes cinema critics a restless and uncertain lot, a group of tipsters swapping guesses and hunches, is the knowledge that impressions begin to bore them before they have been absorbed.

Well, since 1931, several things have happened. First, recording on the sound-track is much clearer and more intimate. Musical scores can sound like a concert performance. What is more, and perhaps worse, is that they can be amplified to volumes of lushness unknown to any concert hall. Next, the trend especially in comedy has been towards the inconsequential, depending for a slow-timed inflection. There never was an era in the movies when genre work was less likely. We are on top of the players all the time. In 1931 Hollywood was editing a little more aloofly, less lap-dissolves and angles, they had not begun to file away as useful tricks the devices that were basic principles to the Russians. Since then the move to merge the audience into the screen, to make the effort of looking on less and less painful, has gone along briskly. When Charlie Chaplin started making pictures we were normal men and women looking from a far distance at the antics of creatures jerking their sawdust hearts around in another, practically a puppet, world. Since then they have become more like us and move at the distance of ordinary conversation. We're no longer an audience, we're just pals.

In the early Chaplins, he looked like a normal man because everybody else looked insane. But since 1915 projectors have been scrapped, the camera rose from its bed and walked, we have been seeing eight more pictures to the second than we used, and though we are fooled the way we always were – the screen is still black half an hour in every hour – yet the action has slowed down and accepted us as a norm. All this has been fine for Myrna Loy and Greta Garbo and for Robert Riskin and Frank Capra. But it has made the Chaplin figure become increasingly grotesque . . . it has made the Chaplin talent *look* like a period piece even when his psychology and feeling were subtler than his contemporaries'. But all his films had a unity and a style because it seemed, as the years went by, that he wisely kept his art within the limits of its first technical shape. He triumphed by making no concessions – where other men kept their cameras still from lack of imagination, he kept his still from conviction, from the conviction that the peepshow movie was the best for him. 'They are indecent because they have no distance', he once said of the players in a typical Hollywood piece of two years ago. If, performing some gesture, the camera was forced to pan or tilt to take it in, he would prefer to send his camera back and keep it still, framing the whole act. And, in truth, that miraculously compact extravagance of mime could best be seen when you could see the whole figure. In light values, too, he kept on the other side of the Hollywood fence. Cartier-Bresson has excellently noted his 'bad' photography in a protest against the banal excellences of the latest Hollywood films; and indeed the 'funny man would dissolve in that suave lighting, which brings a Garbo to life'. And he had many unforgettable scenes, lit with exquisite understatement, providing an aura for his miming to etch itself in. As late as *City Lights*, the contrast with the current commercial film was startling. Where it was smooth, expensive, illuminated, his film was lit cheaply and vaguely in a world somewhere between Rembrandt and Hogarth, ready to move poignantly into one, to tear cheekily into the other.

Well, for the first time in Chaplin's history, we have a Chaplin film that looks and sounds as if it came from only one place – from Hollywood. Prosperity has turned the corner and flashed its diamonds along Easy Street. And the street can't take it. Nor can the little man, who, suddenly caught by suave lighting, like a romantic aeroplane spotted by a searchlight, crystallizes out into something solid and functional. In *City Lights* the music, brilliantly amateur, snatched a little Tchaikovsky and Beethoven from memory and orchestrated them for a small-town band. In *Modern Times*, the themes are as good as ever but they have been orchestrated fatally by Mr Alfred Newman, United Artists' accomplished and probably inoffensive music master. And the product is a purring ocean of harmony, lush and symphonic. Whereas all that Charlie Chaplin needs is a tango band or a drunken cornet. For much of his charm is that air of a child honestly and successfully being the little gentleman. Give him a tin trumpet and the child's skill is more amusing . . . give him a grand piano and he is far from an adult.

Since he has yielded these twin integrities – the looks and the sound – he has yielded much of his strangeness. I am aware that this is possibly the most serious lament to make about a Chaplin film, and I have taken some trouble to verify my anxiety. Maybe, I thought, there never was a characteristic oddity and his movies flickered and 'rained' no more than anybody else's. In the last day or two I have seen again *The Cure* (1917), *The Pawnshop* (1917), *The Vagabond* (1917 – and some of it fresh as magic), *City Lights* (1931); and with them Harold

Lloyd's *Just Neighbours*, and Harry Langdon's *Saturday Afternoon*. The Lloyd was terrible, without character of any sort, he might have been any amiable young American. *City Lights*, the most relevant test, has long stretches of mawkish wistfulness that *Modern Times* has not, though it has its share. The swallowed whistle incident I found helplessly funny, funnier than anything in *Modern Times*. But the production had the Chaplin setting, the lighting of the streets, of the embankment; the brilliant orchestration of the boxing match with three or four dithering strings. And there was a form in it and un-flagging continuity.

Modern Times is inexplicably an anthology of gags rather than the progress of an episode. This again is a remarkable defection. For, as Paul Rotha has rightly insisted, Chaplin's continuity was always simplified by dint of great labour. I am personally so mystified by this sudden sprawling and redundancy that I suspect another, and a clumsier, hand has done it. Perhaps Mr Joseph Breen, the Censor, may be the real villain, for practically as the film was catching the boat six sequences were ordered to be trimmed for ribaldry. It was charm-ing, harmless stuff and since it is unfair to Chaplin to lay at his door all the blame for not realizing the Chaplin myth (which I have tried to ignore), it is with relish that I single out Mr Breen, Mr Newman, and some third person, possibly the assistant director, for the unexpected, and fatal, flaws in structure, lighting, sound, and style.

Since Mr Chaplin has broken with his old convention in other ways, it is bewildering to find that he has not broken with a habit of un-necessary sub-titles. I was prepared to accept these along with the saccharine, coy conception of the girl (which always does for his fantasy sweetheart). But when half the film has shiny labels of 1936, it's hard to notice lots of torn ones showing from 1915. Things like 'cured of a nervous breakdown but without a job he leaves the hospital to start life anew', where the caption comes first and the pantomime afterwards. All through there is this double statement for an incident that his pantomime could confidently cover. It sinks to unbelievable carelessness on captions like – 'She stole a loaf of bread . . . !', 'No, she didn't . . . I did' . . . when the words are afterwards elaborately acted.

Again, the whole first section of the film destroys at one stroke the Chaplin stand against a restless camera. He swings and pans and dissolves as glibly as the rest of them. And from too close a range, the camera has the effect of making much of his pantomime seem muscle-bound. I am not pretending that Mr Chaplin is a unity any more than anybody else, any more than Dickens, say, with whom he has much in common; and it is possible to deplore their too easy pity of the workers, their Little Nells and little waifs, and yet to bow down and worship before a clear-eyed and irresistible invention. But let us have them as they come, and not even as Mr Graves might rewrite them, or Metro-Goldwyn-Mayer remake them. You may, by Heaven, be M.-G.-M. Or you may, by the grace of Heaven, be Charlie Chaplin. But you cannot be both. And I must point the issue by saying that *Modern Times* is like Chaplin the actor directed and produced by M.-G.-M.

This sentence, my positively final sigh, will hint, too, the fact that the success of this film is Chaplin the actor. For one thing, Mr Chaplin has kept his promise that he was about to extinguish Everybody's Little Ray of Sunshine. The tragic comedian is no more. This time, when a policeman pushes him about in the street he does not creep away, forlorn and spiritual. He turns and with a precise Latin viciousness indicates that he is on his way and will not be man-handled. The whole character has said goodbye to pathos, and that's very fine with me. He has gained, instead, an absurd perkiness, a mood that translates itself into gesture as a rhythm of alert petulance.

He sprinkles his food with dope which he thinks is salt and the cheerfulness, curiosity and increasing suspicion with which he yields to its effect is, in my mind, the best thing in the film. His ridiculous, athletically certain miming when he shouts 'Now we'll get a real home'; the parody of the suburban home; his determination to get back into jail . . . all these are blameless and show his pantomime to be as swift, delicate, and inimitable as it has ever been and as it, presumably, always must be till the day he dies. Only in the rehearsing, the song, the fine gypsy impudence of the song itself, and once in the dope scene does his pantomime leap away from a logical frame. But nowhere is there a moment of that absorbed insanity, that pure fantastic invention that came to him sometimes in a moment of grief and still recalls the Oceana Roll in *The Gold Rush* – far and away the most beautiful comedy he has made and the only profound one, for it should be said with firmness and regret that *Modern Times* is never once on the plane of social satire.

Robert Forsythe
If you have had fears, prepare to shed them; Charlie Chaplin is on the side of the angels. After years of rumours, charges and counter-charges, reports of censorship and hints of disaster, his new film,

Modern Times, had its world première (gala) last week at the Rivoli Theatre, with the riot squad outside quelling the curious mob and with the usual fabulous first-night Broadway audience gazing with some doubt at a figure which didn't seem to be quite the old Charlie. For the first time an American film was daring to challenge the superiority of an industrial civilization based upon the creed of men who sit at flat-topped desks and press buttons demanding more speed from tortured employees. There were cops beating demonstrators and shooting down the unemployed (specifically the father of the waif who is later picked up by Chaplin), there is a belt line which operates at such a pace that men go insane, there is a heart-breaking scene of the helpless couple trying to squeeze out happiness in a little home of their own (a shack in a Hooverville colony). It is the story of a pathetic little man trying bravely to hold up his end in this mad world.

Chaplin's methods are too kindly for great satire, but by the very implication of the facts with which he deals he has created a biting commentary upon our civilization. He has made high humour out of material which is fundamentally tragic. If it were used for bad purposes, if it were made to cover up the hideousness of life and to excuse it, it would be the usual Hollywood product. But the hilarity is never an opiate. When the little man picks up a red flag which has dropped from the rear of a truck and finds himself at the head of a workers' demonstration, it is an uproarious moment, but it is followed by the truth – the cops doing their daily dozen on the heads of the marchers. In the entire film, there is only one moment where he seems to slip. After he meets the girl and gets out of gaol for the third time, he hears that the factory is starting up again. What he wants most in the world is a home, where he and his girl can settle down and be happy. It is the same factory where he has previously gone berserk on the assembly line. From the radical point of view, the classic ending would have been Chaplin once again on the belt line, eager to do his best and finding anew that what a man had to look forward to in that hell-hole was servitude and final collapse. Instead of this there is a very funny scene where Charlie and Chester Conklin get mixed up in the machinery in attempting to get it ready for production. Just when they have it ready, a man comes along and orders them out on strike. At this point I was worried. 'Uh-huh', I said to myself. 'Here it comes. The usual stuff about the irresponsible workers, the bums who won't work when they have a chance.' But what follows is a scene of the strikers being beaten up by the police and Charlie back again at his life of struggle. Except for that one sequence the film is strictly honest and right. It is never for a moment twisted about to make a point which will negate everything that has gone before.

If I make it seem ponderous and social rather than hilarious, it is because I came away stunned at the thought that such a film had been made and was being distributed. It's what we have dreamt about and never really expected to see. What luck that the only man in the world able to do it should be doing it! Chaplin has done the entire thing himself, from the financing to the final artistic product. He wrote it, acted in it, directed it, cut it, wrote the music for it and is seeing that it is sold to the distributors who have been frantic to get it. It is not a social document, it is not a revolutionary tract, it is one of the funniest of all Chaplin films, but it is certainly no comfort to the enemy. If they like it, it will be because they are content to overlook the significance of it for the sake of the humour.

And humorous it is. Chaplin has never had a more belly-shaking scene than the one where he is being fed by the automatic machine, with the corn-on-the-cob attachment going daft. The Hooverville hut is a miracle of ruin. When he opens the door, he is brained by a loose beam; when he leans against another door, he finds himself half-drowned in the creek; when he takes up a broom, the roof, which it has been supporting, falls in. He comes dashing out of the dog house for his morning dip and alights in two inches of water in a ditch.

Religion comes off a trifle scorched in the scene where the minister's wife, suffering from gas on the stomach, comes to visit the prisoners in gaol. There are hundreds of little characteristic bits which build up the picture of Mr Common Man faced by life. To the gratification of the world, Chaplin brings back his old roller-skating act, teetering crazily on the edge of the rotunda in the department store where he is spending the night (one night only) as a watchman. He gives the waif (splendidly played by Paulette Goddard) her first good meal in months and a night's rest in a bed in the furniture department. His desire to get away from the cruel world is so strong that he deliberately gets himself arrested, stoking up with two full meals in a cafeteria and then rapping on the window for the attention of a policeman when he nears the cashier's desk.

From the standpoint of humour, however, the picture is not a steady roar. The reason for it is simple. You can't be jocular about such things as starvation and unemployment. Even the people who are least affected by the misery of others are not comfortable when they see it. They are not moved by it; they resent it. 'What do you want to bring up a lot of things like that for?' That Chaplin has been able to present a comic statement of serious matters without perverting the problem into a joke is all the more to his credit. It is a triumph not only of his art but of his heart. What his political views are, I don't know and don't care. He has the feelings of an honest man and that is enough. There are plenty of people in Hollywood with honest feelings, but, with the distributive machinery in the hands of the most reactionary forces in the country, there is no possibility of honesty in films dealing with current ideas. It is this fact which makes *Modern Times* such an epoch-making event from our point of view. As I say, only Chaplin could have done it. Except for the one scene I have mentioned, he has never sacrificed the strict line of the story for a laugh. That is so rare as to be practically unknown in films. *Modern Times* itself is rare. To anyone who has studied the set-up, financial and ideological, of Hollywood, *Modern Times* is not so much a fine motion picture as a historical event.

Graham Greene

I am too much an admirer of Mr Chaplin to believe that the most important thing about his new film is that for a few minutes we are allowed to hear his agreeable and rather husky voice in a song. The little man has at last definitely entered the contemporary scene; there had always before been a hint of 'period' about his courage and misfortunes; he carried about with him more than the mere custard pie of Karno's day, its manners, its curious clothes, its sense of pathos and its dated poverty. There were occasions, in his encounters with blind flower girls or his adventures in mean streets or in the odd little pitchpine mission halls where he carried round the bag or preached in pantomime on a subject so near to his own experience as the tale of David and Goliath, when he seemed to go back almost as far as Dickens. The change is evident in his choice of heroine: fair and featureless with the smudged effect of an amateur water-colour which has run, they never appeared again in leading parts, for they were quite characterless. But Miss Paulette Goddard, dark, grimy, with her amusing, urban and plebeian face, is a promise that the little man will no longer linger at the edge of mawkish situation, the unfair pathos of the blind girl and the orphan child. One feels about her as Hyacinth felt about Millicent in *The Princess Casamassima*: 'she laughed with the laugh of the people, and if you hit her hard enough would cry with their tears'. For the first time the little man does not go off alone, flaunting his cane and battered bowler along the endless road out of the screen. He goes in company looking for what may turn up.

Modern Times: Chaplin and Paulette Goddard

What *had* turned up was first a job in a huge factory twisting screws tighter as little pieces of nameless machinery passed him on a moving belt, under the televised eye of the manager, an eye that followed him even into the lavatory where he snatched an illicit smoke. The experiment of an automatic feeding machine, which will enable a man to be fed while he works, drives him crazy (the running amok of this machine, with its hygienic mouth-wiper, at the moment when it has reached the Indian corn course, is horrifyingly funny; it is the best scene, I think, that Mr Chaplin has ever invented). When he leaves hospital he is arrested as a communist leader (he has picked up a red flag which has fallen off a lorry) and released again after foiling a prison hold-up. Unemployment and prison punctuate his life, starvation and lucky breaks, and somewhere in its course he attaches to himself the other piece of human refuse.

The Marxists, I suppose, will claim this as *their* film, but it is a good deal less and a good deal more than socialist in intention. No real political passion has gone to it, the police batter the little man at one moment and feed him with buns the next: and there is no warm maternal optimism, in the Mitchison manner, about the character of the workers: when the police are brutes, the men are cowards; the little man is always left in the lurch. Nor do we find him wondering 'what a socialist man should do', but dreaming of a steady job and the most bourgeois home. Mr Chaplin, whatever his political convictions may be, is an artist and not a propagandist. He doesn't try to explain, but presents with vivid fantasy what seems to him a crazy comic tragic world without a plan, but his sketch of the inhuman factory does not lead us to suppose that his little man would be more at home at Dneipostroi. He presents, he doesn't offer political solutions.

The little man politely giving up his seat to the girl in the crowded Black Maria: the little man when the dinner-bell sounds tenderly sticking a spray of celery into the mouth of the old mechanic whose head has been caught between the cog-wheels: the little man littering the path of the pursuing detectives with overturned chairs to save his girl: Mr Chaplin has, like Conrad, 'a few simple ideas'; they could be expressed in much the same phrases: courage, loyalty, labour: against the same nihilistic background of purposeless suffering, 'Mistah Kurtz – he dead'. These ideas are not enough for a reformer, but they have proved amply sufficient for an artist.

Otis Ferguson

Modern Times is about the last thing they should have called the Chaplin picture, which has had one of the most amazing build-ups of interest and advance speculation on record. Its times were modern when the movies were younger and screen motion was a little faster and more jerky than life, and sequences came in forty-foot spurts, cut off by titles (two direct quotes here are 'Alone and Hungry' and 'Dawn'); when no one, least of all an officer of the law, could pass a day without getting a foot in the slack of his pants, when people walked into doorjambs on every dignified exit, stubbed toes everywhere on the straightway and took most of their edibles full in the face; when tables and chairs were breakaways, comedy was whiskers and vice versa, and heroes manœuvred serenely for minutes on abysses that were only too visible to the audience. It is in short a silent film, with pantomime, printed dialogue, and such sound effects as were formerly supplied by the pit band and would now be done by dubbing, except for Chaplin's song at the end. And not only that: it is a feature picture made up of several one- or two-reel shorts, proposed titles being 'The Shop', 'The Jailbird', 'The Watchman', 'The Singing Waiter'.

Part of this old-time atmosphere can be credited to the sets. The factory lay-out is elaborate and stylized, but not in the modern way or with the modern vividness of light and shadow; the department store might have been Wanamaker's in its heyday; the 'dance' music is a cross between Vienna and a small-town brass band, twenty years old at least; the costumes are generally previous; and as to faces and types, Chaplin has kept a lot of old friends with him, types from days when a heavy was a heavy and Chester Conklin's moustache obscured his chin (still does). Above everything, of course, is the fact that the methods of silent days built up their tradition in group management and acting – in the first, a more formal explicitness, so that crowds gather jerkily from nowhere, emphasized players move stiffly front and centre, the camera does less shifting; in the second, actors tend to underline their parts heavily and with copious motion (see the irate diner, see the hoity-toity wife of the parson, see Big Bill and the rest).

Modern Times has several new angles, principally those of the factory and the occasional off-stage reports of strikes and misery (the girl's father was shot in a demonstration). But they are incidental. Even in taking René Clair's conveyor-belt idea, for example, you can almost hear Chaplin, where Clair directed a complex hubbub, saying to one of his old trusties: You drop the wrench, I kick you in the pants, you take it big, see, and we cut to chase, got it? It has the thread of a story, Chaplin's meeting up with the orphan girl, very wild and sweet, and their career together. For the rest it is disconnected comedy stuff: the embarrassing situation, the embroilment and chase, and the specialty number, e.g., the roller skates, the completely wonderful song-and-dance bit, the Chaplin idyll of a cottage and an automatic cow, beautiful with humour and sentiment. These things and the minor business all along the way – in gaols, cafeterias, with oil cans, trays, swinging doors, refractory machinery – are duplicates, they take you back.

But such matters would not call for discussion, if all together they did not set up a definite mood, a disturbing sense of the quaint. Chaplin himself is not dated, never will be; he is a reservoir of humour, master of an infinite array of dodges, agile in both mind and body; he is not only a character but a complex character, with the perfect ability to make evident all the shades of his odd and charming feelings; not only a touching character, but a first-class buffoon and I guess the master of our time in dumb show. But this does not make him a first-class picture-maker. He may personally surmount his period, but as director-producer he can't carry his whole show with him, and I'll take bets that if he keeps on refusing to learn any more than he learned when the movies themselves were just learning, each successive picture he makes will seem, on release, to fall short of what went before. The general reaction to this one anyway is the wonder that these primitive formulas can be so genuinely comic and endearing.

There has been a furore here and there in the Press about the social content of *Modern Times*, and this could be skipped easily if Chaplin himself were not somehow confused (see his introduction to the film) over its worth as corrective comment. Well, the truth is that Chaplin is a comedian; he is back to type again, the happy hobo and blithe unregenerate, a little sad, a little droll. Whatever happens to him happens by virtue of his own naïve bewilderment, prankishness, absurd ineptitude and the constant support of very surprising coincidence. He couldn't keep a job or out of gaol anywhere in the world, including the Soviet Union – that is, if he is to be true to the Chaplin character.

And Chaplin is still the same jaunty wistful figure, pinning his tatters about a queer dignity of person, perpetually embarked on an elaborate fraud, transparent to the world but never very much so to himself. He brings the rites and dignities of Park Avenue to the gutters of Avenue A, and he keeps it up unsmilingly until it is time to heave the pie, to kick the props out, to mock with gestures and scuttle off, more motion than headway, all shoes, hat, stick and chase. With him it is all a continuous performance, played with the gravity, innocence and wonder of childhood, but with ancient wisdom in the matters of sniping cigar butts and tripping coppers into the garbage pile. He is pathetic with the unhappiness of never never succeeding, either in crossing a hotel lobby without at least one header into the spittoon, or in eating the steaks, chops and ham and eggs that are forever in his dreams; and yet he somehow cancels this or plays it down; when the ludicrous and debasing occurs, he picks himself up with serenity and self-respect, and when it is time for heartbreaks he has only a wry face, a shrug, some indication of that fall-to-rise-again philosophy that has made hoboing and destitution such harmless fun for his own special audience, the people of America. His life on the screen is material for tragedy, ordinarily. But on the screen he is only partly a citizen of this world: he lives mostly in that unreal happy land – you see the little figure walking off down the road toward it always into the fade-out – where kicks, thumps, injustice and nowhere to sleep are no more than a teasing and a jolly dream (Oh, with a little pang perhaps, a gentle Woollcott tear), and the stuff a paying public's cherished happy endings are made of.

Cecelia Ager

There used to be a time in pictures, a long time ago, when waifs were running wild. A waif was an unfortunate creature, simple and virtuous and pretty, in rags and with a sunny disposition. Then waifs went out and the modern girl with back-talk came in, so much back-talk that it's mighty soothing to meet up with Paulette Goddard, a good, old-fashioned waif in *Modern Times*.

It's no cinch to be 'a waif' in a Chaplin picture. Chaplin's no skimpy waif himself, but Miss Goddard, peeling off even the black cotton stockings that used to be a waif requisite and skipping about barefoot, submitting to photography in the harsh and revealing sunlight of her many outdoor sequences, whisking around in make-up of no especial tenderness, her dark hair realistically lank and unkempt, is nevertheless so cheerful, her beauty and vitality so genuine, her good humour so honest, even though she must realize deep down in her feminine heart that she'd knock 'em dead with her looks in any other kind of pic – she's such a good sport about the whole thing, that she finishes a waif stand-out on her own against the best waif competish in the world.

Then too, the fact that she goes for waif No. 1 all through, who also proves himself, once and for all, pictures' most sympathetic creation, the fact that she sticks and doesn't wander off with some big handsome guy adds plenty to the sympathy she grabs off for herself.

Annotated Index